COURAGEOUS SOULS

COURAGEOUS SOULS

Do We Plan Our Life Challenges Before Birth?

BY ROBERT SCHWARTZ

Published by Whispering Winds Press

Second edition 2007

Printed and bound in the U. S. A.

10 9 8 7 6 5 4 3 2

QUANTITY DISCOUNTS are available on bulk purchases of this book.
Please contact the publisher at:
Whispering Winds Press
www.CourageousSouls.com
e-mail: CourageousSouls@yahoo.com
Whispering Winds Press has printed this title on
50% postconsumer recycled paper.

Courageous Souls: Do We Plan Our Life Challenges Before Birth?
by Robert Schwartz

Cover Illustration by Jared McDaniel, Studio430.com
Book Design & Typesetting by Jill Ronsley, SunEditWrite.com

~

Publisher's Cataloging-in-Publication data
Schwartz, Robert M., 1962-
Courageous souls: do we plan our life challenges before birth? / Robert Schwartz.
    p. cm.
    ISBN 0-9776794-5-4
    ISBN 13 978-0-9776794-5-4
1. Spiritual life. 2. Soul. 3. Life change events. I. Title.
BL624 .S375 2006
248.420--dc22
Library of Congress Control Number: 2005910974

Dedicated to

Jon
Doris
Jennifer
Penelope
Bob
Sharon
Pat
Valerie
Jason
Christina

and
Their loved ones

and
My family

At each shift of the paradigm, the impossible presents its impeccable credentials...
and the unthinkable becomes the norm.

Rabbi Michael Berg
Becoming Like God

Should you shield the canyons from the windstorms,
you would never see the beauty of their carvings.

Dr. Elisabeth Kubler-Ross

Contents

Acknowledgments

FOREMOST, I OFFER MY HEARTFELT thanks to the many individuals who shared their stories with me. Without you, this book would not have been possible. It takes both bravery and great generosity of spirit to offer your story to the world. Your willingness to speak so candidly of your most difficult challenges has inspired me and is deeply appreciated.

To Deb DeBari, Glenna Dietrich, Corbie Mitleid, and Staci Wells, thank you for giving your time, energy, and considerable talents to this undertaking. Truly, no words can express my gratitude. Your compassion and sensitivity touched the lives of all those with whom we spoke—and mine as well. It has been my joy and my privilege to work with you.

To Marilu Wilson Peña, thank you for your wonderful channelings, generosity, and warm encouragement. To Judy Goodman, thank you for sharing your knowledge and insights with me.

To Carol Bergmann, your friendship, warmth, and unwavering support have meant more to me than you know. Thank you for being there. Thank you for caring.

Thank you to Sue Mann for your brilliant and detailed editing, to Jared McDaniel for your skill in creating the cover, to Jill Ronsley for your wonderful interior layout and typesetting, and to Edna Van Baulen for transcribing the sessions and for your enthusiastic support.

I am ever appreciative of the assistance and kindnesses of so many others, including Katelyn Daniels, Marissa Milagro, Kathy Long, the members of the Ashland Writers Group (and particularly Beth Hyjek for the extra time you took to offer your thoughts), and Ellen and Doug Falkner.

Finally, to the guides, angels, masters, and others in spirit who lighted my path, I offer my gratitude for your wisdom and love. The creation of this book has been a true partnership and a wondrous journey. Thank you for taking it with me.

*P*rologue

ON FEBRUARY 25, 1969, Christina, a twenty-year-old administrative assistant in the department of political science at Pomona College in Claremont, California, went to the department's basement mailbox to pick up her employer's mail. As she touched a package in the mailbox a bomb detonated, hurling her across the room. Dust and soot filled the air; six-foot splinters of wood shot like arrows into the cement wall behind her. Flames from the explosion scorched Christina's face, leaving her temporarily blind. The blast severed two fingers from her right hand and ruptured both eardrums.

Christina planned this experience before she was born. And she knows why.

*P*reface

IN MAY OF 2003, I was leading an unfulfilling life as a self-employed marketing and communications consultant. Although I enjoyed some of my work, I did not derive deep satisfaction from any of it. I often felt that if I were to fall off the face of the Earth, my clients would hardly notice; they would simply plug someone else into my role. More important, my life was not a unique expression *of my soul.* A spiritual but not a religious person, I longed to make a contribution to the world that would be "uniquely me," but I had no idea what that might be.

I had exhausted the usual routes one explores to find meaning and purpose. I was lost and floundering. Then, an inspiration came to me: why not consult a medium? Although I had a strong belief in God, I had never (as far as I knew) directly experienced the metaphysical. I felt I had nothing to lose. I researched mediums and selected someone with whom I felt comfortable.

My session with the medium took place on May 7, 2003. I remember the exact date because on that day my life changed. I told the medium very little about myself, describing my circumstances only in the most general terms. She explained that each of us has spirit guides, nonphysical beings with whom we plan our lives prior to incarnation.

Through her I was able to speak with mine. They knew *everything* about me—not only what I had done but also what I had thought and felt. For example, they referred to a specific prayer I had said to God some five years earlier. At a particularly difficult time I had prayed, "*God, I can't do this alone. Please send help.*" My guides told me that additional nonphysical assistance had been provided. "*Your prayer was answered,*" they said. I was astounded.

Eager to understand the suffering I had experienced, I asked my guides about the major challenges I had faced. They explained that I had planned these challenges before birth—not for the purpose of suffering, but for the growth that would result. I was shaken by this information. My conscious mind knew nothing of pre-birth planning, yet intuitively I sensed truth in their words.

Although I did not realize it at the time, my session with the medium triggered a profound spiritual awakening for me. I would later understand that this awakening was really a *remembering*—a remembering of who I am as an eternal soul and, more specifically, what I had planned to do on Earth.

For the next few weeks I continued with life as usual, although the information from my guides was constantly on my mind. I did not know what to do with it. One afternoon I took a break from work and went for a walk—and had an experience even more profound than my session with the medium. *I suddenly felt overwhelming, unconditional love for every person I saw!* No words can adequately convey the power of this love. It was of an intensity and depth I had never experienced and did not know was possible. For each person—the mother pushing her baby in a stroller, the cab driver waiting for a fare, the child playing at the corner, the barber cutting hair behind the window of his barbershop — I felt pure, limitless love.

Though I had never before heard of such an experience, I knew intuitively what was happening: *I was in enhanced, immediate communion with my soul.* In effect my soul was saying to me, "*This love is who you are.*" I now believe my soul gifted me with this experience to facilitate the work I would soon begin.

I became obsessed with reading about spirituality and metaphysics. As I read I thought often about pre-birth planning. All my life I had viewed my challenges as nothing more than meaningless suffering and their occurrences as random and arbitrary. Had I known that I'd planned my challenges, I would have seen them rich with purpose. That knowledge alone would have greatly eased my suffering. Had I also known *why* I'd planned them, I could have consciously learned the lessons they offered. Feelings of fear, anger, resentment, blame, and self-pity would have been replaced by a focus on growth. Perhaps I might even have been grateful for the challenges.

During this period of intense study and inner exploration, I met a woman who is able to channel her soul and who agreed to let me speak with her soul about pre-birth planning. I had no knowledge of channeling and was taken aback when she went into a trance and another consciousness, one clearly distinct from hers, began to speak through her. I spoke with her soul for fifteen hours over the course of five meetings.

These conversations were thrilling. They verified and complemented my reading and study. Her soul told me in detail about her own pre-birth planning: the various challenges that had been discussed and the reasons some were selected. Here I had direct, specific confirmation of a phenomenon of which very few people were aware. Because the pain in my life had made me extremely sensitive to—and intensely motivated to relieve—the suffering of others, I was excited by the potential healing an awareness of pre-birth planning could bring to people. I knew that the information I had discovered could lighten their suffering and imbue their challenges with new meaning and purpose. As a result I resolved to write a book about the subject and to share its significance with others.

My enthusiasm for my new path was, however, tempered by the uncertainty of letting go of the old. Though unfulfilling, it was at least comfortable and familiar. Nevertheless, I was sustained—indeed, compelled to go forward—by the importance of the work, the opportunity finally to express myself in unique ways that would be of service to the world, and the certainty of knowing that came from directly experiencing my soul.

At first I thought the idea for the book had originated in this lifetime. In truth, however, I had simply remembered my own pre-birth planning. By working with several gifted mediums and channels, I discovered I had planned not only to write a book on this subject but also to interview at least one of the people whose stories appear on these pages. In all I had dozens of sessions with mediums and channels, during which I spoke with many wise beings in spirit about my challenges and about pre-birth planning in general. In this book I offer to you what they have taught me.

I now understand why I had planned certain challenges for myself: I wanted to take the journey those who read this book may also take. I, too, at times felt victimized by the universe and blamed others for the "bad" things that happened to me. I saw my challenges as pointless, empty suffering and doubted my worth when I did not rise to them in the way

I would have liked. But with my knowledge of pre-birth planning, I now realize that an entirely different perspective on life challenges is possible. In writing *Courageous Souls*, I set out to teach what I had most needed to learn.

It takes a great deal of courage to live the plans you made before you were born. My desire, my most fervent wish, is that you recognize the tremendous courage you show in every moment of every day when, with each breath, you reaffirm your decision to embrace and learn from your own challenges. Within that recognition, you will find your soul.

Introduction

TO RESEARCH THE PRE-BIRTH PLANNING of life challenges, I collaborated with four extraordinarily gifted mediums and channels. Together we obtained information about the pre-incarnation plans of dozens of individuals, ten of whom share their stories in this book. In this introduction I will explain how I found these individuals, how the mediums and I researched their pre-birth planning, and mediumship and channeling in general. The conceptual underpinnings of pre-birth planning—that is, the reasons why we as souls choose to incarnate and experience challenges—are then presented in chapter 1.

Finding Interviewees

People replied to messages I posted to Internet news groups and bulletin boards. In some instances I asked specifically for individuals who were aware of (or at least open to) the possibility of pre-birth planning. On other occasions I expressed an interest in finding those who could talk about their challenges in a metaphysical context. At times I simply asked for people who wanted to discuss the underlying spiritual meaning of the difficulties they had faced. I sought variety and balance in their experiences and backgrounds.

Generally, interviewees said they were motivated by a desire to help others who face the same challenge. Of the ten eventually selected for this book, three used pseudonyms, and all said they would like to hear from readers. You will find their contact information in appendix A.

Eight of the ten interviewees planned their life challenge as a primary experience; that is, they sought the challenge from the initial stages of their pre-birth planning and they knew the challenge was highly likely to occur. One (Doris, chapter 2) planned her challenge as a secondary experience, meaning that its occurrence would be determined by her response to a primary challenge. Another (Bob, chapter 4) did not select his challenge during his initial pre-birth planning but instead created a new life blueprint at the soul level after an unexpected event at birth. Of the many pre-birth plans I examined, these were the only ones in which the challenge was not designed as a primary experience. I included these stories as important illustrations of how we as souls are aware of and use potential forks in the road for personal growth.

As you read the stories, you'll probably wonder whether you planned your own life challenges. My research suggests that the vast majority of life challenges are indeed selected. In general, the more profound the challenge the more likely it was chosen before birth. If a particular experience is important enough for you to ponder whether you planned it, then it is likely you did. One important exception, however, concerns experiences our intuition warns us to avoid. Unplanned challenges can occur when we ignore our intuitive promptings; therefore, internal "danger signals" are to be acknowledged and honored at all times.

It is not, however, my intent to suggest that all life challenges are planned, either as probabilities or as possibilities.

When we incarnate we have free will, and we can exercise our free will to create challenges that were not part of our pre-birth planning. The operative word is *create*. I believe we are the creators of everything we experience, and unplanned challenges occur when we vibrationally draw them to us because we need the wisdom they can engender. (In such instances intuition would not guide us away from the learning we need.) Our growth derives from the experiences themselves, regardless of whether or not we planned them. Therefore, this book will be most helpful if you focus on *why you might have* planned a particular challenge in your life, not on *whether* you did.

The question of *why* will be addressed as you read the stories of others' pre-birth planning. In their planning you may hear echoes of your own. I would suggest you not limit your reading only to those stories dealing with challenges you or your loved ones face, even if you are in crisis. Challenges that appear to be quite different from one another may have been planned to teach similar lessons or result in similar growth. You may find your *motivations* as a soul in the story of someone whose life is, at least on the surface, nothing like yours.

The Stories

Each story begins with an interview in which the individual and I focus on a specific life challenge. These interviews should be read carefully. Often, they contain details that appear at first to be unrelated to the challenge but that in the sessions with the mediums prove to be essential for a full understanding. I have not related complete personal histories; therefore, there may be no reference to certain blocks of time in the person's life.

To make this book as helpful as possible, I focused on common life challenges and organized the chapters by type of challenge. In some respects the stories build on one another, and the first stories provide basic information about metaphysics that will help you better appreciate subsequent stories. I therefore encourage you to read them in order.

Of the many mediums and channels with whom I have worked, I consider the four on these pages—Deb DeBari, Glenna Dietrich, Corbie Mitleid, and Staci Wells—to be among the most talented. Each has conducted thousands of readings over the course of her career. Their contact information is presented in appendix B. I have had personal sessions with all of them, and they were extremely accurate in providing information about my life they could not have known without true psychic abilities, abilities that are different for each. As Corbie explained to me, mediums and channels are like professors at a university: each has a particular specialty. If you attend a faculty cocktail party, you would not approach the biology professor with a sociology question, nor would you ask a scholar in the English department to solve a mathematical equation. Rather, you would recognize their various areas of expertise and appreciate what each has to offer.

Each interview is followed by one or more sessions with the mediums. I had told the interviewees that I would like to begin by asking the medium, "Was this challenge planned before birth, and if so, why?" They had agreed that this was a sound starting point, and further inquiries grew out of the response to that question. In some instances they permitted me to handle most, if not all, the questioning during those sessions.

Generally, when medium Staci Wells did not conduct the primary reading, I asked her and her spirit guide to do a supplementary reading. This reading served three important functions. First, it provided another confirmation that the life challenge had indeed been planned. Second, it offered additional information about that planning. Third, because Staci has the rare ability to visualize and listen to our pre-birth planning sessions, all her readings (whether primary or supplementary) provided *actual conversations* from them. This dialogue afforded a remarkable glimpse into the nonphysical realm, one in which we were privy to the hopes, feelings, and motivations of souls. As you will see, these conversations focused exclusively on the planning of life challenges — not because souls don't plan other aspects of their lives, but because Staci and I asked her guide to bring us only the most relevant portions of the discussion. Interviewees were present for primary but not supplementary readings, though supplementary readings were always done with the person's consent. Before each reading I provided Staci with the interviewee's name and birthdate, which her spirit guide needed to access information about that person.

In the pre-birth planning sessions that Staci hears, souls speak in the first person; however, in two channelings not conducted by Staci, a soul refers to itself as "we." Staci's spirit guide explained that the souls saying "I" are focused on the one life that is being planned, whereas the souls saying "we" are focused on their many previous incarnations.

Following the sessions with the mediums, each story concludes with my commentary. In these commentaries I draw upon my study of pre-birth planning and metaphysics, including the many conversations I had with nonphysical beings like spirit guides and angels, to expand upon the sessions.

Both the personal interviews and the readings with the mediums were edited for clarity; syntax was amended to enhance readability.

Mediums and Channels

Mediums and channels receive information in a variety of ways. If they are *clairaudient*, they hear the thoughts of nonphysical beings. (I use the term *Spirit* to refer to such beings; by contrast, I use *spirit* to refer to the nonphysical realm.) When a medium or channel "tunes in" to a non-physical consciousness, it is much like setting the dial on your radio. Just as every station is at a particular wavelength, so, too, is each being with whom they speak. At such times true telepathic communication takes place. If mediums or channels are *clairsentient*, they have the ability to feel the emotions of others. *Clairvoyance* is the ability to visualize things that have happened or will happen; *claircognizance* is an inner knowing, often in the form of a feeling. Channels are adept at "stepping aside" so that another consciousness may speak directly through them. Deb, Glenna, Corbie, and Staci have combinations of these abilities, which elicited valuable information about the interviewees' pre-birth planning.

Certain words have particular significance when used by mediums and channels. When they say, "I get," "I sense," or "I feel," they may be picking up information through one of their psychic gifts. People often say "I feel" when expressing an opinion. Mediums and channels, however, may use the word *feel* to denote perception beyond the five senses.

Mediums and channels communicate with a variety of beings, including spirit guides. A spirit guide is a highly evolved, nonphysical entity who in most (but not all) cases has had many physical incarnations. Through these incarnations, they have acquired great wisdom that now allows them to act as guides to those of us on the physical plane. Spirit guides speak with us in the same way our souls do: through inspiration, feelings, ideas, and intuition. When we have a "gut" feeling about something or when we "just know" that something is so, these are often communications from either our guides or our souls (also referred to as the "higher self"). One example is the person who decides not to board a plane because he or she has a "bad feeling" that something will happen and thus avoids a fatal accident. Spirit guides, who are well aware of our life plans and whether or not they include plane crashes, can create such feelings in us. It is said that Spirit whispers to us; meditation is a powerful way to quiet the mind so we may hear those messages. Experienced meditators are able to hear the inflow of nonphysical energies into the body, something they describe as sounding like the wind.

Soul Planning

Prior to birth, we have in-depth conversations with our spirit guides and the other souls with whom we will share our incarnation. We discuss the lessons we hope to learn and the ways in which we will learn them. When Staci accesses these discussions and the places in which they are held, she sees certain commonalities: a room in which the incarnating souls gather to talk; a smaller, adjoining room from which the guides monitor the planning, coming forth when called upon for advice; a black-and-white "chessboard" or "flowchart" used to map if-then scenarios in the life to come. The squares on the chessboard are developmental stages in the individual's life.

When Staci and I first began our collaboration, I incorrectly assumed that these images were metaphors placed in her mind by her spirit guide for concepts and processes beyond human understanding, but her guide later told me that these things exist. He explained that in the nonphysical realm, thought is literally and instantly creative. There is agreement among all involved that the pre-birth planning will be conducted in a certain place and will use certain tools like the chessboard. This mutual agreement, expressed in thought, brings into being the items and locations Staci sees.

In one session, Staci provided the following information about the place in which souls conduct pre-birth planning:

> In this particular building, there are eight floors and eight planning rooms on each floor. I am told [by Spirit] that this is because eight is the number of karma and destiny. The eight vibration was planned for this building so that it would best serve its intended purposes.
>
> This building is one of eight laid out like flower petals in a circular shape. The buildings are rectangular. They are each eight floors, eight planning rooms within each floor. They tell me there are twelve such groups of buildings on the other side, most of which are used for planning lives on Earth. They say that many souls prefer to come back to the same building, the same floor, and the same room if possible. It gives them a feeling of comfort and stability, and from that one place they're more able to sense their evolvement in each lifetime and the time in between lives.

When Staci's spirit guide conveys to her conversation from pre-birth planning sessions, he is accessing the Akashic Records, though he prefers the term "Book of Lives." This is a complete record of our every experience, act, word, and thought. When mediums provide their clients with information about past lives, they are often tapping into the Akashic Records. The great American psychic, Edgar Cayce, used these records in the thousands of readings he conducted.

As mediums see and speak with beings in spirit, they often describe them as male or female, but souls are actually a combination of male and female energies. When Deb sees an interviewee's "deceased" loved one the way the person appeared in physical life, it is because that consciousness chose to appear that way. When Staci sees a male or female soul in a pre-birth planning session, it is because that soul is creating—in a sense trying on—the energy of the upcoming incarnation (which Staci and her spirit guide refer to as "the cloak of the personality"). The same is true when a spirit guide appears as male or female. Guides have both male and female energies, but they may identify more strongly with one or the other and, therefore, choose to appear in that form.

In the planning sessions, nonphysical beings use some distinctly modern terms. Following one session with Staci, I asked her spirit guide if he had actually said *self-esteem* or if it was the closest approximation available in Staci's mind. He confirmed that he had. At times spirit guides and other nonphysical beings spoke without using our rules of grammar. Staci's guide told me, "We do not always speak in ways that you would consider to be grammatically correct."

The realm of spirit, in which we plan our incarnations and to which we will return when they are complete, is accessible to us now through mediums and channels. The equivalent of spirit guides in human form, they are compassionate, sensitive, and insightful pathfinders to the other side.

CHAPTER 1

⌒⊙⌒

Pre-birth Planning

YOU MAY FIND THE CONCEPT of pre-birth planning — particularly the planning of painful challenges — astonishing. I know this feeling well. For most of us, this notion presents a new and radically different way of looking at the world and our purpose in it. The more traumatic our challenges, the more difficult the concept may be. My understanding, acceptance, and eventual embrace of the idea occurred slowly and in stages, particularly in regard to the most painful aspects of my life. With each stage I felt the healing of old wounds. Anger and resentment faded and were replaced by feelings of peace and joy. I saw a beauty in life that previously eluded me.

My purpose in writing this book is not to persuade you of the absolute reality of pre-birth planning, but rather to offer, in a spirit of helpfulness, an idea that has been profoundly helpful to me. I ask only that you consider its possibility. You need not be convinced of the idea to benefit from it. You need only ask, "What if? What if I really did plan this experience before I was born? Why might I have done that?" Simply asking these questions gives new meaning to life challenges and launches a journey of self-discovery. That

19

journey demands no particular beliefs regarding spirituality or metaphysics, only an interest in personal growth and the acquisition of wisdom.

On these pages you will read the stories of ten courageous individuals. You will learn what they planned before birth and why they planned it. The process of understanding pre-birth planning may be likened to viewing a sculpture. If you want to truly appreciate a sculpture, you would not view it from only one angle. Rather, you would walk entirely around it, pausing in various places to look from a new perspective and observe the nuances that are now suddenly visible. Each story is one such perspective. By viewing pre-birth planning from ten angles, you'll arrive at a more complete and integrated understanding than only one or two perspectives or a purely theoretical discussion would allow.

I strongly encourage you to read the stories with your heart. The heart has a higher form of knowing, a greater wisdom, than the mind. Intellectual analysis will carry you only so far. These stories are meant to be *felt*. When you as an eternal soul planned your current life, you were not concerned with what your mind might come to know. Instead, you wanted to experience the feelings that would be generated by life in a physical dimension. Life challenges are a particularly powerful means of creating feelings, which are, in turn, vital to the soul's self-knowing. These feelings cannot truly be comprehended by the mind; in fact, the mind is a barrier. In many ways life is a journey from the head to the heart. We plan life challenges to facilitate this journey, to break open our hearts so we may better know and value them.

Empathy is a key that unlocks the door to the heart and makes possible an understanding of these stories and their spiritual meaning. Just as it took courage for the people in this book both to plan their challenges and to share them with you, it will take courage for you to empathize. I believe that empathy heals. If you seek healing, you may find your courage well rewarded.

This chapter provides you with the information you need to appreciate the stories' metaphysical aspects. If you are unfamiliar with metaphysics, some of these ideas may strike you as unusual, just as they once did me. I ask for your patience. They will have greater meaning and validity as you see them applied in the stories—and still greater meaning and validity as you apply them to your challenges. This chapter will also give you an overview of the commonalities I found in the interviewees' life blueprints. With this roadmap you will have a framework in which to incorporate the wisdom they share.

Why We Incarnate

The planning we do before birth is far-reaching and detailed. It includes but goes well beyond the selection of life challenges. We choose our parents (and they choose us), when and where we will incarnate, the schools we will attend, the homes in which we will live, the people we will meet, and the relationships we will have. If you ever felt you already know someone you just met, it may well be true. That person was probably part of your pre-birth planning. When a place, name, image, or phrase seems oddly familiar the first time you see or hear it, that familiarity is often a vague remembrance of what was discussed before incarnation. In many planning sessions, we use the name and take on the physical appearance we will have after birth. Such practices help us recognize one another on the physical plane. The feeling of déjà vu is often accurately attributed to a past-life event, but many déjà vu experiences are memories of pre-birth plans.

When we enter the Earth plane, we forget our origins in spirit. We know prior to incarnation that we will have such self-induced amnesia. The phrase *behind the veil* refers to this state of forgetfulness. As divine souls, we seek to forget our true identities because remembering will give us a more profound self-knowing. To obtain this deeper awareness, we leave the nonphysical realm—a place of joy, peace, and love—because there we experience no contrast to ourselves. Without contrast, we cannot fully know ourselves.

Picture, if you will, a world in which there is only light. If you never experienced darkness, how well would you comprehend and appreciate light? It is the contrast between light and dark that leads to a richer understanding and, ultimately, a remembering. The physical plane provides us with this contrast because it is one of *duality*: up and down, hot and cold, good and bad. The sorrow in duality allows us to better know joy. The chaos of Earth enhances our appreciation of peace. The hatred we may encounter deepens our understanding of love. If we never experienced these aspects of humanity, how would we know our divinity?

Imagine you are originally from a place in which the most exquisitely beautiful music ever created plays. This music is rapturous, resplendent. As long as you have lived, you have always heard it. It has never been absent, nor has any other music ever been present. One day you realize that because you have always heard it, you have never *really* heard it. That is, you have never really known it because you have never known anything else. You decide, therefore, that you would like to know the music truly. How might you accomplish this?

One way would be to go to a place where the music of Home does not exist. Perhaps a different music plays, a music that contains jarring notes or strident passages. This contrast would instill in you a new appreciation of the music you always heard at Home.

A second way would be to go to a place where the music of Home does not exist and recreate it from memory. The experience of composing those magnificent sounds would give you an even deeper understanding of their beauty.

A third possibility exists, one that is much more challenging but that also holds the greatest promise. It occurs to you that a truly profound knowing can be gained by going to a place where the music of Home does not play and once there recreating it *but only after you have forgotten what it sounded like.* The experience of remembering and then composing the extraordinary symphonies of Home would produce the richest, fullest, and most expanded knowing of their inherent grandeur.

And so bravely you travel to the world that offers the third option. There you hear music that you, lacking memory, believe to be the only music you have ever heard. Some songs are lovely, but many strike your ears as dissonant. These harsh tones foster within you a desire—and ultimately a resolve—to create original music.

Soon you begin to write your own compositions. At first you are distracted by the loud music of your new world. Over time, however, as you turn away from the external blare and listen to the melodies in your heart, your musical creations grow in beauty. Eventually you compose a masterpiece, and when it is finished you remember something: the masterpiece you wrote is *the very same music* that had played at Home. And this recollection triggers yet another: *You are that music.* It was not something you heard outside yourself; rather, it *was* you, and you *were* it. And by creating yourself in a new place, you now know yourself—truly know yourself—in a way that was not possible had you never left Home.

This is the experience the soul desires. A soul is a spark of the Divine; a personality—a human being—is a portion of a soul's energy in a physical body. The personality consists of temporary traits that exist only during the physical lifetime and an immortal core that reunites with the soul after death. The soul is vast and goes well beyond any one personality, yet each personality is vital to and dearly loved by the soul.

Importantly, the personality has free will. Life challenges may therefore be accepted or resisted. Earth is a stage on which the personality enacts or deviates from the script written before birth. We choose how we respond—with anger and bitterness or with love and compassion. When we recognize that we planned our challenges, the choice becomes clear and much easier to make.

While we are in our physical bodies, our souls communicate with us through feelings. Feelings like joy, peace, and excitement indicate we are acting and thinking in ways that are consistent with our true nature as loving souls. Feelings like fear and doubt suggest we are not. Our bodies are exquisitely sensitive receivers (and transmitters) of energy that tell us through feeling whether there is a match or a mismatch between who we really are and the ways in which we are currently expressing ourselves.

Why We Plan Challenges

Life plans are set up so we experience who we are not before we remember who we really are. That is, we explore the discordant sounds in our earthly lives before we recreate the symphonies of Home. This pattern became quite clear to me as I conducted research for this book. I refer to such life blueprints as "learning-through-opposites" plans.

For instance, a deeply compassionate soul who wishes to know herself as compassion may choose to incarnate into a highly dysfunctional family. As she is treated with a lack of compassion, she comes to appreciate compassion more deeply. It is the absence of something that best teaches its value and meaning. A lack of compassion in the outer world forces her to turn inward, where she remembers her own compassion. The contrast between the lack of compassion in the physical world and her inner compassion provides her with a more profound understanding of compassion and, therefore, herself. From the perspective of the soul, the pain inherent in this learning process is temporary and brief, but the resultant wisdom is literally eternal. There is a component of learning through opposites in every story in this book.

Remembering who we really are — majestic, transcendent, eternal souls — is one way to surmount our life challenges. For example, people who define themselves as the body will feel great anguish if their bodies are severely damaged. Others whose bodies endure the same damage but who define themselves as the soul will experience far less torment. Because our challenges call us into recollection of ourselves as souls, the very event that initially caused suffering may ultimately alleviate it. This expansion of self-concept from personality-body to soul may or may not reduce our pain, but it can certainly ease our suffering. Such awakening is both a purpose and a profound benefit of life challenges. It revitalizes our passion for life, the passion we felt before we incarnated. It is, quite simply, cause for celebration.

As we awaken or respond positively in other ways to our challenges, we carve an "energetic pathway" that makes it easier for others to cope with—and heal from—their challenges. This idea is based on the premise that we are all energetically connected to and affected by one another. The stories in this book suggest that each of us has an impact that far exceeds our knowing. Our ability to affect the world so forcefully is equally a wonderful opportunity and a great responsibility.

Each of us is a seed that was planted within our world's current vibration. When we raise our own frequencies through the growth produced by life challenges, we raise the world's frequency from within. Like a single drop of dye added to a glass of water, each person alters the entire hue. As we create feelings of joy, even if we do so while living alone on a mountaintop, we emit a frequency that makes it easier for others to be joyful. As we create feelings of peace, we resonate an energy that helps to end wars. As we love we make it easier for others, both those whom we meet and those who will never know of us, to love. Who we are is therefore far more meaningful than anything we may ever do.

In chapter 7 you will meet Christina and her spirit guide, Cassandra. Cassandra had this to say about the energetic pathway:

> When a specific life challenge is accepted, one can receive healing energy from those who have blazed a trail. The path of light is paved with compassion and healing love that raises the frequency of the person traveling the road [behind them].
>
> Learning and healing from a specific life challenge raises the auric field of the one who has survived a challenge. Others in their presence know they have something that bathes them in hope and faith. The experience need not be the same; just the healing frequency can carry the

soul forward, but the receiving soul must be prepared to receive. Even if the physical form [of the receiver] does not change or "heal" by Earth standards, the soul moves to new heights.

Suffering is a gift of immense proportions both to the soul and to the chosen others who are allowed to assist that soul on its healing journey. The language of suffering is a frequency of its own. It comes in the eyes, hearts, and minds of those who are there. It is profound and mundane all at the same time. See it, believe it, and impart love and compassion to those in need. Small acts of consciousness and kindness make healing possible. Thoughts of beauty and grace can be projected out and perceived even remotely by those who can benefit.

Just as our energetic impact radiates throughout this dimension, so, too, does it extend throughout other dimensions. You will see references to "higher" and "lower" dimensions. *Higher* does not mean better, nor does *lower* imply worse. These terms refer simply to frequency. Higher dimensions vibrate at faster frequencies than ours and are therefore nonphysical, but they overlap and incorporate lower dimensions. In short, all is one. For this reason our individual frequencies, whether those of love or fear, emanate endlessly outward, affecting both nonphysical beings and other people who may seem to be "elsewhere" and quite separate from us.

As you read the stories, it is helpful to bear in mind the limitations of language in discussing some of these concepts. For example, I will at times refer to people "coming from" the spiritual realm when they incarnate and "returning to" that realm after the death of the body. These words and others like them are intended to indicate a change in perception, not place. They are not meant to suggest separation between dimensions. Incarnation does not literally remove us from our eternal Home; rather, it simply limits our capacity to see the nonphysical part of it. Death, then, is the dissolution of the veil that screened the nonphysical realm from us.

The concepts of *oneness* and *separation* are important in order to understand fully why we choose to experience life challenges. When we are in spirit, we have a continuous awareness of our inseverable link with all other beings. We know we are one with one another and, indeed, with the entirety of creation. Unqualified compassion and empathy are our very nature. Although we have individual identities, we do not perceive that we are separate from other individuals. This fundamental concept is paradoxical to the human brain, which, by design, perceives the illusion of separation. When we as souls project a portion of our energy into physical bodies, we intentionally restrict our focus to that of the body, thereby blocking our perception of oneness. That we are capable of narrowing our perceptual range allows us to plan lives in which we play pre-scripted roles and thus provide challenges for one another. We hope we will respond to these challenges with love. If we are able to do so, after a physical lifetime we will return to spirit with a deepened understanding of the compassion, empathy, and oneness that we temporarily screened from our own awareness.

As the stories indicate, we plan life challenges to accomplish certain goals. One common objective is healing; specifically, the healing of "negative" energies left unresolved from past lifetimes. Let's say, for example, that a person was consumed by fear during one incarnation. At the conclusion of that lifetime, the individual may carry traces of the energy of fear. This is particularly true if the person died while experiencing great fear. The low frequency energy of fear cannot be carried fully into the high frequency nonphysical realm where the soul resides, yet an energetic residue may still cross over. The individual feels this lingering energy and is motivated to plan a new life in which it will be healed through the expression of love.

We also plan challenges to balance karma. Karma is sometimes conceptualized as cosmic debt, but it may also be described as unbalanced energy with another individual. Typically, we have karma with members of our soul group — others at the same evolutionary stage with whom we have shared many lifetimes. In those past lives, we have played the roles of husband, wife, daughter, son, brother, sister, mother, father, beloved friend, and mortal enemy to the same souls. (I recall the true story of a father who was reading a bedtime tale to his young daughter. As he finished, she smiled and said, "Daddy, remember when you were my child, I was your mommy, and I read bedtime stories *to you?*")

One soul in the group may, for example, have had an incarnation in which many years were spent taking care of someone who was physically ill. If the soul who played the role of caretaker then plans a life with the challenge of illness in it, the soul who received the caretaking may seek to balance that energetic exchange by offering caretaking. In body, however, neither soul will remember the plan. The one who chose to be the caretaker may feel burdened by the need to care for another person, perhaps even viewing it as punishment for misdeeds in a past life. In truth, however, there is no punishment, simply a desire to balance karma. Similarly, because we have scripted the roles we play, we are not victims. No one is to blame; in fact, there *is* no blame. The universe does not punish us by making "bad" things happen. Like gravity, karma is a neutral, impersonal law by which the world operates. If we stumble and fall, we do not blame gravity or feel victimized or punished by it. When we realize that karma works in the same way, feelings of blame, victimization, and punishment in regard to life challenges dissipate. In their place we may find an understanding of what we had hoped to learn and an abiding appreciation of the challenges that expand our souls.

An understanding of karma helps us to move beyond judgment, particularly in regard to those who have experienced major traumas or "setbacks" like drug addiction or homelessness. Usually, these individuals are living their incarnations and balancing past-life energies just as they had planned. Their lives, sometimes labeled "failures" from the viewpoint of the personality, are often unqualified successes from the viewpoint of the soul.

Most souls plan life challenges to be of service to others. This desire is a fundamental aspect of our true nature as eternal souls. When we are in spirit and aware of our oneness with one other, we view service as a basic purpose of life and see opportunities to serve as wondrous blessings. Like souls who are balancing karma, many of those who appear to be struggling with life are actually performing acts of service. A soul may plan, for instance, to experience alcoholism so that others may express and thus know themselves more profoundly as compassion. Some of society's harshest judgments are meted out to alcoholics and others who gift us with the very experiences we sought. If only more people knew this!

A *lightworker* is someone whose life plan is particularly service oriented. Broadly, the term applies to anyone who is committed to helping others. Though one does not have to plan great challenges to be a lightworker, many lightworkers have done just that with the intent of surmounting those challenges for the benefit of society as a whole. This type of life blueprint is no better (or worse) than any other. Indeed, given the large number of incarnations each of us plans, many will play this role at some point.

Naturally, we plan life challenges in part for our own personal growth. As souls we learn a great deal between incarnations, but the lessons become more deeply instilled in us when we concretize them on the physical plane. Learning while in spirit is similar to classroom work; life on Earth is the field study in which we apply, test, and enhance that knowledge—a powerful experience for the soul.

Ultimately, regardless of the specific challenges they contained, every life blueprint I examined was based on love. Each soul was motivated by a desire to give and receive love freely and unconditionally, even in those instances when the soul had agreed to play a "negative" role to stimulate another soul's growth. Many souls were also motivated by a desire to remember self-love. Literally, we *are* love. I base this statement not only on my research, but also on direct, personal experience—the revelation of my soul described in the preface. Life challenges give us the opportunity to express and thus know ourselves more deeply as love in all its many facets: empathy, forgiveness, patience, nonjudgment, courage, balance, acceptance, and trust. Our earthly experience of ourselves as love may also take the form of understanding, serenity, faith, willingness, gratitude, and humility, among other virtues. Love is the primary theme of pre-birth planning and, therefore, the primary theme of this book.

As we enter the physical plane, we are love temporarily hidden from itself. When we remember who we really are, our inner light, our love, shines forth for all to see.

That, I believe, is why we are here.

CHAPTER 2

∽∽

Physical Illness

A IDS IS ONE OF THE most feared illnesses of our time. As I write these words, more than one million Americans are HIV positive, and more than forty million people worldwide have HIV or AIDS. Approximately eight thousand people die each day from this disease. The treatment may exact a terrible physical and emotional toll, and the stigma complicates and strains relationships with caregivers and loved ones. Could it really be that some souls want to have this experience?

When I decided to write about pre-birth planning, I knew immediately that physical illness was one life challenge I would examine. Given that virtually every human being will face health challenges, the importance of the topic was undeniable. I wanted to know if souls chose before incarnation to experience physical illness. One question in particular called to me: do souls plan to have specific illnesses, and if so, why?

Jon Elmore's Story

Jon remembers the exact date when his life changed: January 23, 1997. On that day he was diagnosed with AIDS. "They identified me by a code number," he told me. I wondered how it felt to have an illness viewed by society as so shameful that it requires the patient to have a number instead of a name. As I would soon learn, shame was a theme in Jon's life.

Jon was born in Livingston, Alabama, a town of 2500 people, in 1956, a time of social upheaval and racial intolerance in the South. As a child, Jon, who is Caucasian, watched news reports of the marches in Selma, where fire hoses and German shepherds were used against African Americans who wanted to vote.

As a young adult, Jon told his father about his sexual orientation by showing him a "Dear Abby" column in which Abby congratulated a man for his enlightened attitude toward his child's homosexuality.

"What are you trying to say?" Jon's father asked.

"Well … I'm trying to say that I'm gay."

His father burst into tears. "You realize you're Jon Elmore, and the line stops with you? I can take you up across the river. You can get with a woman, and you can have you a good time."

Jon tried a different approach with his mother. One television network had been advertising a special daytime news show featuring an interview with a homosexual man. *("He's young. He's successful. And he's homosexual! We're going to talk to him and his parents.")* Jon asked his mother to remind him to watch the show.

While Jon watched the program in the den, his mother sat a few feet away at the kitchen table. She was "doing what she did to relieve stress—playing solitaire," Jon recalled. "Every four seconds I could hear those cards click. She'd put one down and click. Click. CLICK. It kept getting louder and louder," he said with a laugh. I imagined the tension in the air and the look of intense concentration on his mother's face as she tried to focus on the cards.

"I was secretly hoping she would come into the den and sit with me, but that didn't happen," Jon said sadly.

At school Jon's classmates, who were aware of his sexuality, taunted him. He was called "fag" and pushed around. Once, a teacher pulled him aside and said, "Jon, you're a man. Why don't you act like one?"

Jon told me the religious climate in which he grew up was equally intolerant of his sexuality.

"In which religion were you raised?" I asked.

"Methodist."

"What is the Methodist view of homosexuality?"

"That it is a sin against God."

"What religion were most of the people in Livingston?"

"Baptist."

"What is the Baptist view of homosexuality?"

"You're going to burn in Hell," Jon laughed. "The Baptists are on a warpath."

"Jon, what's striking to me," I said, "is that you had shame in your personal life—through school, family, and religion—*and* you chose to incarnate in a place where an entire race of people was being shamed publicly." My research had clearly indicated that souls choose their parents and the time and location of their birth. "There's shame both in private and public," I added. "It's everywhere."

"It's everywhere," he agreed. "It never stopped. I was incarnated in a family of shame, in a place of shame, in an era of shame." Jon also said he had felt shamed by the harsh words of more than one romantic partner. Although I did not know it at the time, that aspect of Jon's past would take on much greater significance when we later obtained information from Spirit about his pre-birth planning. AIDS is part of the pattern of shame that Jon either witnessed in the South or experienced firsthand. When he received his diagnosis, "it was a feeling of, 'Well, I got what I deserved,'" Jon said somberly.

Despite feeling that he deserved it, he was nevertheless stunned. "I got in my van. I remember driving down the street, seeing people going about their business. You never notice that, but I *saw* these people. It seemed like everyone was moving through molasses. They were crossing the street. They were going into drug stores and grocery stores and talking on the sidewalk. I passed fire stations. The firefighters were doing something with their equipment. I've got all the windows rolled up. I started screaming, *'Don't you know the entire world has just changed?'* For me it really had."

At one point, Jon became critically ill. While hospitalized he had a near-death experience.

"It's kind of foggy," Jon said, "but I remember being in a room. It was dark. I was surrounded by a lot of other people. It was like a big cocktail party. There wasn't any noise, and there wasn't any conversation, but I could sense that there were a lot of people who weren't of the same realm that I was. I felt I could join them, or I could not. I distinctly remember choosing not to. It was an internal decision. It was like, 'I don't want to stay.'"

Jon chose life. Not just the physical continuation of it, but a new type of life.

"After you've been bumping butts with the Angel of Death, you get a little appreciation for where you've been," Jon said. "I stopped feeling ashamed. I did. What I discovered was that as close as I had come to dying, I didn't want to."

"Jon," I asked, "how did AIDS and your near-death experience help you to overcome shame?"

"What other tribulation could I face that is as long a journey through shame?" Jon replied. "The best way to treat your fears is to kiss them on the nose, and they disappear. Almost dying helped me to realize that They — with a capital *T* — don't have any power over me anymore. We all know who They are. Neighbors and teachers and all of these people that come out of the woodwork from time to time and jabber at me. They don't exist anymore.

"All I want is to live and live in truth," he added.

"Jon, what would you like to say to someone who is experiencing shame?"

"The shaming words were solid, immovable events in my life. What do you do with the solid and immovable? You build on it."

Jon's Session with Glenna Dietrich

As a channel, Glenna Dietrich enters a trance in which the consciousness of another being speaks through her. Some channels are fully aware of every word spoken by the channeled entity; others have a vague awareness of what is discussed though they are not able to recall specific words. Glenna, by contrast, has virtually no memory of the conversations. After our sessions she was curious about how they went and what had been discussed. A very caring person, she always wanted to know if they had been helpful.

It is immediately clear when Glenna begins to channel. Her voice softens slightly; cadence, tone, and diction all change noticeably. Sometimes, as with Jon's session, more than one nonphysical being is present and speaks through her.

"We are three to see you, as you are three," began the channeled entity. "We are not of the material world, but of the spiritual realm—as you consider it, behind the veil. Two of us have not been in human material form as you are. We are from the angelic realm. We remain nameless to you, as all our names are not pronounceable. So we appear in your minds only as colors in vague shapes and more as feeling."

I marveled at the fact that we were now speaking with angels. Through Glenna we were reaching across the veil to the nonphysical world. There was a sweetness in the angel's tone that I found soothing. The angel's greeting reminded me that beings in spirit often communicate with us through feeling, and that mediums frequently see the colors of both nonphysical beings and the human aura.

It was common in these sessions for the discarnate beings not to use names. Every being, whether physical or non-physical, is energy. The term *energy signature* denotes that every consciousness is identifiable by its unique energy. The angels were able to recognize Jon, Glenna, and me—and one another—by virtue of that energy.

"One of we three has been in an incarnated state many times," continued the angel. "And this being will now communicate with you directly."

"Yes, I have been incarnate in your realm 867 times," said the second angel. "These are the times that I have spent in human bodies. There have been any number of times when I have chosen to spend my incarnate time in bodies other than human. Truly, I have chosen to be one of your [Jon's] guides as you have incarnated. We have been

together many times in many incarnations. We have been
sisters. We have been mother and daughter. We have been
enemies who have murdered one another. And we have
been dear friends.

"In each time you and I have decided where we will meet
and in what circumstances we will bring opportunities for
one another to have those beautiful growth experiences. We
are truly what those in your realm consider to be soulmates.
Two souls of very similar vibration — a frequency at which
we both have a *color* and a *sound* that are similar.

"I wish to say to you that I am proud and happy at the
many steps you have made forward in this incarnation.
There are many things you have proven and many energies
you have brought forth. I have stepped beside you. And at
times I have been in front, encouraging you during those
times you considered to be the darkest. Yes, my energy is
familiar to you. I wish for you to remember, dear one, the
beauty of your soul, the incredible light that can come into
your heart. It is difficult to be that shining light when most
around you desire only darkness. It is the true healer, the
true sage, who remains sage amongst those who are not
awake. Take heart and remain at courage."

To me the angel said, "We have heard your questions, but
we wish that you pose them to us one at a time."

"Thank you," I began. "Did Jon plan before birth to have
the experience of AIDS in this lifetime, and if so, why?"
Prior to the session, Jon and I had agreed we would begin
with the central question. He was as eager as I to hear the
answer.

"Yes, certainly," replied the angel. "There are no
heavy energies in this realm [the nonphysical] to impede
progress, to inhibit the ability to see forward. The
between-times [periods between incarnations] are spent

assessing and planning for what the soul considers to be the next step, the next level or plateau. The answer to your question is yes.

"Truly, that which has been discussed was the release of the genetic parent and belief system from the soul group in which Jon considers himself a part of a family." (As we would soon learn, the angel was referring to a past life of someone in Jon's soul group. In that lifetime the incarnate personality took fear-based actions that caused a complete forgetting of its origins as a soul—something no soul in Jon's group had experienced previously.) "Indeed, all members of the soul group came to agreement that Jon would take the essential burden and, despite those so-called distractions or things created by illusion, begin nonetheless to shine, to become that light and begin to see and understand the truth about himself.

"Those [souls] who come together to assist one another imbue their personalities and their perceptions of Jon in a way that brings about the obstacles he must overcome in order for his truth to become apparent to him." (As you will see in medium Staci Wells's supplementary reading for Jon, the angel was speaking of members of Jon's soul group who agreed before birth to shame him as part of his life challenges.) "It is almost like an obstacle race. The more times you come to the same obstacle, the easier it is to catapult yourself over it, crawl under it, or shimmy around it until finally it becomes second nature. When Jon no longer sees himself as less important, less loving, less delightful, less sacred than those around him, the obstacles of this human will fade."

With these words, the angel conveyed a primary purpose of life challenges: to show us how our thoughts and feelings create our reality. Challenges are mirrors that reflect to us our feelings about ourselves. In that sense, they are gifts. Wisdom allows us to recognize them as such.

"Indeed," the angel explained, "the body itself is being used to bring about this awareness, to shine light on where healing is needed. And because this has great impact on his soul family and this [nonphysical] realm, it is brought about in an extremely intense and very powerful method so that all may benefit from truths that are uncovered. If another obstacle had been brought up, the victory would not be as great."

Here we had it: confirmation that Jon had specifically planned the experience of AIDS, not just for his own learning but also for the growth of his entire soul group. As sessions with other interviewees confirmed, the progress we as personalities make on the Earth plane expands both our individual souls and every soul in our group.

"Could you please say more," I inquired, "about how the experience of AIDS helps Jon to grow?"

"It is the necessity of seeing oneself as you truly are," replied the angel, "and believing in one's own truth, one's own identity. It has to do with the belief that all love is deserved, that unconditional love is deserved. As the soul group involved sets forth only conditional love that needs to be experienced in a particular way—a conforming, a tradition—the [Jon's] nonconformity leads them to withdraw their love. In this way Jon's belief about himself is formed: that he is not deserving of love in an unconditional amount, but only to be loved when he performs in a set way, when he meets others' expectations and others' approval. Confusion sets in, and the personality that develops in the small child becomes broken apart, split. The disease of AIDS is about splitting a desire for unconditional love with the belief that one does not deserve it.

Therefore, healing comes and is completed when the soul of Jon shines through and the personality of Jon sees that light and believes that to be himself."

The angel had beautifully stated the heart of the spiritual growth process on Earth: self-love is kindled when we cease to think of ourselves as limited, flawed personalities and instead remember that we are transcendent beings. To recognize this inner light is to change thought patterns and, by extension, physical health.

"How did Jon's soul plan for its light to shine through, and how did Jon's soul know that would happen?" I asked.

"All incarnations in your realm," answered the angel, "are designed to move across the baser levels of darkness. There is a vibration of hatred. The vibration of separation from God, the vibration of nonacceptance, the vibration of fear—these things all exist there as hidden levels of a frequency we would equate to sound. It has an effect on human bodies that is unbeknownst, unseen, not measurable.

"You who are in that realm believe that that is you, that you are fear, that you are hatred and nonacceptance. And so you are able to murder one another. You are able to abuse and exploit one another. You act on baser frequencies. As the soul enters the body, the clarity for the most part disappears, and as a human, you begin to believe that you are the body. You cease to remember that you are the soul. This is part of the plan, because to forget your divinity and through many trials remember the truth brings about great power, solidifies beliefs, and uplifts that frequency to higher levels."

(Jon would later say of this remark, "That is exactly the kind of power I have been seeking. I have been making noticeable strides in reaching for that entity I know is inside me. The experience of AIDS has brought me to believe that my body is threatened but my soul and my being and my awareness are not.")

"Does this answer your question?" the angel asked me.

"Yes," I said, though I still wanted to understand how Jon's soul could know, or why it felt, that Jon's life plan would bring about such tremendous growth. "Were specific events planned into Jon's life that would allow the light of his soul to shine through and be recognized by his personality?"

"There have been many events implanted [by the soul] and experienced by Jon that he may or may not recall that are synchronistically involved in opening that awareness to that light," answered the angel. "This is a gradual process. The human body vibrates at very low frequencies. At higher frequencies a revelation of truth commences. The body is incapable of accommodating higher frequencies at a fast rate. So, people allow themselves only glimpses into the higher frequencies and in that way acclimate the body in tiny increments, making it possible for the cells to accumulate light and bring about higher frequencies in a very gradual way."

The angel was helping me to understand how physical illness could stimulate spiritual healing. Even so, I wondered why such healing would be needed in the first place. "The shame Jon is trying to heal—the belief that he is not deserving of unconditional love—where did that originally come from? How was it created?" I asked.

"Within the bloodline in that spirit group, it was designed in an individual who was part of organized religion. A religious dignitary of magnitude. That individual's personality was imbued with calculated imbalance. As this imbalance manifested in that human's body, it became a mental illness fraught with many fears. As this ancestor acted on these fears, they became very powerfully intact, not only in his body but also in the bodies of his offspring."

I had learned in other sessions that action on the physical plane concretizes emotion, making it more deeply a part of our being. It is for this reason that subsequent incarnations are often designed for healing. That which is created in the physical is most readily healed in the physical.

"It was a calculated drop into darkness," continued the angel, "into a vibration so low it had not been experienced by this soul group previously. So in this experiment, genetically through the DNA, this code [the energy of fear] was passed and truly became a far-reaching code that many other soul groups adopted, seeing that it was useful in descending into lower levels of frequency." The angel was referring to the desire of souls to experience contrast in order to arrive at a deeper self-knowing. "The further distance from the truth of one's being, the darker it becomes and the lower the frequency.

"As the soul group through incarnations makes its way through this murky, heavy energy, it clears. [The soul group] becomes cognizant once again of the light, the truth. Its awareness becomes stabilized. Those beings, when eventually they leave this wheel of reincarnation and move into other realms, take with them knowledge of that descent from the light. Does this answer your question?"

"Yes, thank you." I replied. "It sounded as though you said that the souls in Jon's soul group asked him and that he agreed to be the one with AIDS, and that the others were incarnating around him to judge him, reject him, and not provide him with unconditional love. Is that correct?"

"That is correct," answered the angel.

"That seems to be a risky plan, because Jon might adopt the beliefs of those around him and conclude that he is in fact not worthy of unconditional love."

"Yes, he has in many incarnations. It's part of the healing of his own soul."

"Does the soul group continue to use this kind of plan until there's an incarnation in which the individual concludes that he *is* worthy of unconditional love?"

"That is correct."

We had now come to the timeless issue of human suffering. I did not want the angel to feel challenged by my next question, but the suffering in my own life had been so profound at times that I simply had to understand the necessity for it. In many ways my need for such understanding had propelled me to set up this session.

"Why do it that way?" I inquired. "Why not design a pleasant life with plenty of unconditional love? Wouldn't that be an easier way to learn that one is deserving of it?"

"A balance is obtained by experiencing both the light and the dark," said the angel. "All individuals who incarnate into your realm experience being both the light and the dark in some incarnation. One may choose to become that individual who exterminates an entire tribe of humans. One may choose to abuse children. All of these things create a level of learning and knowing. This is truly the realm in which there exists a polarity of good and bad. Finding the balance between the light and the dark, the good and the bad, brings you out of that realm, moves you away from the sense of duality, and creates within you instead a belief in All That Is." The angel was referring to the divine nature and unity of all that exists in the universe.

"Does that mean Jon's soul group is healing shame through both pleasant, loving incarnations and more challenging ones like the experience of AIDS?"

"That is correct," said the angel. I felt comforted to hear of the balance in the life-planning process.

"You mentioned earlier a lower frequency," said Jon, now asking his first question. "How can I raise that frequency?"

"I would say to you, Jon, that the highest frequency in the universe is that of love. And so to hold that frequency for yourself as long as possible, whenever possible, is the secret."

"What would you say to someone with AIDS," I asked, "who is trying to understand the deeper spiritual meaning?"

"Remain very open in your heart," the angel said softly. "Follow that which comes only from the heart, and in this way many healings will occur on levels that are beyond your understanding."

I would hear similar words from Spirit many times in other sessions. When we close our hearts, we block energies—primarily the energy of love—from healing us. For this reason, the emotional hardening of the heart leads to its physical hardening.

"Of those in Jon's soul group," I asked, "why was he the one chosen to experience AIDS?"

"It was his turn," the angel told us.

"It's just that it was his turn?"

"Yes."

"What else is important to understand about the experience of AIDS?"

"It is a plague of your time," replied the angel, "that points to a pattern of self-hatred among humankind, a culmination of centuries and generations of movement away from

Spirit, movement away from light, and a belief in the self as the body and separate from All That Is."

"Is it accurate, then, to say that AIDS is healing humanity?"

"That is correct," said the angel.

∾

Though Jon's session was not the first in which I had participated, and though I had already heard Spirit confirm that other interviewees had chosen and planned their life challenges, I was nonetheless stunned by what we were told. Jon had *elected* to experience AIDS—and we had learned *why.* I wondered how many people with AIDS, or any disease for that matter, view their illness as a punishment from God or the universe, or at best a form of pointless suffering. The conversation with the angels had made clear that Jon's experience, though painful, is deeply meaningful. In fact, it is transformative.

Jon described the session as eye opening. "It made me realize that there is much more goodness inside me than I gave myself credit for. I now have a stronger sense of purpose than I've had in years." He also said that his soul is prompting modifications to his personality in the same way a tailor alters a suit. "The chalk marks are disappearing and the garment is becoming more formfitting. The soul is the purest form of me that can be."

Staci Wells's Reading for Jon

Though I refer to her as a medium, Staci Wells, like Glenna, has the ability to channel. At times her spirit guide speaks through her and she retains only a slight awareness of what was said. At other times her consciousness remains at the forefront as she repeats what he says or as she describes visual images and sensations.

As I discussed in the introduction to this book, Staci has the remarkable ability to see and hear pre-birth planning sessions. I often felt that I had been transported to another world, that I could almost reach out and touch the souls who were present. To bear witness to these conversations was a true gift from Spirit. Staci and I, and by extension all who read these words, have been given a glimpse into both another dimension and an intensely personal process. Here, souls were discussing their most intimate hopes for their own evolution and, at times, openly acknowledging the disappointments of past lives. Staci's guide could not present this information to us without the permission of the souls involved. I thank them now for their openness in making us part of such an intimate experience.

Over time it became clear that Staci's spirit guide is a highly evolved being. I was honored to collaborate with him. Because he chooses to present himself to Staci in male form, I use masculine pronouns.

"I'm seeing a pre-birth conversation between Jon and his father," Staci began. "Great love was spoken between these two individuals. I see him and his father as souls but looking a lot like the bodies they inhabit in this lifetime. His father is telling him how much he loves him. It's apparent that Jon has already decided to experience homosexuality. There is talk here about experiencing a grave illness that could even lead to death. These things have already been decided."

Though I had worked with Staci previously, I was again amazed as she repeated word for word the conversation:

Jon's father:	I will not shame you.
Jon:	I need to experience this [shaming words]. I need to hear you say this to help me find myself. The shame will strengthen my will and give me the courage I need to face my destiny.
Jon's father:	All right then, I agree to do this because I love you. [Jon's mother is at his father's side. His father reaches out and draws her close to him.] We agree to patronize you as well.
Jon's mother:	I agree to love and care for you, to cherish you throughout your life. There is a possibility I may push you away. It will be very difficult for me; however, I will accept this challenge *for you.*

"Previous lifetimes had themes of trying to become emotionally and financially independent," Staci continued. "Jon spent four lifetimes in a row being very poor, one of them in a Third World country. In his continuing quest to rise to this challenge, to construct a sense of self that is strong and supportive, he entered into an agreement with his parents and certain other individuals to beat him down psychologically so that he would be forced to find strength within himself and build his own character."

Staci had just described a classic learning-through-opposites life plan. In such a plan, the individual chooses before birth to experience the lack of what he or she most wants to understand and appreciate. Commenting on Staci's reading, Jon later told me, "I believe that I chose the exact opposite type of life I actually want [now as a personality] in order to know compassion for others." For much of his life, he said, he thought his suffering was punishment for being cruel to people in past lives. He now knows this is not the case.

"There is something else I'm picking up," said Staci. "Jon picked this time to enter into embodiment to experience a revolution in consciousness and the sexual revolution. He wanted to be alive at this time, as part of this generation, so that he could experience both.

"He also has a history in past lives of not being able to use good self-control in romantic relationships or even relationships with family. He is still working on that in this present lifetime. He planned to contract the AIDS virus through someone he should have known better than to be with and through risky behavior, both of which pertain to not using self-discipline." Jon later told me that Staci was right on target here and that "self-control and self-discipline are rather foreign to me."

"I see somebody now in Jon's pre-birth planning session who was one of his schoolteachers," said Staci. "She identifies herself as artistic. In this present lifetime as his teacher, she was working on strengthening her more aggressive characteristics in order to balance the artistic temperament. She was developing the male energy within herself and allowing it expression. Whatever she said to him [that shamed him] was through her own filter. She was the perfect person to make this agreement with. Jon had known her from other lifetimes very, very long ago, lifetimes that we would consider to be third or fourth century A.D."

Staci's words reminded me that the soul seeks balance in all things, including the expression of male and female energies. Some people I had interviewed had difficulty in previous incarnations expressing either male or female energy. They had planned a subsequent lifetime to practice that skill.

"Were there any other conversations with people who shamed Jon?" I asked Staci.

"I'm told that Jon's classmates were not soulmates in the sense of having made a soul-level agreement with him," she replied, echoing the words of her guide. "But they were impressed by their guides to say things. Their guides were working in concert with Jon's. They were given phrases, things to blurt out. I just asked if that was every time it happened, and I was told, 'Yes, that was every time, and they would likely have no recollection of this.'"

I was surprised by this information. I had not yet heard that spirit guides influence people in their speech. Nevertheless, it was consistent with other sessions in which I learned that our guides work diligently to ensure we have the experiences we planned before birth, even when those experiences are painful. Though perhaps unpleasant or difficult to comprehend when viewed from the perspective of the personality, this idea takes on an entirely different meaning when considered from the viewpoint of the soul. As souls, we know that life is a drama on the Earth stage and that we can be permanently harmed no more than an actor can be by another actor's lines.

I wondered who else in Jon's life might have agreed to shame him. "What about romantic partners?" I asked.

Staci paused as she tuned in to another part of the pre-birth planning session, a conversation between Jon and a man who had been his romantic partner earlier in this lifetime.

Man: I don't want to do this. I don't want to treat you that way.

Jon: But I want this. I want certain phrases to be said. I want a certain attitude that will motivate me. I want this.

"Jon wants to rise above these statements because these are things he had thought about himself in previous lifetimes," Staci explained.

Jon: I love you so much that I will forgive you. I will not carry it in my heart when I pass out of this lifetime. I will not blame you, and there will not be new karma made that will require us to have another relationship in another lifetime in which I work on forgiveness.

Man: To make such statements and hold such attitudes is childish. [Pauses as he considers Jon's request.] I will agree to what you ask, but there must be love between us. We must experience love.

Jon later told me, "And we did. We did experience love."

"I'm seeing a change in people," Staci continued. "This man is turning around to talk with others. I'm being taken to the agreement *he* has to get HIV from somebody. He is talking with a group of souls who are all going to be sick in this same way. They are saying that in addition to their individual lessons that will be learned from this experience, they're also agreeing to do this to teach their elders a substantive lesson in tolerance and unconditional love. This goes beyond the personal issues to something much larger in this particular soul group. I see this man turning back to Jon.

| Man: | There is an issue larger than all of the personal benefit of contracting this illness. We can teach our elders, honor them, and provide them with a valuable opportunity to experience, learn, and grow. |
| Jon: | I agree, but I also need to experience this as part of my resistance to change and to learn to use more intelligence and act wisely, romantically." |

I now realized the magnitude of what Jon's soul group had undertaken. They were working for the benefit of the masses. They intended to be of service to humanity by increasing tolerance in the world. They would bear the brunt of society's judgments so that those making the judgments could choose instead to express and know themselves as unconditional love.

Staci and her guide had provided a clear picture of how and why a soul might plan before birth to contract AIDS. But what about individuals who had developed AIDS without a pre-birth plan to do so? What role, if any, does the soul play in those instances?

"I had a friend who died of AIDS who did not come into this lifetime with that plan," Staci said in reply. "He chose it."

"Chose it at the level of the soul or the personality?" I inquired.

"On the soul level. But he chose it while in the physical body."

"So the soul wanted to pull its energy out of the incarnation?"

"Yes."

"Why?"

"My friend was feeling unloved and had felt unloved since birth. He did not want to commit suicide in the sense of doing himself in. He wanted to do it this way because it would give him a lot of love and attention during the time he was sick. His higher self [soul] agreed to what his personality felt. His personality was so filled with sadness, lack of forgiveness, and remorse. It was the simplest way for his soul to get out of this life."

"How does a soul prompt a personality to get AIDS?" I asked.

"There were already behaviors in place that led to an easy opportunity from any number of partners," Staci answered.

I still could not understand just how this would occur. "But it sounded as though the soul had control over whether the personality would get AIDS. How would the soul control that?"

"When we sleep at night, we do a lot on the soul level. This was the decision that came about when he was asleep."

"In other words the personality goes into lightbody during the night, meets with the soul, and agrees to do something when awake to contract AIDS?" The term *lightbody* is used to describe our appearance when we are in spirit. It is a literal description: our luminous bodies are made of light.

"Yes," she said.

"Staci, beyond what we've discussed with Jon, what are the main reasons why souls plan to experience a major illness in a lifetime?"

Abruptly, Staci's speech slowed and became more deliberate. For the first time in this session, she was channeling her spirit guide verbatim. It was as though he knew we had come to the end of the reading and wanted to offer his concluding remarks.

"There are many [reasons], including selflessness and selfishness," he said. "Major illnesses can be used to make major modifications within oneself and one's belief system, values, and judgments. Sometimes it is a form of karmic balancing."

"What would you like to say to people who have an illness or care about someone with an illness and are trying to understand the deeper spiritual meaning?" I asked.

"Use a great deal of love. And I would remind your readers that although it may seem burdensome to be the one who is ill or caring for the one who is ill, it is a stepping-stone to something else. It is a rung on the ladder of evolvement."

∽

Jon had formulated a brilliant life plan. Like all souls, Jon had the option to incarnate in any location at any time. He chose a place and a period of history in which the shame in society mirrored the shame in his heart. By selecting the South at a time of great racial intolerance, he designed a life that would give birth to a profound understanding—and eventually a profound healing—of shame.

The shame in the world around Jon reflected to him the shame in his personal relationships. He could not have planned much more challenging circumstances. He chose a small town in which anonymity would be impossible, thus requiring him to conceal his sexuality. He surrounded himself with members of religions who were not accepting of his true nature. He chose parents—members of his soul group—who would actively and powerfully judge him.

To these challenges he added perhaps the most shame-producing illness of our time: AIDS. Jon did not paint the canvas of his life with soothing pastels. With courage, he chose bold, vibrant, and often harsh colors to create a dramatic picture that would reawaken him to the beauty of his soul.

Jon's parents are no less beautiful than he. Reluctantly, they played the roles he requested and scripted, their sole motivation that of love. The same love drove a former romantic partner to accept an equally difficult part. Indeed, he accepted that role only on the condition that he and Jon experience love. The souls of Jon's intolerant father, judgmental mother, and shaming partner *are* love. It is for this reason that Jon's discussions with them in the pre-birth planning session focus on love, both as a motivation and as an experience. When Jon eventually reunites with them in spirit, he will thank them for roles well played.

Spirit is love. The universe is love. We are love. When we look beyond the personality to the eternal soul within, we recall who we really are. The temporary loss of that identity and its subsequent rediscovery—and the contrast between the two—give the soul a more profound self-knowing and self-appreciation. For the soul, this kind of stark contrast cannot be obtained or understood without a physical incarnation. For the personality, the rediscovery of oneself as love results in the physical and emotional healing that Jon has begun to know.

The entire soul group benefits from this experience. After this lifetime is complete, Jon will return to his soul group with a wealth of feeling-knowledge about shame, particularly how that feeling contrasts with the magnificence of the soul. Jon will share this wisdom with all in his group. It will become part of them, and together they will advance on the evolutionary spiral. The suffering Jon endures while on Earth is evanescent; he and his soul group will carry the wisdom forever.

Self-forgiveness is the touchstone of Jon's healing in this lifetime. He must forgive others for their intolerance, but the greater challenge is to forgive himself for believing what others said to and about him. When Jon learned he was HIV positive, he felt that he deserved the illness. Such was the depth of his shame. Only through his near-death experience did he realize he wanted and deserved to live. Prior to that experience, Jon had traveled far from any awareness of his inherent worth. The contrast between that darkness and the life to which he returned triggered a recollection. He was no longer defined by the harsh words of his father, the judgments of a teacher or schoolmates, or the shaming by ex-lovers. He was no longer defined by AIDS. The healing journey is one of *remembering.* Jon awakened from his brush with nonphysical life with an internal, intuitive remembrance of his immeasurable value. Only by courageously embracing darkness can we understand and fully appreciate the light.

Much of the darkness we experience on the physical plane is the result of our belief in separation. We believe that we are individuals, distinct and separate from one another and from Spirit. We believe, as the angel said, that we are our physical bodies. The persuasiveness of the illusion is necessary for physical incarnations to provide rich lessons in spiritual growth. If we did not perceive separation, life would lack the gravity it needs to be our teacher, and we would lack the motivation we need to be its pupils.

By experiencing AIDS, Jon provides all of us with an opportunity to let our true selves emerge. This gift is offered by many of those we judge most harshly. The alcoholic, the drug addict, the person with AIDS—each presents us with an opportunity to move beyond the judgments of the personality to become living expressions of tolerance and compassion. Jon and others in his soul group planned the life challenge of AIDS in part to teach those divine virtues to society. Rather than condemn, we might instead thank such individuals for being our teachers. Experiencing AIDS or any life challenge for the purpose of teaching others is a gesture of selflessness. In some instances that selflessness may balance selfishness from past lives. In all instances it is a gesture of love.

To express love when our true nature is hidden from us—by our own design—is the fundamental task of life. We meet that challenge and awaken from self-induced amnesia when we realize that the personality is a temporary cloak. Jon has pulled that cloak aside to reveal the infinitely loving, eternal soul underneath.

LIKE JON, DORIS EXPERIENCED A catastrophic illness—breast cancer. Although the illness is different, its origin and role in personal growth are not. As you will see, Doris's cancer sprang from her thoughts and feelings about herself, just as Jon's illness stemmed from his. Physical illness, therefore, reflected aspects of themselves in need of healing.

As I write Doris's story, only a few days have elapsed since a close friend told me she has breast cancer. I was stunned by this news; my friend, as far as I knew, had been in perfect health. Though her prognosis is favorable, she is currently very ill from chemotherapy. Suddenly, my desire to understand why such things happen is even greater than usual. Can I uncover something—anything—that will help my friend and others in similar circumstances? Why did my friend and Doris encounter this challenge? Did Doris, like Jon, choose before birth to experience a major illness? If so, why? If not, could Doris's pre-birth planning explain why the cancer had occurred or how Doris might grow as a result of it?

Doris's Story

"She could touch you very gently, then, like a lightning strike, backhand you enough to crack your neck."

That was how Doris described her alcoholic mother.

A pivotal incident with her mother occurred when Doris was sixteen. Inexperienced and curious, Doris and her friends had purchased a package of condoms. They had taken them to Doris's bedroom, where they had inspected and played with them. Eventually, they had put the package in Doris's bureau and had forgotten about it.

Several days later, Doris came home from school to find her mother, drunk, in her room. "She had ripped all the clothing out of my closet," Doris said. "Five of my six dresser drawers were on the floor. She was standing there very dramatically with her hand on the last drawer. She ripped it out, broke it, held up the package, and said, '*What's this, whore?*'" For weeks thereafter Doris's mother called Doris "whore" and "slut."

"I figured she's probably right," Doris said sadly. "I was still a virgin, but I went out and very clinically got rid of my virginity, feeling I didn't deserve it. After that I took to heart the idea that sex was the only thing I was worth."

Doris internalized other derogatory comments from her mother. Though she had by her own description a "Dolly Parton figure" when she was younger, Doris was not over-weight. Nevertheless, when her mother told her she was fat and unattractive, Doris believed her. Doris also recalls that as she was preparing to leave for college, her mother asked, "Do you want a breast-reduction operation before you go? You won't look so freakish."

"You never knew what she was going to do next," Doris added.

Doris remembers feeling alienated from her family not only as a result of her mother's verbal abuse but also because the family was Jewish.

"I always felt like I'd gotten on the wrong bus. The religion held no sense of belonging."

As I listened to her speak, I was mystified by her child-hood reaction. Why would a young girl feel so out of place in the only religion to which she had been exposed? Doris made no mention of Jewish beliefs or customs being forced upon her. Unexpectedly, I would soon discover the answer.

Doris was in her mid-thirties when she received her first diagnosis of breast cancer. "I went into the kitchen where my roommate was standing," she recalled. "I looked at her and said, 'I have cancer.' She dropped a glass into the sink and shattered it. Then she flew to me and held me. Neither of us could believe it.

"I knew I wasn't dying," she added matter-of-factly. I wondered how Doris could have been so sure. That, too, would soon be revealed.

Doris underwent radiation treatment and a lumpectomy. As the surgery was being performed, she traded jokes with her doctor. She asked the operating room staff to play a particular station on the radio so she could hear her favorite rock bands.

After the procedure, Doris thought cancer was behind her. It wasn't. Twelve years later she was diagnosed with cancer in both breasts.

"I still had not dealt with my feelings about myself and the whole sexuality issue," Doris observed. "I was still having very bad bouts of self-judgment. I was a successful author. I had been traveling all over. But there would always be a little voice inside me … "

Doctors told Doris that a double mastectomy would be necessary. A few days later, the full impact of the doctor's words hit her.

"I had a meltdown," Doris said frankly. "All of a sudden in my mind came the words, *'They're going to cut your breasts off.'* I panicked, and I cried."

Despite her fears about her own health, Doris tried to comfort others about theirs.

"I had the habit of sitting down [in the doctor's waiting room] next to whoever was most pissy. To one girl I said, 'Hi, what's with you?' She looked at me like I had three heads and said, 'I have cancer.' I said, 'Me, too. What flavor is yours?' Then she was less defensive, more willing to be reached out to."

After her double mastectomy, Doris felt a sense of relief. "I was so glad it was done, because I wouldn't have to worry anymore. There wouldn't be the holding my breath every time I had a mammogram.

"I was afraid to look at the 'new girls.' My husband said, 'You look like a girl, honey. It's okay.' They're much more in proportion to my frame. Taking the breasts took a pair of distorting glasses from my eyes, and I was able to see myself in a more real viewpoint. All of my mental torment was gone."

Doris's feelings about herself changed even further when she learned just how many people had been praying for her. Many sent words of love and support and told her how she had inspired them.

"There was incontrovertible proof of how much I had done, how many lives I had touched," she said joyfully. "There was no way I could deny any longer that I was a good and loving person who made a huge difference in the world.

"It took a crescendo for me. It doesn't have to for everybody."

Doris can now see other ways in which the illness brought about growth and healing. "I was very uncomfortable with feminine power. I didn't trust it, just as I didn't trust females. I never learned how to play manipulative girl games — I hate them — or love gorgeous clothes. I hate makeup. If I would go into a restroom, I wouldn't be in there fluffing and primping. But I had to turn to other women for support [when ill]. I got to really respect what we're made of."

"Doris," I asked, "what did you learn about who you are?"

"I'm one tough cookie with a wellspring of compassion for the human condition. I love being human. I intuit the human experience well, and I use it well. I'm grateful that I will be able to use this to stretch out my hand to other women and say, 'Come on, you can cross this bridge.'

"I never felt like a victim of cancer. I never felt like it was done to me. I felt like I chose it, always. I was always looking for the gift."

"Doris, what would you like to say to someone who has breast cancer?"

"When I describe my double mastectomy and reconstruction to people, I tell them that it was a great one-stop surgery. Six hours — three for the demolition work and another three for the front-end realignment. Hearing that description, most people start laughing. Find the humor. Play with it. Dance with it. There is nothing that says you have to wring every drop of misery out of this."

∾

In part I chose to speak with Doris because she is clairaudient; I hoped she would obtain information about her own pre-birth plan. What I never anticipated was the startling way in which she would use her psychic ability during our conversation. To provide a second connection to the nonphysical realm, medium Staci Wells joined us for this exploration.

I had expected Doris to relay the words she was hearing from nonphysical beings, most likely her spirit guides. I was taken aback when she immediately entered a trance and began to channel. I was even more surprised when I learned the identity of the being who was speaking.

As we began, I felt an intense surge in energy in Doris's voice. The channeled entity spoke with a tone of considerable authority. With the first words, the pattern of speech changed dramatically. Doris's personality was clearly no longer present. She had left, and in her place was a new and as yet unidentified consciousness.

Doris's Channeling

"This soul [Doris] has had a fear of its own power and—these days we will call it—a fear of success," declared the channeled being. "The combination of the two can be very difficult. This spirit has more of a challenge within a female structure than a male structure. When housed in a male body [in past lives], it was on most occasions rather graphically macho, civilized to a greater or lesser degree, but definitely believing the male is superior. As a result there has been difficult sexual karma on both sides of the equation. When in a male body, women are not respected or given equality. When in a female body, sexuality is often the first line of defense—sex as weapon, sex as bargaining chip.

"During this life, we presented opportunities to trip triggers. The physical form is exaggeratedly female. The planned situation with the mother-daughter monad was that of a mother who was very jealous of her daughter and presented a test by accusing the daughter before she had lost her virginity of being of loose morals. At that point, the door could have swung either way. This spirit could have proved the mother wrong and stayed virginal for many years. Or, as she did, she believed that her mother must know something about her that she did not. From that point in her life, she set herself up with sexuality as the bargaining chip and often the sole commodity of which she felt she had control.

"Because of that situation, her self-image was extremely toxic. This then set up the secondary test in terms of power and success. She believed that she was unable to do anything that did not have sexuality as its basis and be a success. We expressed the cancer as a focal point of what occurs when one refuses correct sexual energy.

"This personality knew that it was not to die from the first incident of cancer and therefore went through surgery and radiation with little if any fear. But the self-loathing and difficulties with self-image were not resolved. Therefore, we brought about a second bout of cancer, which caused a crisis of faith, but yet was walked through.

"When the self-loathing was then compounded with aging, while at the same time her teaching had come to fruition and she was embarking on her life's work, it was decided that the objects of derision, pain, and self-loathing were best removed so that she could continue her work unencumbered. Therefore, she received the [second] diagnosis, at which point the physician felt that removal of the breasts was the wisest course of action. The response to this has been extremely positive, and we are pleased."

In my experience with channeling, I had found that each nonphysical being had a particular energy. In this instance I felt great strength. The power of the energy was compounded by the succinct yet comprehensive explanation that had been provided. This being was aware of the larger picture and had presented it with a certain emotional detachment; yet, there was also caring in the voice. One thing was clear: Doris's body had reacted to her feelings about herself. Our cells hear our thoughts, and they respond to them.

Had my interview with Doris been one of the first in my research, I may have thought Doris had been punished with breast cancer for believing her mother or for refusing "correct sexual energy." Instead, I knew this was not the case.

What may feel like punishment from the perspective of the personality is an opportunity for growth from the viewpoint of the soul. As the angel in Jon's story said in regard to Jon's feelings of shame, illness serves "to shine light on where healing is needed." Given the personal growth Doris had described, it seemed that her body, like Jon's, had acted as a springboard to heightened self-awareness.

The use of *test* by the channeled being suggested that much of the experience had been planned, although I did not yet have any indication why. But before pursuing that line of inquiry, I wanted to find out who was speaking.

"You've used the word *we* several times," I said. "Who is 'we'?"

"We are an oversoul. We encompass all personalities. The personalities do not die. They are a part of the great chorus. We leaf through them together with our guides as we plan the life as a painting in three dimensions, a collage."

Because I knew that the soul contains all personalities from all incarnations, I understood that *oversoul* was being used as a synonym for *soul.* I was shocked by this announcement; never had I imagined that Doris would channel her soul. Doris was therefore providing an extraordinary opportunity to talk directly with a soul about the plan for an incarnation. And now that I knew who was speaking, I focused on the meaning of Doris's breast cancer.

"Am I correct in understanding that the lessons Doris could have learned to prevent the breast cancer are self-love and correct use of sexual energy?"

"That is correct. And also the element of accepting the female form without judgment."

"What things were planned into her life that could have taught those three lessons and prevented the cancer?"

"The key incident was the episode with her alcoholic mother at the age of sixteen. At that point karma was neutral. But when she accepted her mother's definition of her as a whore and worth nothing further, then she walked onto the more known path. She did not attempt to see if her mother would have been incorrect."

"Was that incident something that was planned with the mother's soul prior to birth?"

"Yes."

Doris's soul had just confirmed something I had seen many times, including Jon's story: those who most challenge us do so at our behest. These roles are agreed upon before birth, with the souls who play "tormentor" doing so out of love and often deferring their own learning until another lifetime so we may have the growth experiences we seek.

"When this lifetime was being planned, why did you choose those three lessons to work on?" I inquired.

"This soul has many good qualities as a teacher, as a leader. But as we explained, when this soul is in a male incarnation, sexuality is often used to dismiss those with whom it is not at parity. The lack of self-love is a more minor threat that when in the male incarnation does not often come up for discussion. We wish to ensure that karmic threads are completed within the next three to four lifetimes. Therefore, this life was packed rather full."

"You said that you brought about the episodes of breast cancer. How did you do that?"

"Certain parameters were set in motion. Think of a lever in an elaborate mechanical piece. We set a balance piece on that lever which could either be held in place by positive thought and acceptance or dislodged through toxic thought and feelings. The toxic thought and feeling changed the biochemistry and awoke the possibility of the cancer."

"Was there a genetic predisposition toward breast cancer that was triggered by the thought patterns?"

"Yes, but if you look at the hereditary background of both parents, there is no incidence of breast cancer previous to this point. However, mutation is possible."

"When you set up that plan, it seems to me you were taking a risk because Doris could have responded negatively to the breast cancer. She could have become angry or embittered."

"There is no pass or fail with life. It is simply choosing your lesson. We would have accepted all possibilities. None would have been incorrect."

Here, Doris's soul conveyed a perspective I was to hear many times. From the viewpoint of the soul, no event or course of action is "bad." All is simply experience, and every experience teaches and offers seeds of growth.

"When you plan a life, you are shown the most probable path, correct?"

"Yes. We are shown, let us say, the major artery on the freeway. Exits are also pointed out, [minor] arteries and detours. All are a part of the road. One does not have to drive every inch of asphalt."

"Were you also shown scenes from lives in which Doris responded less positively than she actually has in this lifetime?"

"Yes," said Doris's soul. "That is why there is no risk. What does not happen in one dimension will happen in others, if necessary."

"The other dimensions...are those physical dimensions?"

"They are real dimensions. Can you touch them? Probably not. They are not dreams unless this is a dream. They are as real as this, though *physical* makes it a limited statement."

"Are there other dimensions for every decision that a person makes? Because that would be an infinite number."

"Do you feel that the universe is not big enough to hold these?"

"I believe it's big enough," I said. "But how do you as a soul experience an infinite number of choices and an infinite number of dimensions?"

"We do not see ourselves as limited. Therefore, there is room for all of it. When you are not in [linear] time, there is no need to rush. There is no time for all of it."

The soul's use of *no time* was an intentional way of pointing out that time is an aspect of our physical dimension. It is an illusion, a means of instruction, a way to have certain experiences that are not possible without its perception.

The comment that souls do not see themselves as limited is of great significance. Thought is literally creative, both in the nonphysical realm, where it manifests instantly, and on the physical plane, where thoughts become physical reality if they are of sufficient frequency and strength over time. Belief—specifically, the belief that one is not limited—empowers thought. The combination of focused thought and a belief in oneself as unlimited is potent enough to move mountains.

I wondered about the relationship among the dimensions in which Doris's soul was active in an unlimited way. "Is the Doris in this dimension influenced by the other Dorises that made different choices in different dimensions?" I asked.

"That is possible, yes."

"How would that happen?"

"It depends most on the enlightenment. If one is locked down tightly into this dimension, it is, if you will, like trying to touch a person through several layers of winter coat. When one is more aware of one's interdimensional possibilities, it is easier to touch and therefore understand other possibilities."

"Can you give an example of how this Doris has been influenced by another Doris in another dimension who made a different decision?"

"When she was first diagnosed, without reason there was a knowledge that she would not die. This is because there might have been a touch from the universe where indeed the cancer had been more serious and there was death. We do not seek to repeat. Therefore, there was the inner knowledge that on this plane, death from this cancer was not planned."

"You've mentioned the three lessons for Doris to learn: correct use of sexual energy, acceptance of the female form, and self-love. Can you explain how the cancer experience has helped Doris to learn these things?"

"Doris has through this cancer found that sexuality is now a minor 'talent' when one must concentrate on healing. Brought to the fore are creativity, courage, resolution, acceptance of opportunity, faith in others. When the mind and heart are full of these things, sexuality as weapon and tool tends to be shoved aside and forgotten.

"The acceptance of the female form. Doris has now realized that there is a saying 'form follows function,' that form is not simply to convey her gender and sexuality, that secondary characteristics do not make her more or less of a female or more or less desired. Therefore, the emotional charge with the body has been disengaged.

"As she has worked through her cancer and inspired others, the seeing of herself by others who gained from her courage and kindness allows her to understand that there is much about the self to love."

"You said earlier that you want to resolve all karma in the next three or four lifetimes. What happens after that?" I asked.

"She will be very busy. There is much teaching that this soul fragment has asked to do."

"Will this teaching be on a nonphysical dimension?"

"No, we are speaking of the physical dimension. Just as it is easier to study in a clean and orderly environment, when one is not distracted by one's own karmic assignments one can teach more fully. Eventually, this soul will take its place as a spirit guide. But there is still much to learn and savor on the human plane."

"Is it true in general that the personality can learn certain lessons in perhaps less painful ways, and if the lessons are not learned, the challenges become greater?"

"This is a common usage, though we would point out it is not the sole usage. There are advanced souls who are willing to come down with great challenges, though they do not require them karmically. But they are willing to be the impetus, the linchpin, the trip trigger for others who, viewing their own karmic difficulties, will then respond for their own lesson."

"This puts me in a difficult position as the writer of this book," I said. "I'm not sure that telling people they may have developed cancer or faced some other challenge because they didn't learn lessons earlier is a particularly helpful thing to say. On the other hand, if that's how things work, I need to say it."

"Not learning a lesson is not failure," declared Doris's soul. "Think of it more as choosing to learn it on a different path. Anything can be judged, and anything can be seen from a non-judgmental and compassionate level."

"Could I offer input here?" asked Staci, who had been listening quietly thus far.

"We are pleased," replied Doris's soul.

"It [life lessons] is something that a soul chooses before entering this life, along with choosing the possible outcomes. Isn't the soul presented with ramifications of choices during the planning session before being born?"

"That is correct," confirmed Doris's soul. "There is no fear of failure during the planning stages, because there is no separation. Humans, because they believe in separation—us versus them, right versus wrong—feel that to not go in one direction means the other direction has to be lesser, that difficulties are given because one has flunked the exam. We say that a soul who has chosen this [other direction] is one of great strength, maturity, and courage."

"It seems to me," I observed, "that the soul is often teaching the personality—which is part of the soul—something the soul already knows. For example, we've talked about one of Doris's lessons being self-love. My concept of a soul is that a soul *is* love. It's as though you're teaching yourself something you already know. Can you help me to understand that?"

"Yes," said Doris's soul. "The soul knows that all is one but casts itself from that [knowledge] so that it may feel separation and learn to come Home. Also, the lessons that the personality brings back to the soul are incorporated to understanding the greater human experience. While souls know that they are love and that they are loved, to learn the fullness of it we experience the lack of love, so that we may understand self-love from all facets and all directions."

Those words reminded me of the angel in Jon's story, who said that for the same reason Jon had wanted to experience a lack of love. It seemed that both Jon and Doris had designed learning-through-opposites life plans.

"What happens after Doris's life is over?" I asked. "Is it correct to say that her energy will be reunited with you, and yet at the same time she will retain her individuality?" Based upon other conversations with Spirit, this was my understanding.

"Yes. Certain aspects of the personality do dissolve upon transition, but the closer one comes [while in body] to one's true soul, the more easily the personality is retained."

"Then is it ever correct to say that one person was another person in a previous life?"

"There are fragments of the soul which move from one personality to another. For instance, in this [Doris's] body, there is a substantial fragment of that soul spark which was placed in the body of a male German soldier ninety years ago."

I inquired about a new subject. I knew from my research that souls can have more than one incarnation on Earth simultaneously. "How many physical incarnations do you have at this time?"

"On this plane, there are two."

This revelation made me wonder how many lives her soul was living on nonphysical dimensions. "How many are on other planes?" I asked.

"An infinite number. They are born and die, grow and fade, as nexus points are reached."

"How much of your time, if I may use that word, is devoted to overseeing the two personalities on Earth and guiding them?"

"There is always contact. The thread is always there with love and compassion, but the personality is there to better its own information and bring it back."

"What other activities are you engaged in?"

"We, too, serve as guides and mentors for others, and we seek our own melding with the Absolute. There are many experiences for which a human would have no words or comprehension."

"Is your growth dependant upon how well the physical personalities learn their life lessons?"

"It is not a matter of how well they learn them. It is simply a matter of what they bring back. The more information they can bring back, then the—it is not quite right, but we will say—more rapidly we complete that which we seek."

"Am I correct in understanding that when you were planning the lifetime for Doris, you could have chosen any time period and any geographic location?"

"Time is a web, not a line. That is correct."

"How and why did you choose the United States at this time?"

"It was coordination with other souls. Because that was a part of our planning that had flexibility, we agreed with the United States. With the teaching aspect of what this soul is being asked to do, the United States is a logical choice, having more freedom and a greater physical sphere of influence than many other countries. This soul tends to be placed in countries that are at the forefront of a given period. For instance, the German officer was part of the end of the German empire. An English knight was a player at the time of the War of the Roses, which changed dynastic lines. There are other lives which are less at the forefront. The one immediately before this one was a relatively innocuous life in the United States in Chicago. When the soul is meant to play a larger role, it is to our and its advantage to place itself where there is the highest degree of world attention."

"But you could have selected Atlantis, ancient Egypt, or the United States in the year 3000."

"Yes."

"Could you also have selected a different physical planet?"

"Yes, but we are finding that this soul works extremely well in the bipedal human form, and therefore Earth is a favorite school building."

Staci interjected. "I had glimpses of the lifetime in Germany. This experience with breast cancer has also served to help the personality essence from that lifetime dispel guilt."

"This is correct," replied Doris's soul. "There are two lessons from that lifetime which are directly addressed in this life. The first is a strong streak of anti-Semitism, which is why the personality [Doris] was based in a Jewish family and yet never felt as if this was a correct placement. Upon reaching an understanding, the life in Germany—that karmic knot—was undone.

"This was also a life where as a male there was a great difficulty with intimacy with women. There were three women of import in the life of the German soldier. The first being a girl [he met] in his early twenties of whom he was very fond and had hopes, but his hopes were very cruelly dashed. There was a second, physical-release situation when this personality was an engineer in Africa, and there was an enormous amount of guilt and self-loathing for crossing the racial barrier. The third incident was with a girl to whom he was engaged a month before he was killed. Interestingly, if you put a picture of the fiancée next to this personality's [Doris's] maternal incarnation, you will find that the fiancée and the mother look extremely alike."

"Wasn't that personality in Germany a part of the war effort? A pilot?" Staci asked.

"Yes," said Doris's soul.

Staci explained, "The breast cancer goes back to alleviating guilt from taking the lives of innocents. It was repressed by the personality while it was alive, although the feelings were there. It was only after crossing over into death that the personality was not forgiving of itself to the extent where it could release all emotional burden."

"This is correct," confirmed Doris's soul.

Staci's insights had provided the last pieces of the puzzle. Feeling we had now arrived at a full understanding of why Doris had gone through such a difficult experience, I asked one more question.

"What would you say to someone who has just been diagnosed with breast cancer, does not see a deeper spiritual meaning, and is wondering, 'Why would God do something like this to me?'"

"All is choice. All is perception. This is not to say that the personality has no right to feel fear or grief, but all that is given, even the most difficult, has within it profound seeds of understanding and beauty. The experience of breast cancer may heighten the senses, may bring people into the life that would not have been there had they remained healthy, may perhaps awaken talent and strength they did not know they had. If one sees cancer as a cruelty, then one cannot overcome. One is already defeated. If one can look at the cancer in a neutral fashion the way one can look at fire positively or negatively or neutrally, one is better equipped to hear the lesson that is being articulated.

"Illness is dis-ease. It is a final manifestation of emotional or mental difficulties. It is simply another layer of learning.

"There is no fault involved. This is no punishment. This is no sign of lack of love on the part of God, your guide, or your angels. This is part of the human existence, as are the need for sleep, hot, and cold. As humanity learns to express itself on a higher vibrational level, illness will no longer serve a purpose and therefore will diminish."

"Thank you for talking with us today."

"Thank you for allowing us to teach in another venue. You are complete. We are complete."

Doris's Pre-birth Planning Session

Following the conversation with Doris's soul, I asked Staci to access Doris's pre-birth planning session.

"I am in a room with many souls," Staci began. "The ones I am focusing on are Doris and her mother. The soul of the mother is agreeing to make a sacrifice. She is really quite a loving and generous soul, but is agreeing to play a part that has been scripted for her [by Doris's soul]. There are certain aspects of the personality of the mother that are there for the mother's own growth, but there is some conversation about how the mother's soul will soften parts of herself and harden other parts to help Doris accomplish what she needs. I keep hearing the word *sacrifice*, as if she's putting off some of her major goals for one additional lifetime.

"The odds of developing the cancer were presented to Doris as a byproduct of certain choices she might make in dealing with certain karmic issues. It was laid out to her both by being talked about and on a board. I see Doris looking down at the floor. I see her three spirit guides around her. On the floor, I see the board. It is a diagram of a path to be taken and turns that can be made along the path. It demonstrates what choices cause what consequences.

"I see Doris shaking her head yes, that she has a greater understanding of the concept they are presenting. I see her actually agreeing to handle the breast cancer should it come up and agreeing also that it will serve as a wake-up call.

"I am told that Doris comes from a group of teachers. That is her primary purpose in how she wants to be of service to others."

∼

Like Jon's illness, Doris's breast cancer resulted from her thoughts about herself, thoughts that were triggered by an event she had planned before she was born. Like waves crashing upon a shore, our thoughts wash powerfully over our bodies. And as the tides shift each grain of sand, so do our thoughts swirl in and around each cell, impressing upon them the energy they carry. Though it may seem that our thoughts occur in response to physical reality, in truth they create it. In the human form, each cell is an individual consciousness that responds to the voice of the mind. That voice echoes through our bodies like a cry in a mountain canyon, and our cells heed the call.

When we plan our lives, we are aware of the power of thought to affect the bodies we will inhabit. We know, too, that our responses to our planned challenges may take the form of thoughts that generate illness. For this reason both Doris and her mother displayed great courage in planning their lives. Doris sought to heal her unresolved energy of loathing for both females and the female form, and her mother sought to make that healing possible. From the perspective of the soul, her mother's harsh words were said in love because they mirrored to Doris aspects of self in need of healing. Prior to birth Doris knew those words would be painful to hear. She also knew that her reaction to them could lead to breast cancer. Her bravery and desire to heal herself were so great that she selected this life plan, not in spite of these challenges but because of them.

There are many types of hurtful words and ways in which one person can shame another. Given what Doris sought to heal, it is not coincidental that she chose a "Dolly Parton body," that her mother commented repeatedly on her weight and breast size, or that the pivotal incident at age sixteen entailed shaming with the words *whore* and *slut*. Doris's life blueprint is a specific form of challenge to self-love. Her mother's judgments of her character and appearance were designed to show Doris the specific judgments she held of women in her past lives. As Doris's soul said, women were not respected or viewed as equals in those lifetimes. The energy of those judgments could have been released and healed by choosing self-love in the face of her mother's condemnations. When Doris chose instead to internalize her mother's words, the trip trigger — the planned potential for breast cancer — was activated. Just as there are many forms of verbal wounding, there are also many forms of cancer. The development of breast cancer was no more coincidental than any other part of Doris's life.

As Doris's soul told us, her cancer is neither a failure nor a punishment. From the perspective of the personality, suffering is bad, and learning quickly is better than learning slowly. For the soul there is no "badness" in any experience, and the time it takes to learn something like self-love is of no importance. The soul is always aware of its eternal nature, and it operates in dimensions in which there is no linear time. Consequently, the soul cares about growth, not the time required for growth.

The duality we see in the world — right/wrong, good/ bad — sits in marked contrast to the neutrality of the soul.

Although the personality tends to judge everything that flows by on the river of life, the soul sits quietly and contemplatively on the riverbank, observing with detached compassion and nonjudgment. A profound inner peace results when we remember this neutrality. In large part the purpose of this book is to facilitate a shift from personality-consciousness to soul-consciousness. To make this shift is to cultivate a protective detachment from potentially hurtful life events. This detachment does not eliminate such events, but it can reduce the suffering they engender. To the personality, judgment is the natural consequence of suffering. To the soul, suffering is the natural consequence of judgment. When we awaken and recall that we are immortal souls who cannot be harmed, we release our judgments of life challenges. In their place we embrace a neutrality that reduces suffering and magnifies joy.

As we expand our self-concept from personality to soul, we grant ourselves a more accurate self-understanding. We also shift our focus from the pain caused by life challenges to the wisdom and growth they offer. When we saw pointlessness, now we see purpose. When we saw a punishment, now we see a gift. When we saw burden, now we see opportunity. Never again the victims of life, we become the recipients of its many blessings.

In Jon's story the angel told us that AIDS is healing humanity. Similarly, from the soul perspective Doris's cancer is a form of healing, not illness. As Jon and Doris release shame and self-loathing and choose instead to love themselves, they make it easier for every person on Earth to replace self-judgment with self-love. That is, they create a vibration or resonance of love that radiates well beyond their immediate sphere. It is said that the flutter of a butterfly's wings can cause gale-force winds on the other side of the globe. In the same way, Jon's and Doris's decisions to love themselves have far-reaching energetic effects. As we shift from the perspective of the personality to that of the soul, we recall a truth we knew before we were born — that our actions, words, and thoughts impinge upon the entire world. By surmounting the challenges we planned before birth, we create a resonance that heals humanity.

When we plan our lives, we choose to "work" with other souls whom we love very much and who love us. Like Jon's parents, Doris's mother knew before birth there would be painful conflict with her child. Only a soul who truly loved Doris and was committed to Doris's evolution would agree to bear the brunt of her anger. In this way our greatest tormentors are often those with whom we share the most love when in spirit. When this lifetime is complete, Doris will thank her mother for the growth she fostered, and Doris's mother will thank her for the opportunity to have been of service. Gratitude toward those who have most challenged us — and thus most stimulated our evolution — is a soul-level perspective we can adopt while still in body. When we make that choice, we remove blame from our lives. Without blame forgiveness becomes possible, and with forgiveness comes healing.

As Staci pointed out, Doris's mother agreed to defer some of her growth to help Doris. It is common for souls to put their learning aside to be of service to others. From the level of the personality, it is difficult to imagine that some of those who "mistreat" us are actually engaged in a form of service. It may be even more difficult to see that the so-called mistreatment entails sacrifice on their part. These concepts, which are so familiar to us before birth, are forgotten when we incarnate. To remember them is to know self more profoundly and in ways that are not possible without a physical incarnation.

Doris has made the most of the challenges. She wanted to learn self-love. She did so by internalizing the enormous outpouring of love from family and friends who reached out during her illnesses. She wanted to respect women in a way she had not in previous lifetimes. By experiencing a form of cancer that is almost uniquely female, Doris was forced to rely on other women for emotional support. She saw their strength and respected them for it. She wanted to experience sexuality in a more loving way. The need to heal the cancer brought out personal talents like creativity and courage. When focused on them, Doris no longer had a need or desire to use sexual energy as she once had. When she returns to spirit, she will rejoice in the beauty of this lifetime. The suffering will seem but an instant in "time"; the wisdom will be hers forever. When she eventually takes her place as a spirit guide, the people she guides will be the beneficiaries of it. You or I might be among those people.

Little in life is what it appears to be, and much is the opposite. In Jon's and Doris's stories, we have seen that illness is healing. By the same token, feelings of powerlessness, which often result in the face of serious illness, are actually the byproduct of a life designed by an enormously powerful being. Our power to plan our lives and create the growth experiences we seek is immense. That power extends to planning lives that include physical illness. As souls, we are aware of this reality. As humans, we lose sight of it—by design—until illness and other life challenges call us into remembrance. We then recall that only the most powerful of creators could conjure a world in which we appear to be powerless, one rich with wondrous opportunities to rediscover ourselves and thus reclaim our power.

CHAPTER 3

⟨∾⟩

Parenting Handicapped Children

HAVING A HANDICAPPED CHILD IS one of the most heartbreaking challenges one can face. Beyond the desire for their children to be happy and healthy, parents naturally want them to have better lives than they themselves had. When a child is born with or later develops a handicap, there is often anger at the universe. Why, we wonder, would this happen to an innocent child? Parents who give birth to a handicapped child may also blame the partner or themselves for "faulty" genes. Their anguish is profound.

When I decided to research this life challenge from the perspective of the parent, new questions arose. If some souls planned to be handicapped from birth, presumably they would coordinate their life blueprints with their parents'. Do souls, then, actually agree to be the parents of handicapped children? If they do make such plans, do they *desire* the experience or is it more of an acquiescence to another soul's planning? If the former, what does the experience offer that will make such suffering worthwhile from the perspective of the soul?

Jennifer Stewart's Story

"I know that I was chosen for my benefit and their benefit," Jennifer said about being the mother of three children, two of whom are handicapped. She spoke with utter conviction.

"My son, Ryan, is sixteen. He has Asperger's Syndrome. That's a new name for what really is high-functioning autism. He also has bipolar disorder and ADD [Attention Deficit Disorder]. The bipolar, which did not manifest until he was a teenager, involves violent mood swings ranging from 'I'm happy, everything's wonderful' to 'I'm in the depths of Hell' as far as depression or raging anger.

"My younger son, Bradley, is eleven. He has much more severe, straight autism, and he is legally blind. He has a very rare condition with his eyes, ocular albinism, which is like being an albino except just in his eyes."

Jennifer has been divorced for seven years and is raising the boys on her own. She explained that children with Asperger's are often called "little professors" because they fixate on one or two special interests. With Ryan it's weather and politics. He adores his weather radio and corresponds daily by e-mail with a local TV weatherman. He also e-mails politicians regularly, giving them suggestions.

"I show him all the positive things," Jennifer told me. "I say, 'You have abilities nobody else has.' If you ask most people when's the last time you had your eyes examined, they may say, 'I think it was last year.' My son could say, 'It was May 24th [of last year].' He's got that ability with dates," she said proudly.

Like others with Asperger's, Ryan sometimes speaks in a monotone and avoids eye contact. As a result, other kids shun him. Recently, Jennifer took Ryan to see his therapist.

"She asked if he had any friends. He said no. She asked if he had ever had any friends. He said no. That broke my heart," Jennifer said quietly.

Jennifer's son Bradley has a vocabulary of about twenty words. Until recently conversation was limited to yes or no questions. Bradley also communicates through sign language. Two years elapsed between the time Jennifer learned that Bradley was blind and the moment when he was diagnosed as autistic. "God gave us time to digest one thing before the next," Jennifer said. "I was always grateful for that."

When he was younger, Bradley threw violent temper tantrums, often banging his head against objects. He became particularly distraught when something unexpected occurred. If Jennifer went grocery shopping with Bradley, he had a tantrum if she returned to a previous aisle. The only way to prevent an outburst was to continue forward through every remaining aisle, then go back through each one in reverse order. Jennifer also found that she could not purchase gas with Bradley in the car. If she turned the ignition off, he thought they were getting out of the car. If they didn't, a tantrum ensued.

Like his brother, Bradley has an unusual ability. "Music is his talent," Jennifer said. "It's amazing. He can hear a song once or twice—"Twinkle, Twinkle, Little Star" or the Mickey Mouse Club song—and play it on a keyboard."

Jennifer told me that when she was first coming to terms with her boys' handicaps, she was afraid to cry.

"Why?" I asked.

"I thought, If I cry, I'll never stop."

"Jennifer, did you ever ask God why?"

"No, I never did because I knew there was a reason. Somehow, deep down somewhere, I must have known something about the autism. I took psychology in high school. They showed black-and-white films about autism. I was fascinated. Then I took psychology again in college and wrote a paper about autism. When I heard there was going to be a movie [*Rain Man*] about it, I couldn't wait. This was way before Bradley. Somehow, subconsciously, my soul was preparing me for it. I knew. Of all the things to be strangely interested in … "

"You mentioned you were chosen partly for your own benefit. What is the benefit to you?"

"Patience. I had to learn so much more patience. And I would not have met the fantastic parents I have met. The support group online. There are people, places, things I never would've gotten to know."

"What have you learned about yourself?"

"I always knew I was a strong person, but it just reaffirms that, 'Gee, Jennifer, you must be one tough cookie.' Not only do I function, but I'm completely at peace. When my father, who is a worrier, will say, 'What's going to happen with Bradley or Ryan when you're dead?' I say, 'Dad, all we have is today.' The things people worry about usually don't happen."

I asked Jennifer to talk about her third child, Sarah, who is twenty-three. She told me that Sarah and Bradley look very much alike and that both have blond hair, even though no one else in the family is blond. They were also born on the same day. That "coincidence," which had no meaning for me at the time, would later prove to be significant in Jennifer's session with the medium.

"Sarah has always been crazy about them [Bradley and Ryan]," Jennifer said. "I tried to give each child attention, but it is difficult. Children that are 'normal' sometimes get the short end of the attention stick. I've asked her. She says, 'No, I never felt resentful. I always knew they needed your attention.'" As Jennifer and I would soon discover, Sarah's pre-birth planning explains her remarkably positive attitude.

Jennifer feels the attention she has shown her sons has made all the difference in the way they respond to their challenges. Bradley, for example, enjoyed a major break-through one year ago.

"He finally got his DynaVox, this talking device that's programmed," Jennifer said excitedly. "He tapped me on the shoulder as I was driving. He pushed the button that said 'fish.' Then he pushed the button for 'feed.' I thought, *Oh my God, are we having a conversation?* I asked if he wanted to feed our fish tonight. He said yes. I was like a kid in a candy store! I asked him all kinds of questions. 'What would you like for dinner tonight?' He pushed 'pizza.' We actually had a whole conversation! It was the first time."

Jennifer's Session with Corbie Mitleid

Prior to the session with medium Corbie Mitleid, I felt reasonably certain that Jennifer had planned her experience. I suspected that one or more of Jennifer's previous incarnations accounted for her apparently strong desire to be the parent of handicapped children. Had she not sought such an experience, she probably would not have *two* handicapped sons, and each probably would not have multiple physical challenges. Jennifer's early and at the time inexplicable interest in autism also hinted strongly at planning on the soul level.

Corbie began the session with her customary prayer. "Mother/Father/God, thank you for this profound opportunity for service today. Surround us with Your unconditional white light of love, protection, compassion, wisdom, and truth. Let only truth be spoken. Let only truth be heard. Let me be a clear mirror to bring Jennifer, Rob, Bradley, and Ryan the information they seek today. And may I remain always head, hand, and heart completely in Your service. In the name of the Christ this is done. Amen."

With those words Corbie had requested from Spirit the guidance we would need. She had also established our intent. On a spiritual level, intent is of great significance because it directs the flow of energy. By asking to be a "clear mirror," Corbie had in effect requested that the filter of her mind be minimized. Her intent was not to let personal inclinations color the information she would receive.

"Jennifer," Corbie began, "Spirit is showing me the 1930s. It's a newspaper office of people scurrying back and forth, papers in their hands, clackety-clack of typewriters. You are one of the people at the desk, one of the reporters. You were doing a story people did not want to hear. Primarily, you were receiving information about the Final Solution. There was frustration on your part. You were banging on every door, sitting in hallways for hours waiting for meetings that always got put off. But you knew that these people [Jews] had no voice and that you had to be the voice. You were banging on the American public, on Congress, on everything that you could to get people to finally realize what was happening. You were not Jewish. You could have ignored this and done well simply doing the society page, but you had a profound fear of being shoved away or not heard. So this was something you did for the entire world.

"You had connections in Europe. You were told about the camps being built, the disappearances, and what the Jews were really being put through, which the American public at that point wanted to stay blissfully unaware of. You shuttled between New York and Washington, D.C. quite often. Your offices were in New York. You were with one of the smaller, more independent, more feisty newspapers.

"You did what you could to get people in Washington to see what was happening, to offer some aid, raise our quotas for immigration, anything. But you were patted on the head and told, 'Yes, I'm sure. Europe's been around a long time. They can take it,' pretty much keeping you at arm's length. Nobody wanted to get involved. Nobody really believed that World War II was going to occur. Not yet.

"The sense I'm getting is that the children were in Europe. Your boys were on the opposite side of the fence—Nazis.

"The lesson for all of you is communication. You had spent your life trying to communicate to others that this kind of desecration of the soul needed to be stopped. At that time your sons, who were also brothers, spent their time working propaganda.

"Oh boy!" exclaimed Jennifer. "That's amazing, because my older son has lived and breathed politics since he was a little child!" Jennifer was confirming something I had seen frequently in my research—that souls often carry certain interests into multiple lifetimes.

"The reason Ryan and Bradley chose to come back communicatively disabled—or coming through a 'cracked megaphone'—is to learn what it is like to have the truth and be unable to communicate it, since before they had the truth and deliberately buried it," Corbie explained.

With these words, Corbie had provided us with a glimpse into the motivation of Ryan and Bradley's souls. At the end of each physical incarnation, the soul has a life review. There, Ryan and Bradley would have seen that they had distorted truth on behalf of the Nazi war machine. They had therefore planned subsequent lives in which they could learn the value of truthful communication. They had sought their handicaps to foster their spiritual evolution.

"You again [in this lifetime] have the truth and are doing what you can to bring it forward," Corbie told Jennifer. "You have agreed to walk them through their challenge in a sense just to show how big your soul is. You are further along the road than they are in terms of soul age. They're still young souls. You're at a mature stage. When you are a mature soul, it is the emotions, the understanding of personality, and who you are that are important as opposed to worldly power."

Souls of vastly different ages incarnate on Earth. As a general rule, younger souls design incarnations in which they explore third-dimensional subjects like power or survival. Older souls, by contrast, in the physical world tend to be less interested in conquest and more interested in emotions. They know intuitively that growth occurs through emotion. (Although it is beyond the scope of this book, I would refer interested readers to the Michael System. "Michael" is the name given to a consciousness that is channeled by a number of people around the world, a consciousness that discusses life blueprints in the context of soul age.)

"Is there anything regarding my daughter, Sarah?" Jennifer inquired. "I ask because she and Bradley were born on the same day and they've always had this connection."

"I will share what I immediately saw," Corbie answered. "My [deceased] father stepped into the picture and waved. I know exactly what that means. My father and I share a birthday. I was his thirty-fourth birthday present. He is pointing to the phone, pointing to you, and nodding. Sarah and Bradley have been around together a lot of lives, but generally as best friends. Bradley knew he would need a friend as a sister this time, so she agreed.

"Very often, when we have a soul that has partnered [with us] up and down the line and that knows us that well—like a soulmate, because soulmates are the core team, not just the one person you fall in love with and marry—they will choose to do relationships like parent-child, siblings, husband-wife, teacher-student. In this case, Bradley needed someone he could depend on to speak for him if he got too frustrated, and she will do that. When he can't say something, she has a good intuitive sense of what it is he wants." Now I understood what Corbie's father had meant: Sarah serves as Bradley's "phone line" to the world.

"Corbie," I asked, "how is Jennifer's soul growing as a result of helping the boys learn to communicate?"

"Jennifer's soul is going into what I call teaching mode," Corbie replied. "When you are a mature soul—especially if you are going to flip to old [soul], go up that level—you can't leave 'school' without passing the baton. What she is learning at this point is how to teach another soul."

Corbie's point echoed my own understanding: a soul in its last incarnation on Earth will design a life in which it passes its accumulated wisdom and knowledge to others, and doing so is, in fact, a requirement for graduation from Earth school.

"Let me explain souls," Corbie continued. "You have fingers. You have a palm. You have arms. Our incarnations are like fingers. They dip down from the main part of our soul and come back up at the end of a particular life. They all connect back into that palm, which is the soul, the completeness of us, which then connects back into God, the arm.

"Jennifer's palm part is reaching down inside this incarnation to teach Bradley and Ryan, who are working on their own personal growth. When much of our personal karma is completed, then we as souls are willing to come to help others."

Seen in this light, Jennifer's experience as the parent of two handicapped children could not be misinterpreted as a punishment for her. Given what we had been told about her sons' role in the war, however, it would be possible to misinterpret their handicaps as punishments for them. I knew, though, that souls view karma as an opportunity to balance energy, not as a punishment.

"Corbie, one could infer that Bradley and Ryan's handicaps in this lifetime are a punishment for having been Nazis. Can you speak to that?"

"Just because someone was a Nazi doesn't mean their souls are black and therefore they deserve to be punished. They chose to do that to learn. It's a matter of balance and consequence. If you have a thousand dollars and you choose to spend that thousand dollars on things other than rent and bills, the consequence may be that you're delinquent on your bills and you lose the apartment. Are you being punished? No. It's neutral. Cause and effect. People have to get the idea of punishment out of their heads. Your soul chooses all kinds of things to taste. In one case it's power. In another, it's riches. You can have a lot of money and use it wisely. Or, you can have a lot of money and be greedy about it. It's going to torque people a bit, but neither one is good or bad in terms of how you learn. It's just another chapter in the textbook."

Corbie's explanation confirmed what I had learned: karma is an impersonal law of the universe that serves to maintain order. Without karma chaos would reign. On

Earth conditions often *appear* chaotic because we cannot see the karmic balancing that occurs over multiple lifetimes. Behind the scenes an elegant and perfect balancing is taking place. As souls grow in wisdom over many incarnations, they realize that negative actions, words, and thoughts have effects that must eventually be balanced, and they choose to live in ways that do not accrue additional karma.

"Corbie," I said, "the boys are learning lessons about communication. Why did Ryan choose Asperger's, bipolar disorder, and ADD to learn those lessons? Why did Bradley choose severe autism and blindness?"

"What if somebody chooses an honors Shakespeare course freshman year at school, and somebody else chooses Freshmen Writing 101?" Corbie replied. "You can take the accelerated immersion course, or you can take it two nights a week plus a lab. You're going to learn it either way. The intensity is your choice."

"Even though Bradley has much more severe autism and the blindness," Jennifer interjected, "he is a very, very happy kid. Ryan, believe it or not, even though he's very high functioning, has had a much harder time. Bradley's handicaps are more severe, but his life is easier than Ryan's."

"We'll continue with the college and the lesson thing," said Corbie. "When you choose the course you're going to give yourself down here, you also choose your textbooks. The textbooks may all be valid but have different points of view.

"Bradley wanted to be locked into what he had [severe disabilities] in order to make sure he learned. His is the immersion course, if you will. Ryan is more like the kid in independent study. He knows what he has to do, but he's got less structure in how he has to do it. They will both come out of this life with some hugely valuable lessons.

"This is not the first time Ryan's been in politics. Ryan is a leader. It's his natural bent. There are some lives where he can't lead. Also, we have male and female lives. Ryan's female/male energy is a little stronger female to male. Those lives [as a male] are always tougher for him."

I had seen similar challenges with others. Often, someone who has had a preponderance of male incarnations will have difficulty with a lifetime as a female, and vice versa. As souls evolve they seek balance in their male/female aspects and design incarnations in which they learn to express the energy that is less familiar to them.

"Ryan's had quite a few psychic experiences in the last year or two, and Bradley has, too," said Jennifer. "Is that just their particular souls, or is it related to their handicaps?"

"The majority of kids coming in now are what they call Indigo children," Corbie answered. "Indigo children are the next version of *Homo sapiens*. They are better wired than we are in terms of being able to access other dimensions. It doesn't mean we can't do it, but it's like with an old computer — sometimes you have to attach an extra modem or juice up the batteries. Indigos are a modern laptop computer. They have all the wiring. They can access what they have more readily."

There was a pause that suggested our session with Corbie had run its course.

"Corbie," I asked in conclusion, "what would you like to say to parents of handicapped children?"

"Honor them," Corbie replied. "Honor their choices. Do not look up at God and say, 'Why me?' It's not punishment. Remember, there's a fully functioning soul in there that does not have speech problems, doesn't have spina bifida, can see, can hear, can think. They chose a very ill-fitting suit with a seam sewn wrong, but what inhabits the suit is *purpose*."

Staci Wells's Reading for Jennifer

To obtain additional information, I asked medium Staci Wells to conduct a supplemental reading for Jennifer. As usual, I provided Staci with names and birthdates—the information her spirit guide would need to retrieve the relevant information and present it to her. I also told her the nature of the boys' handicaps.

We began with a few moments of silence as Staci entered a trance. "There's talk here about being independent and having a challenge that would cause her to stand on her own two feet," Staci announced.

She then began to channel the conversation.

Jennifer: Why does this have to be done in such a difficult way?

Spirit Guide: It is your choice to learn at the hands of others and experience growth through your relationships, both difficult and serene. To fulfill the parental role for these boys is a very high purpose and a way to honor them. This will fulfill your desire to be of service in a way that you have not experienced.

"Although I don't yet see the two boys in her planning session, I have the awareness that she knows them but hasn't talked with them yet. They are part of her soul group. Her soul group is a rather evolved one. These are souls who live by higher ideals and like to take on great challenges.

"Having these boys in her life will serve as an unconscious reminder to stay grounded and centered. The choice is either to cope in that way or by going in the opposite direction and not living up to her responsibilities. She wants to take the higher path.

"Let's see if I can move forward to when Jennifer actually talks to Ryan and Bradley." There was a long pause as Staci shifted her focus to another part of the planning session. Her reading for Jennifer was proceeding in a typical fashion: Staci's spirit guide usually took her to general, "big picture" information before presenting more specific details.

"She has been Bradley's mother in another lifetime, so he feels very comfortable with her. It's important that his mother be somebody he is already comfortable with because of the choices he's made about blindness and being a very sensitive child.

"I hear him talking to her about fears he has. The fears stem from a previous lifetime where he spent his entire childhood in an orphanage in England. He never knew a mother's love. He was beaten and abused emotionally. It scarred him for that life. He did not want to experience anything like that in this lifetime. He did not want to put himself out in the world where he might be hurt again. He said that he needed to live a physical life again in this way so he could let go of the memories of being trauma-tized. He felt that if he could live one lifetime being cared for and not being thrown out into the brutal world, that would help him release the trauma. Also, Bradley's choice of blindness was so that he wouldn't have to see the cruel-ties in the world.

"Jennifer, in her always giving, loving way, agreed to this. Jennifer has a history of giving and doing for anybody she cares for just by being asked. She feels this is the right way to give to somebody you love. So, she agrees.

"Now, let me see if we can move on to Ryan." Again there was a pause as Staci shifted to a different portion of the pre-birth planning. "I see the soul of Ryan talking with Jennifer. He points out that his imbalances will remind her to take responsibility for others in a very serious way. Every time he acts up, it is a challenge to her to stay calm and focused on what really matters. Since her greatest challenge in this lifetime is to build a very strong sense of self, having Ryan in her life will keep her focused on that karmic challenge.

"I'm asking my guide to show me specifically the purpose these challenges will serve for Ryan." I waited expectantly as Staci listened to her spirit guide's words. "Ryan has lived seven lifetimes as a very studious, intelligent individual. One lifetime was as a male scientist. What I hear is that he had grown tired of living so many lives of educational and scientific pursuits. He wanted to be the 'imbalanced' one and experience what that was like.

"I am asking why these specific choices [handicaps] were made." Another pause as Staci's spirit guide spoke to her. "Due to the disabilities, there is no expectation of Ryan to live a life of achievement. That burden is taken off him; his mind is free to explore whatever he wants. His autism is just enough of a handicap that he wouldn't be expected to perform. Jennifer is willing to give him this life because she has spent several lifetimes following whims. So, she understands his need to experience this. Not only does it serve her purpose, but also she understands his need to feel a release from responsibility. He wants a great deal of personal freedom, and she gives him this by agreeing to be his mother."

Staci became silent. I assumed she was listening as her guide presented additional information to her. I was therefore surprised when she suddenly began to channel him. I was delighted by and grateful for the opportunity to talk

directly with this wise being, just as I would be each time
he appeared in future sessions.

"There has long existed a challenge to this soul to stay
focused in life," Staci's spirit guide said of Jennifer. Staci was
now speaking much more slowly and somewhat haltingly. "It
is felt that this situation, appearing as if it is forced on her in
that it is a responsibility from which she cannot escape, will
force her to narrow her focus in life and give up personal
freedom that would otherwise be far too tempting to her, as
it has been in past lives when she was not serious about life,
when she gave herself over to pleasures and temptations that
do not make for a satisfying life. She realizes, as her guides
have said to her, that too often she gives in to temptation.
So, she agreed to have children and to go it alone, especially
in terms of sharing the burden with the husband."

Earlier, Corbie had seen a lifetime in which Jennifer had
developed a skill—truthful communication—that would
be of value to her sons. Staci's spirit guide was now referring
to some of Jennifer's other past lives. When souls plan lives,
they generally do so in response to their previous incarnations; usually, a few specific lifetimes have the greatest
relevance to and impact on the planning.

Feeling that I now had an understanding of why Jennifer,
Ryan, and Bradley had planned their lives as they had, I
decided to expand my inquiry.

"What else motivates souls to plan lives as parents of
handicapped children?" I asked.

"Handicaps are chosen by souls because it gives them
opportunities they would not normally have," replied the
spirit guide. "Sometimes, it gives souls a different way to
learn the same lesson they've been working on [in previous
lives]. Often, it is [chosen as] a challenge to the caretaker to
show compassion, mercy, and love. Souls choose to honor

other souls by making themselves the vehicle through which they can be born. They choose to care for those souls by allowing them, the handicapped children, to live this life as they wished — less involved in the ordinary, everyday functions of life. It is a unique opportunity for the handicapped child, and it is an opportunity for the parent to show love. These agreements are made out of love."

"When parents have a handicapped child, they sometimes feel guilty or blame themselves or their genetics. What would you say to those people?"

"Self-blame is actually self-pity. That is not where the focus should be. The focus should be on the child. Everything is for a purpose. What you feel is a disadvantage is a challenge that can often turn out to be an advantage. Remember, this was planned. That will shift your perspective. Blame, guilt, and shame serve no purpose and hold you back from progress. Instead, see it as an opportunity. See this child and your life from a higher perspective."

I thought about Bradley's temper tantrums, particularly the way in which he became upset if something he had anticipated did not take place. "Jennifer has to be very precise in her use of language with Bradley," I told him. "What would you say about the issue of communication with handicapped children?"

"It is impossible to communicate clearly and concisely without a sense of self-worth and self-confidence. When parents communicate with each other, accepting all that they are and all that they feel, they communicate better with others. As children grow and discover their own self-worth, they challenge their parents to do the same.

"Jennifer wanted to be less spontaneous in this lifetime. In the past her lives were overly spontaneous and she did not discern the best choices for herself. When her children demand that she follow through on every word she speaks, the children are helping her to work on this lesson.

"Too often, words are said cavalierly without thinking of the impact they will have. Handicapped children remind parents to make their communications clear and thoughtful."

⟡

Jennifer, Ryan, and Bradley's story shows us that there is no blame or fault involved in giving birth to a handicapped child. Generally, children choose their handicaps before birth for the growth that will result. Similarly, the souls who plan to be their parents choose that experience for the learning it will engender.

To some extent, such planning is based on past lives. In response to an emotionally harsh lifetime in which he was raised in an orphanage, Bradley designed a life in which he would be safe, nurtured, and supported. His decision to heal the residual fears and trauma of that life is not surprising; the soul seeks healing in subsequent incarnations. Ryan desired a rest from the intense pressures of seven previous lifetimes. By creating lives in which they are challenged to communicate their truths to the world, both Ryan and Bradley sought to balance the karma created by their actions during World War II. In her lifetime during the war, Jennifer had a fear of "being shoved away or not heard." Perhaps she, like Bradley, sought to heal a residual fear and thus agreed to be the mother of two children who would at times push her away and not be able to hear her. Fears veil our remembrance of ourselves as eternal souls. If we avoid those fears, the veil grows thicker. If we embrace them, we pull aside the veil to reveal the brave soul who planned the opportunity for fear to be removed.

Some of our pre-birth planning is based simply on a desire to have new experiences. Ryan, for example, sought not only a rest but also the opportunity to experience imbalance. The imbalances he feels in this lifetime—for example, the sharp mood swings of bipolar disorder— contrast with both previous incarnations and the life he knows when in spirit, a life of perfect, divine balance. In the larger picture, his current experiences create both balance and his appreciation of it. Without imbalance, Ryan cannot fully know balance. As a soul he will leave this lifetime with a deeper understanding of its beauty. This experiential understanding is a gift from his physical life and from his mother, who agreed before birth to make that life possible.

Jennifer, Ryan, and Bradley also choreographed their lives to learn certain lessons. All three are learning the importance and value of communication, with Jennifer deepening the understanding of truthful communication that she demonstrated so admirably in her last incarnation. It was with wisdom that Ryan and Bradley selected her to be the teacher of this lesson. By teaching Ryan and Bradley to communicate, she is engaged in an act of service to their souls. As she serves them with compassion and unconditional love, she advances along the evolutionary spiral from mature to old soul.

Whether handicapped or not, children are their parents' teachers, and Ryan and Bradley teach Jennifer even as they learn from her. Through them Jennifer grows in patience, recognition of her self-worth, the ability to lead a disciplined life, and the capacity to remain centered and grounded. In addition to direct teaching, children further their parents' growth through the people they bring into their lives. This, too, is by design. When we plan our lives, we arrange the circumstances that will bring to us the other souls with whom we wish to work. When I spoke with parents of handicapped children, all commented on the extraordinary people they met as a result of their children's handicaps—people they felt they already knew. In all likelihood, they did. There is often a special bond that goes well beyond the commonality of having handicapped children.

As we have seen, Ryan and Bradley chose very different obstacles through which to teach Jennifer and challenge themselves. Some souls are more inclined than others to choose great challenges. Souls who have tendencies in this regard will, like Ryan, seek balance over the span of many lifetimes. If Ryan and Bradley choose to continue working on lessons of communication, they may well design incarnations in which communication comes more easily or in which they are gifted communicators.

At some level we are able to remember the souls we planned to meet and the life challenges we selected. Jennifer's fascination with autism in both high school and college is a vague recollection of her pre-birth blueprint. More than a mere shadow of memory, this interest was also, as she insightfully pointed out, a way for her soul to prepare her for what was to come. Our souls are in constant communication with us, lovingly supplying us with yearnings and interests that lay the groundwork for the future. If we listen closely, we can hear our souls whisper to us of the challenges we had planned.

Jennifer is correct when she says that she was chosen. So was her ex-husband. From the perspective of the personality, it may appear that she was burdened with the challenge of raising two handicapped children on her own. However, Jennifer planned this aspect as well with a soul who loves her and who agreed to give her the experience she sought, just as she agreed to give her children the experience they desired. There are no villains in this script, only souls acting with and out of love. That same love prompted two other members of the family, Bradley and Sarah, to plan a close relationship in which Sarah would intuitively understand and communicate Bradley's needs. In the same way, Sarah's understanding of her mother's need to focus on the boys is an echo of her pre-birth planning.

In the meshing of these life plans is an intricate, elegant coordination of purpose. Motivated by the twin desires of personal evolution and service to others, Jennifer, her ex-husband, Sarah, Ryan, and Bradley chose one another in love, just as other handicapped children and their siblings and parents chose one another in love. Love increases as it is given away. Because souls *are* love, souls expand as they love. The life challenge of parenting a handicapped child is an opportunity to love. Despite its hardships and heart-break, this challenge, so courageously embraced by Jennifer and her family, is therefore an expansion of their souls.

They are all silent heroes. Bradley and Ryan may or may not achieve in ways that society will reward or recognize, yet their accomplishments will be great. Jennifer's patience and compassion may not earn accolades, but her contribution is profound. Far from the world of competition and conquest, neither seeking nor garnering fame or praise, millions of handicapped children and their parents lead lives in which their courage is tested and reaffirmed daily with dignity and grace.

These are lives of quiet magnificence.

CHAPTER 4

❦

Deafness and Blindness

WHEN I CONSIDERED THE MANY difficulties
we as souls could incorporate into a life plan,
I was struck by the magnitude of the challenge
posed by deafness and blindness. We know prior to birth
we will have only five physical senses. We also know the
majority of sensory input will come through sight and
hearing. Why, I asked myself, would anyone choose a challenge that could result in so much struggle? Further, why
would a soul desire a physical life that does not provide
such a significant part of the physical experience? As I
posed these questions, I thought of my young niece who
was born almost totally deaf.

In the United States alone, more than twenty-five million people over the age of eighteen are slightly hearing
impaired. Another six million are severely hearing impaired
or deaf. In this category is Penelope, who has been completely deaf since birth. *If she chose to experience total deafness
from the first moment of physical life, there must be reasons,* I
thought, as Penelope and I started to chat. We conducted
her interview over the Internet by typing our words with
instant messaging.

Penelope's Story

"When I was seven, I asked my mom why I was deaf. I was upset and thirsty for a 'better' answer. I was sobbing. She held me in her arms and explained very calmly that it was not my fault, that God made me who I was—and that was very special. It was my first real, explicit, frustrated moment as a deaf individual. I did not like it. It was almost as if I wanted out."

Now twenty-four years old and engaged to be married, Penelope teaches American Sign Language and English to deaf adults, many who are not American citizens. "I provide a lot of guidance and confidence to those students," she said. Typically, her pupils have had little education. Penelope's teaching suggests the life blueprint of a lightworker—an individual who selects specific life challenges to stimulate both her own growth and that of many people.

As a child, Penelope was plagued by nightmares from which she often awoke screaming. That aspect of her past would later take on great significance in her session with the medium.

Penelope attended a school for the deaf until age nine, at which time her mother opted for mainstreaming her in a public school. Penelope had found the environment at her first school to be accepting and supportive. At her new school, she sometimes needed a sign language interpreter. She had to adjust in other ways as well.

"In elementary and middle school, peers wanted to hang out with me for the sake of being cool and to show off their sign language skills," she told me. "Those were predominantly white schools. So, I was introduced to the world of race consciousness and popularity in one year." Penelope's comment made me wonder why she had elected before birth to be both female and African American in addition to being deaf.

Penelope found high school to be even more difficult than middle school. "I did not feel embraced by my black hearing or deaf peers," she recalled. When she spoke in class in what she describes as her "queer voice," she noticed strange looks on the students' faces. "You know the saying, 'lost in translation'? That worried me. I'm glad I didn't grow any gray hair.

"My most favorite experience of all was at a party. I was trying to pronounce my name after saying hello. *P* is a silent letter. I don't do silent letters. I was probably uttering 'Benelobe.' After I did my best voice impression, this lady turned around and asked my friend if I had a cold. That hurts. That's the last thing I want. But moments like that happen."

Penelope explained that about half the people she meets are able to understand her speech. Often, when someone doesn't understand, Penelope will ask for pen and paper. "You will not believe how many people try *not* to give me a pen and paper. Paper and pen mean more time."

Penelope worries about the information that may be missing when she speaks with people. At times they misinterpret her lack of response. On other occasions they misinterpret her overuse of body language.

Penelope told me that certain behaviors of hearing people are particularly frustrating for the deaf. "People sometimes speak slower than normal. We do not appreciate that. We will ask if we need a slower voice for lip-reading. Or talking LOUD to us. I can tell. Or asking us if we can read. Sometimes, a few of us like to write back 'no.'"

I laughed at Penelope's mischievous sense of humor. In that moment I realized that Penelope had no way of knowing she had made me laugh because our entire conversation had been over the Internet. How many times had she conversed electronically with people and had not been aware of her effect upon them? Prior to my study of pre-birth planning, I would have felt a certain sadness. Now, I knew that these were the types of experiences she had desired.

"What about dating in school?" I asked.

"It was the most painful experience during high school. I felt ready. I felt intellectual. I had so much to share. But communication barriers do not fare well with those high school dudes unless it's about petting and whatnot. I was not interested in that. I wanted to have conversations. I was thirsting for male support and compassion. It hurt me deeply."

Penelope knows that experiences of this sort, though difficult, have made her more empathetic.

"I feel for the people, the unheard (no pun intended)," she said. "My deafness does increase my sensitivity."

I asked Penelope what she saw as the larger purpose of her deafness.

"I knew I was meant to be deaf to better understand the neglected," she replied. "I want to bridge each gap between opposing groups, not just in the worlds of the hearing and deaf, but also any type of cultural boundaries."

I was struck by Penelope's use of the word *knew* when she could have said *think* or *believe*. "How did you know you were meant to understand the neglected?" I inquired.

"It was in my heart. I have intuition. I am literally neglected on the basis of my deafness. I can't help but pay attention to others who have experienced some sort of neglect. I have been drawn to those who are lost, unaccepted, or uncategorized. My soul seems to want to utilize compassion for the forgettable and under-represented."

Penelope's Session with Staci Wells

A few days after our chat, Penelope and I met online with Staci to access information about Penelope's pre-birth planning. Again the conversation took place by instant messaging.

"I will tell you the impressions I see, hear, and feel," Staci typed. "These impressions come to me psychically. They are told to me through my spirit guide, who holds what he calls The Book of Lives [Akashic Records] in his hands, a book that contains all the information about the lives of everyone who has ever lived and who is alive today.

"I feel strongly that deafness is an opportunity for you to explore avenues of growth you have not been able to explore before as well as a link to your most previous past life. Being deaf gives you the opportunity to be more in touch with your inner experience, intuition, thoughts, even the physical symptoms and feedback your body gives you. It helps you to know yourself."

Staci said she had dreamed about Penelope the previous night. It was not unusual for Staci to receive information about someone prior to a session, but this was the first time it had come in the form of a dream. "My spirit guide tells me that I was already adjusting my frequency to yours, so I was open to receiving information about you. I was dreaming about your most recent past life, the one that helped you decide to be deaf in this present lifetime."

Staci had seen Penelope at about age three when Penelope had witnessed her mother being verbally abused by a boyfriend. "This little girl was very, very emotionally sensitive," Staci said. The abuse continued for two or three years. From the dream Staci knew that Penelope's mother in that lifetime is again her mother in this lifetime.

In the previous lifetime, "the abuse escalated and eventually became physical," typed Staci. Once, "in a moment of rage the boyfriend attempted to strangle Penelope's mother with a telephone cord. He wanted to frighten her and bend her to his will.

"One day Penelope was standing with a neighbor outside the apartment in which she, her mother, and the boyfriend lived. Inside, the mother and boyfriend were arguing loudly. Penelope and the neighbor heard items being thrown and smashed. The neighbor put her arm around Penelope to comfort her. Both were paralyzed with fear.

"The boyfriend chased Penelope's mother into the bedroom. She locked the door behind her, leaving the boyfriend outside. The boyfriend had a gun. He kicked in the bedroom door and shot Penelope's mother several times. Penelope heard the gunshots clearly. Her mother bled to death.

"The boyfriend went into the bathroom, sat down on the floor with his back to the bathtub, and cried. At this point, the neighbor took Penelope inside the apartment, where she called the authorities and one of Penelope's relatives. The boyfriend then shot himself in the head. Penelope heard this gunshot, too.

"That is where my dream ends," Staci said. "Penelope, your mother's life was cut short. You missed her for the next ten years in that lifetime. Your own life was cut short as well. I don't think you lived past your thirties in that life. You two made the soul level agreement to be together again in this lifetime and continue the relationship. Your father [in your current lifetime] is *not* the man who shot your mother in that life. That man is *not* alive in this present lifetime.

"The horror, sounds, and screams you heard that day stayed with you the rest of your life. I'm told that you suffered horrible bouts of depression because of it. When you went to sleep at night, and often throughout the day, the sounds of the past would haunt you. I am told that it was your last thought as you passed from that life to be free of those sounds forever, no matter what it took.

"You took your own life in that lifetime. It very much influenced your decision to be deaf in this lifetime. You did not want to re-experience the terror of those times.

"What I want to know, Penelope, is how you are feeling as I've been telling you this. Does this resonate with you? Not just intellectually, but emotionally and physically?"

"The dreams in the night…" Penelope typed in response. "My mom said that I would always scream in my sleep. It would be a little joke. I'm deaf; poor anyone who would have to sleep next to me. I guess that's what's in my subconscious most nights.

"I don't recall my hands vibrating to this level before," added Penelope as she observed a physical sensation that had developed as Staci spoke. "It was so powerful. I had to rub my hands, trying to calm myself down."

"Do they normally vibrate?" asked Staci. "Yes, my guide confirms that. You are still working through it in order to achieve total healing. Working on it at the subconscious level has been the only way you can handle it so far. This is an example of how your physical body expresses your feelings and conflicts, how it gives you signs."

"My fiancé would ask why I become very aggressive whenever I get upset," Penelope replied. "He wanted to know if I had some traumatic experience in *this* lifetime. Now I know. I must break the cycle."

"You become aggressive and physical because of what you saw in that lifetime," explained Staci. "It is still very much in your subconscious."

I asked Staci if she could tell us more.

"I'm being told that it [deafness] enables her to come from a viewpoint of compassion toward people with all sorts of disabilities. It enables her to be more compassionate with animals, which I'm told is something that she enjoys very much. In later years she will reach out to others who are deaf and help them in all kinds of ways, giving guidance of all kinds."

"I also intend to utilize my identifiers (deaf, female, young, ethnic minority) as attention-getters to best share information creatively," offered Penelope.

"Ethnic minority…" said Staci. "I can see that goes along with your *choice* to see things from a more compassionate angle. You experience yourself as being different in a lot of ways."

"Yes!" exclaimed Penelope. "I never felt like I belonged."

"Penelope, how is this experience for you?" I asked, wanting to make sure she was comfortable with her session.

"I feel a sense of relief," she replied. "I have had questions for as long as I can remember. As a human I have just received affirmation. I also feel less alone."

"Staci," I asked, "would it be possible for you to provide the conversation that took place in Penelope's pre-birth planning session when she chose deafness?"

Penelope and I waited a few moments as Staci "tuned in" to the discussion. She then described the planning session in such detail that I felt as though we were actually part of it.

"I am hearing 'thought-conversation,'" Staci typed. "I am also *seeing*. Penelope is in a large room. The walls are high; there are many images on the walls—images from past lives. Her main spirit guide is there along with other guides. I see Penelope sitting cross-legged on the floor; also on the floor are the other souls with whom she will interact in important ways in the lifetime to come. Some of the souls have been with her in previous lifetimes but will remain on the other side while she incarnates. Her main spirit guide stands behind her, directing the proceedings, acknowledging everyone there.

Spirit Guide:　We are gathered here to help Penelope decide on her life that is to be. Many of you have helped Penelope before in other lifetimes and between lives. Penelope still burns from her experiences in her most recent life and seeks healing in the life that is to be. She asks each of you now to join your energy with hers as she decides what she is to be, what she will and will not experience, and how she may best interact with all here in order to achieve her goals.

"They all join 'hands'" Staci continued. "I see the energy pulsing from one to another until it pulses throughout the room like waves that penetrate everyone there.

"The first thing Penelope decides is her body color, as that will be part of the connection between herself and the soul who was and is her mother. As Penelope decides this, I see her soul take on the darker color, 'trying it on for size,' but also adopting it as her own.

"There is thought-conversation between Penelope and her mother, agreements made for her mother to give birth to her and take care of her in ways she could not in the previous lifetime. Penelope expresses to the soul who is her mother that she still feels a great need to be cradled in her mother's arms. There is an agreement made about lots of cuddling time.

"But then the memories of what she witnessed in the previous lifetime spring to her mind, and Penelope asks please not to let that happen again. The man who shot her mother in that lifetime stands up among the crowd and agrees to not inhabit physical form while Penelope and her mother are in physical body. Then he sits back down.

Penelope: But the sounds. I am afraid I will still hear them. I don't want to hear them at all.

Spirit Guide: My dear, you know that they will continue to resonate within your hearing range. Would you prefer to be born deaf so that no sound will ever remind you of those sounds again? You will continue to be influenced by them and by what you saw and experienced, only you will feel them at a deeper, subconscious level, where it will be easier for you.

Penelope: Yes.

Spirit Guide: Wait. [*Holds up his hand.*] Before you agree to this so readily, think on this first: you will continue to be influenced by the atrocities you witnessed in that life because you have told me it is your desire to complete your healing process. You will still feel them, but at a level you will be unable to define for quite some time.

Penelope: Yes, that is what I want and what I wish to do.

"Her energy changes somewhat as she gets more serious. The excitement of being born and living again has now been somewhat overshadowed as she realizes what she will work on. But she agrees and moves on to the next step in the planning process.

Penelope: I want to give to other people in some capacity. I want to expand my ability to be compassionate. In my last life, my ability to express compassion ended when my mother died. I want to care compassionately for many people.

Spirit Guide: You will have the opportunity to use your own experience in the life that is to come to turn your self-knowledge outward and give to others in a kind, compassionate, and caring manner, and to teach others as well.

"There is some talk about volunteering. The neighbor who aided Penelope in that past life will be one of the handicapped people she will work with later [as a volunteer], sometime after the age of 30. Penelope says she wants to do this to give back what was given to her.

"The neighbor stands up and agrees to this. I see her soul image take on the form of someone who has physical disabilities and requires the aid of a cane. I am given the understanding now that the soul image changes during the planning session so that all concerned are better able to recognize each other by sight when they see each other in physical form.

"That's all I'm being given right now. Are there questions?"

I was astounded by both the clarity of Staci's psychic vision and the power of Penelope's pre-birth planning session. Staci's guide had taken her to the portion of the discussion that best explained Penelope's motivations for choosing deafness. Her plan was filled with meaning, purpose, and wisdom.

In my study of pre-birth planning, I had learned that the personality has free will and may adhere to or deviate from the plans of the soul. "Regarding the man who murdered Penelope's mother in the last life," I asked Staci, "was the murder a freewill decision made by his personality, or was the murder planned prior to that incarnation?"

"Let me see what comes to me for an answer... It was known at the time of his planning session that he had spent several lifetimes with issues of self-loathing and rage. He had not yet learned how to achieve self-worth. Penelope's mother said during that planning session that she had been working on relationships for many lifetimes and would welcome the opportunity to work on these issues again—and with him. On a soul level, she freely gave of herself in the spirit of unconditional love.

"The murder was not foreseen or planned. It was indeed a freewill decision made at that time. I do not see that Penelope's mother harbors any ill will against him on a soul level. There is a very clear understanding of what happened and forgiveness and compassion for the issues he was dealing with," Staci concluded.

It occurred to me that a freewill decision to murder would surely create a great deal of karma. "Why did this soul not incarnate now to balance that energy in a way and under circumstances that would not be threatening to Penelope?"

"Because there was no need for what we conceive of as expediency," answered Staci. "There is still plenty of time for that in other lifetimes. The focus of Penelope's life is to heal from that lifetime. Penelope, being very sensitive, would not have been able to heal if he had been in her life. I'm told that one of the things she wanted to heal from the most was her own suicide."

"I know there are many ways for souls to heal while in spirit," I said. "Why did Penelope choose to heal through another incarnation instead of healing while in spirit?"

"I'm told it wasn't either/or. It wasn't instead of. There was some instruction and opportunity to heal on the other side. She did partake in many sessions with her spirit guides and her mother. She came to an understanding of things, but mostly on what we call an intellectual level. There was a need felt for returning to physical embodiment for opportunities to heal in more profound ways. Also, her mother needed to come back to physical form in a certain time frame." (The reasons for her mother's need to do so were not specified. It may be that the souls with whom Penelope's mother wanted to share a life were about to incarnate.) "Penelope very much wanted to be with her, so it was necessary for her to continue healing while in the physical. And her mother welcomed the opportunity to be her mother again and make up for what happened before."

"Staci," I said, "please ask your guide what other aspects of Penelope's story are important to bring out, either for readers in general or specifically for deaf readers trying to understand the purpose of deafness."

Staci had been paraphrasing the words of her spirit guide. She now typed them directly.

"One," he began as he enumerated his points. "One's inner experience is just as real, if not more so, than the outer world. Two. Deafness enables some people to focus on their goals in a better way. Three. Deafness is not a handicap. It is an opportunity. It provides a subtle shift in focus that is necessary for personal and spiritual growth. Four. Deafness is no one's fault. It is a choice. Like every choice, it provides the opportunity to experience life in exactly the way that is needed for one's purpose. And sometimes there is a need to balance that which has been done by the soul. There have been souls who have cut off the ears or limbs of others, who feel the need to punish themselves by incarnating and experiencing deafness, the loss of use of a limb, or disfiguring disabilities. Other times, there is a need for the soul to experience inner harmony. When the soul is sensitive to the extent that Penelope's is, outer forces, sounds, and energies can present challenges to achieving inner harmony. In Penelope's case, it was her soul's desire to exclude any sound that would remind her of the atrocities experienced in the earlier incarnation. Remember that to let go of fear is one of the greatest challenges you experience as humans. Penelope is still working on this challenge."

"In regard to your comment about souls wanting to punish themselves," I asked, "isn't it really more of a desire to develop empathy?"

"Empathy is the greater goal. That is true. But if a soul does not forgive itself, it is stuck. When we [spirit guides] see that, we often see souls choose to punish themselves for what they did. In the end, you judge yourselves. Oftentimes, you cross over [die] with the strong resonance of negative emotions, and that causes you not to see things completely clearly. You see through what you might call 'fear-colored glasses' or 'guilt-colored glasses.' You do not feel compassion for yourselves at that point."

I asked if fear had played a role in Penelope's planning for this lifetime.

"Fear is a carryover in this instance. Penelope died experiencing a state of fear, and so the soul was not able to progress beyond that. She knew that she needed to let go of fear. She still carries unresolved fear from the previous life."

"Thank you for answering these questions," I said.

"You are most welcome," he replied. "You are helping me to fulfill my dharma."

∾

Compassion.

In the many sessions with the mediums, compassion was one of the life lessons mentioned most often by Spirit, along with empathy and unconditional love for self and others. As eternal souls we seek to know ourselves as compassion. This self-knowing, which is really the *feeling* of compassion as both gift given and gift received, comes to us and is deepened by its every expression on the physical plane.

Society views deafness as an imperfection. To be viewed as imperfect by others is to be granted the opportunity to feel compassion for all those deemed by society as "less than." Contrast of this sort does not exist in the nonphysical realm, where all are equal and the iridescent beauty of every soul is self-evident and unquestionable. No soul is "less than"; the very concept is senseless. In the physical realm, this hollow, meaningless notion is temporarily invested with an illusory meaning, one that allows us to understand and experience compassion in a way otherwise impossible.

Penelope planned the experience of deafness in part to know compassion. She feels a great deal of compassion, not only for the deaf but for all who are neglected in any way. She seeks to strengthen connections between the worlds of the hearing and the deaf, between opposing groups, between clashing cultures. Her compassion, borne in a place of silence, speaks loudly to the world as she forges those bridges.

It is not coincidence that Penelope chose to be female and African American. In line with her desire to understand compassion, she elected to be a member of two groups who are often treated with a lack of compassion. Whenever she is treated without compassion, regardless of the reason, her appreciation of and desire for compassion are strengthened.

Women, ethnic minorities, and the deaf have historically been deprived of power. As I listened to Penelope speak, I was struck by the disparity between the considerable power she feels to effect change in the world and the relative lack of power of the groups to which she belongs. By immersing herself in circumstances in which she lacks external power, she created an impetus to develop internal power.

Penelope designed a life of learning through opposites, a common plan on the Earth plane and a path of profound spiritual growth. If she had not chosen circumstances in which she would experience a lack of compassion, she would likely have less opportunity and motivation to cultivate the compassion she now offers to others. If she had not chosen circumstances in which she lacked overt power, she might never know just how powerfully she can affect the world.

It can be challenging to express compassion in the physical, where the ego creates a sense of separation from others and fear sometimes gets the better of us. Such is not the case when we are in the nonphysical. In Penelope's pre-birth planning session, for example, compassion is expressed toward the soul who murdered Penelope's mother in a previous life. There is no anger, hatred, or vengefulness; instead, we see forgiveness and understanding. Notice, too, the compassion and absence of judgment in regard to Penelope's suicide in a previous life. At no point is she criticized or condemned. She does need to complete the learning planned for that incarnation, but those present feel only compassion in regard to the difficulties that led her to end her life.

As souls we do not judge one another. The only judgment in the realm of spirit is the self-judgment that may arise during the life review. We judge ourselves, and we are the only ones who do so. Our spirit guides sit with us as we review our lives and occasionally point out moments at which we could have expressed greater compassion, but even these remarks are made in a loving, nonjudgmental way. Only when we are in body and seemingly separate from one another do we express a lack of compassion through judgment. Those judgments, far from being the results of perceived separation, are actually the cause of it. To release judgment and to love with indiscriminate compassion is to remember who we really are.

Just as compassion is a prominent theme of Penelope's pre-birth planning, so, too, is the desire to be of service. As souls we are motivated by love to help one another evolve, and Penelope's planning session is rich with examples of souls who wish to serve in this way. Penelope designed a life in which she serves humanity, focusing principally on the deaf community. Penelope's mother wanted to be of service to her by providing the love and physical affection that was cut short in the prior life. The neighbor sought to serve Penelope by giving her the opportunity to express compassion. She therefore agreed to take on physical handicaps. The soul who murdered Penelope's mother had such a strong desire to serve Penelope that he agreed not to incarnate at this time, thus deferring his own growth and the balancing of his karma. Love, expressed as a desire to serve others, overflows in Penelope's pre-birth planning session.

The same is true in regard to the planning of the previous lifetime. When Penelope's mother designed that life, she knew the soul who would become her romantic partner might act violently, but she wanted to give him an opportunity to develop feelings of self-worth while in body. At the soul level, her desire to be of service to him was in no way diminished by his history of incarnations in which he had expressed rage. These two souls will in all likelihood plan another incarnation together, a lifetime in which there will be further opportunity for him to choose love over anger.

We love the souls with whom we plan our lives. During our earthly existence, they may be people who complicate matters, cause us stress or worry, or even become our "enemies." When not incarnate the estranged husband and wife, the abusive parent and neglected child, and the warring ex-business partners are loving friends. They care deeply for one another and will often reincarnate together in an effort to master lessons unfinished in previous lives.

Souls need not incarnate to serve in the physical realm. Indeed, as we were told in the session with Staci, discarnate souls were of great service to Penelope in her prior lifetimes. Souls who are in the nonphysical provide tremendous assistance to us by sending love and inspiration. They communicate with us in our dreams and touch us through our emotions when we are awake. Those who love us are with us always, whether or not they incarnate alongside us. The bonds of the heart are eternal.

The neighbor in the previous life will play an important role in Penelope's current lifetime, as will any soul who allows Penelope to express compassion. Learning to accept love and compassion is just as important as learning to express them. Souls plan lives that incorporate physical accidents, illnesses, and physical and mental handicaps—for example, a handicap that confines one to a wheelchair—to create circumstances in which they literally cannot run away from someone who is expressing love. In past lives these souls may have had difficulty accepting caring and tenderness from others. They plan subsequent lives in which they almost require themselves to learn this lesson.

Souls also choose challenges to surmount fear. As Staci's spirit guide indicated, Penelope wanted to overcome the fear that remains from a previous lifetime. In this incarnation, that fear is carried at a largely subconscious level, and her healing is taking place at that level. When we design our lives, we seek healing of many kinds, including the healing of "negative" emotions like fear.

During the course of my research, I came across a young man who in meditation contacted a future self, that is, an incarnation of his soul at a future time. The future self told him that people of the future refer to this time on Earth as "The Fear Ages." Consider the significance of this label. Of the almost infinite descriptors that might be applied to our age, they chose *fear*. Fear is a predominant emotion of our time. It is so much a part of our daily existence that we tend not to notice it. Carried forward from hundreds of prior incarnations, unhealed fear is deeply embedded in individual and collective consciousness. To heal fear we need to experience it — resistance to any energy only makes it stronger — and then choose to move beyond it. Life challenges afford an opportunity to heal those fears, both conscious and unconscious.

Like fear and other "negative" emotions, false beliefs also require healing. If, for example, the soul who murdered Penelope's mother creates a belief while in body that self-loathing is merited or that he *is* rage, then that soul will design future incarnations to learn otherwise. "Less than" is no more accurate a label when applied to self than when it is applied to others. Subsequent lifetimes will use learning-through-opposites plans in which the people incarnating with this soul will mirror his lack of self-worth.

We have noted what is present in Penelope's pre-birth planning, but what is missing from it is as notable: any sense of deafness being negative, "bad," or a form of punishment. Penelope knew that deafness is none of these things. She was wise enough to recognize deafness as a valuable learning opportunity. In fact, she was so eager to choose this life challenge that her spirit guide slowed the process to make sure deafness was what she wanted. At no point does she complain or seek a less difficult challenge. At no time do the other souls express pity over the challenge she will face. Like Penelope, they view it as an opportunity for growth, and they are eager to support her in her quest.

Even now, while in body, Penelope sees the growth that derives from this experience, and she is grateful for her spiritual evolution. The importance of gratitude cannot be overstated. Two tuning forks of similar frequency will strike a sympathetic resonance; that is, they will vibrate in unison. In the same way, gratitude is an alignment of oneself with the frequency of the Divine Mind. Gratitude is an elevated, even sacred vibration, on a par with love, forgiveness, joy, and compassion. Gratitude does not mean that we are "glad" we suffered. It means finding an aspect or consequence of a life challenge to appreciate. Regardless of the nature or severity of our challenges, growth and learning may always result. This expansion of self is to be recognized and treasured.

Most of us listen with our ears. Penelope sought to know herself as compassion and so chose a life in which she would listen with her heart. The heart has a language all its own, and Penelope is mastering its cadence. Many of us listen to outer voices, the voices of people telling us who we are and what we should think, do, and be. Penelope planned a life in which she would listen to her inner voice—the voice of her soul. She heeds that call and is richer for it. Life challenges like deafness puncture the veil that seems to separate us from our divinity. As we embrace our challenges, we emerge from the amnesic voyage with a more profound self-knowing. Penelope's deafness is bringing her Home to this truth.

Bob Feinstein occupies a unique niche in this book. He is the only person whose life challenge, blindness, was the result of an unplanned "accident." (As you will read in a later chapter, we often plan "accidents," or at least the potential for them, prior to birth.) During Bob's session with the medium, I was surprised to learn that Bob had not sought the experience of blindness from the first stages of his pre-birth planning. In fact, he had originally designed a very different life for himself. When the blindness occurred, Bob and his spirit guides adapted to it by creating a new life blueprint.

I have used quotation marks with "accident" because I do not believe there are any true accidents. The universe is finely ordered down to the most microscopic particle, and on some level—sometimes conscious, sometimes not—we are the joint creators of all we experience. We script some "accidents" before we incarnate; together we create others after we are here. In no instance, however, are they genuinely haphazard occurrences.

Initially, I wondered if Bob's story should be included in this book. I thought that perhaps people would be best served by stories of souls who had desired a particular challenge from pre-birth. After further consideration I realized that Bob was a gift from Spirit, which had brought us together to show how souls respond to unexpected events on the Earth plane. This book would not be complete without his story.

Bob's Story

"When I came out of the incubator, I was blind."

That was how Bob's life began. He was three months premature when he was born in December 1949; he weighed less than two pounds. Excess oxygen used in his incubator had caused the cells of his retinas to multiply too quickly, rendering them a mass of scar tissue.

"When I was a little boy," Bob said softly, "my mother never really mentioned that I was blind. I heard the word, but I didn't know what it meant. It wasn't until I was about three years old that I started realizing it was something different about me. I heard things like, 'Turn off the light' or 'It's dark in here,' but it had no meaning for me. My mother would say, 'I see Aunt Sylvia coming.' I would say, 'How do you know?' She'd say, 'I see her.' Then I would ask what that means. She'd say, 'Some people see with their eyes, but you see with your hands.'"

Bob didn't realize just how different he was until he started school. While other kids learned to use pen and pencil, Bob studied Braille and typing. In the classes he took with sighted children, the teachers often began the first day of school by saying, "We have to be very nice to Robert. He's very special." When he touched the books that sighted kids were reading, he was surprised to find they felt like blank paper. He was also surprised to discover that other children could run and ride bicycles without being guided.

"I was very naïve," Bob recalled. "Sometimes kids would say, 'How many fingers do I have up?' I used to say, 'I don't know.' It took the wind out of their sails. Other blind kids would guess and get it wrong, and the kids would laugh. So being naïve in a way served me well."

Although Bob avoided some of the teasing, he still had difficulties with sighted peers. One student who regularly escorted him to the Braille room walked too fast and would not slow down when Bob asked. "They should make other kids do this," the boy complained. "You should walk faster."

Bob experienced challenges at home as well. "My father didn't take much of an interest in me. I think he was very disappointed to have a blind son."

As a result Bob spent most of his time with his mother and aunts, who were loving and supportive. Sometimes Bob pretended to read from print books, making up stories as he turned the pages. "Someone once told me the book was upside down, but my mother never stopped me from doing those things. That's a very good way to bring up a blind child, because it makes them feel more normal. She instinctively knew what to do." When they went shopping, Bob's mother let him touch the merchandise even though he occasionally broke things. She felt it was the best way for him to learn.

Socially, Bob found junior high and high school to be more difficult than the earlier grades. "It was very lonely," he said, sadness in his voice. "Kids would talk about having fun, going places, but I was never included."

There were, however, places where Bob was accepted. When he was fifteen, Bob attended music camp. "This was one of the most wonderful summers I can remember! I always had a friend to walk with." The staff took an interest in Braille music, and Bob played clarinet in the orchestra. He had a good ear and amused his fellow campers by telling them, for example, that a car horn was a B-flat or a door squeak was a high A.

Bob graduated from Oberlin College. "I was proud that I had succeeded in a sighted college, where no exceptions were made for me except those necessary because of my blindness. In my small way I have tried to show that it does not have to be a devastating stumbling block." In college Bob came to terms with his homosexuality, which, as I would soon discover, was part of his pre-birth planning.

One of the great joys of Bob's life was Harley, a Labrador, his companion for eight years.

"Sometimes when I was with Harley, I actually used to forget I was blind because I loved walking with him," Bob remembered. "People thought he wasn't the best guide dog because he was mischievous. One time Harley swiped a chicken cutlet off a guy's plate. Everyone was scandalized! Harley could do no wrong in my book. I was like a doting father." Harley may have saved Bob's life when he prevented him from stepping off a subway platform and falling onto the train tracks below.

I asked Bob to help me to understand what blindness is like. "Bob, how do you conceive of certain objects? A small object you could put in your hand and feel the shape. But something like an airplane—do you have a concept of what a plane or other large objects look like?"

"To tell you the truth, no," Bob replied. "There are a lot of things…you learn the words, but you don't picture them well. Like different animals. I don't really know what they are like because I've never petted them. I don't know what a skyscraper looks like or a skyline or the moon or stars. I don't know what it means that a person is handsome or ugly."

"When you dream, what do you see?"

"My dreams are all voices, like radio programs. One thing that is interesting is that I never dream of walking with a guide dog or a cane. If I have to be somewhere in my dream, I'm automatically there." (Bob's words reminded me that when we are in spirit, we "travel" simply by focusing our attention on the desired destination.) "I don't feel much in my dreams. I don't smell. They're just voices because I've never seen anything. I'm one of the few blind people that has never seen light or dark."

"In your dreams is there ever any reference to your being blind?"

"No … it doesn't matter if I'm blind. If I want to read a menu in my dream—there is no menu. I just know everything that is on the menu. It's me just knowing things."

"Bob, how are the blind different from sighted people?"

"I think we're more sensitive to certain things: touch, smell, kindness. When you're blind you become a barometer of kindness and unkindness because you need it for survival."

I asked Bob how he might be different if he were not blind.

"I have a real feeling for the underdog," he answered, reminding me of Penelope. "If I were sighted, I might be much more snobby, more concerned with money, with the way people look. Those things don't have any meaning to me at all. It is the essence of the person that matters.

"And I think blindness has given me a real love for animals, because I know what it's like to depend on a dog and have a dog use his intelligence to help you. You learn to trust animals. And you learn to trust people in a funny way, because when you are guided by someone, you have to trust them."

Bob's Sessions with Staci Wells

My conversation with Bob had given me a slight understanding of the challenges faced by the blind. Though I could imagine how these challenges might produce tremendous personal growth, I was eager to learn the specific ways in which Bob had hoped to evolve when he planned the blindness. At the time I did not yet know that the original plan for his life had included no such experience.

Medium Staci Wells conducted two readings for Bob; both are combined in the narrative that follows. At various times Spirit asked Staci to stress certain points to me so that I could, in turn, call attention to them in the book. I have inserted [Rob] at those moments to indicate the emphasized ideas.

Like the other life planning sessions Staci saw in our work together, Bob's contains references to the board souls use to design the upcoming incarnation. But unlike all the other planning sessions, Bob's uses two new boards: a transitional board for charting various ways in which Bob might respond to the accident and a final board that contains the new plan for his lifetime.

Prior to Staci's first reading, I informed her that Bob had been born prematurely and placed in an incubator, where excess oxygen had caused his blindness. With clarity and detail, Staci then ascertained both his original and new life plans. We learned that in this lifetime he desired to grow in self-love and self-acceptance. To stimulate this growth, he had originally planned the life challenge of discovering and accepting his homosexuality within the context of a hetero-sexual marriage to a woman named Maureen. When the blindness occurred, Bob and his spirit guides created a com-pletely different plan that would permit him to accomplish the same goals. This improvisation was unlike anything Staci and I had seen. I was thrilled by the opportunity to witness a soul and spirit guides suddenly adapt to a signifi-cant, unanticipated development on the physical plane.

"You are a considerably responsible soul," Staci told Bob as she began to access information. "You experienced lifetimes of great impoverishment in order to forward your spiritual growth. You worked on a lack of ego in those life-times, denying the self and giving the body only what was necessary for a meager existence. You were a hermit monk in Spain. That was to insulate you against the slings, arrows, and injustices of humankind. You walked a long road as part of your mission. You were very thin. You begged for food and lived off the generosity of others.

"That lifetime was the precursor to the choices you made for this lifetime. You rather liked living a solitary life and interacting with people in kind and generous ways. You were a sensitive soul. That was part of why you chose to isolate yourself in that lifetime and multiple previous lifetimes.

"In the planning stage before this lifetime, there was much talk about bringing balance into your being and being part of the world this time around. Now you wanted to interact with people more. You felt very comfortable interacting with the people who were to be your family. You wanted to create a lifetime where you would honor your family and be close with them.

"At the same time, you also vowed to work on a lack of self-esteem that you had developed by going a little too far into the hermit form of spiritual growth. You wanted to retain your emotional independence that you had worked very hard over several lifetimes to attain. It is a challenge in this present lifetime to build your self-esteem from within. You go back and forth between that end of the spectrum and looking to others for reinforcement of who you are.

"There was some discussion about things that would present as challenges throughout your life and various ways you could meet your goals. Your mother giving birth to you prematurely was not expected. The pregnancy was watched [by your spirit guides], but nonetheless the premature birth was news that arrived suddenly. There was surprise.

"The guides were immediately by Bob's incubator side, waiting for him to slip out of body and into that state of consciousness where the spirit or astral body is released. They knew it was going to happen quickly. Some people might say they pulled him out of the body, but they didn't. They wanted me to tell you [Rob] that."

Staci continued. "My spirit guide wants us to start with the chessboard, the planning board. It's a chart on which the steps of growth and development are plotted through one's life, so that the soul has a visual reference. This board is like a flow chart. A flow chart is a question. If the answer is yes, you take one path. If the answer is no, you take a different path.

"When this accident happened to Bob in the incubator ... the phrase I'm hearing is 'back to the drawing board.' Bob and two of his spirit guides got together and went back into the room with the planning board to diagram the alternate path that would be taken to still achieve the soul's goals for this lifetime.

"They're showing me the instant he [Bob] found himself back in spirit in the planning place ... very disoriented by this rapid and huge change and surprised to find himself there. He did not realize what was happening to the infant body. He recognizes his guides, trusts them implicitly, and is totally willing to be guided.

"I'm hearing one of the two guides, who is speaking for both of them, telling Bob that there has been a mishap in a procedure and that Bob's brain has received too much oxygen. Bob appears to be in a state of shock about this — quiet, eyes wide, pupils dilated, numb and glum.

Spirit Guide: The nurse involved in the operation of the tubes attached to your crib, where your physical body is even now, has made an error and has allowed too much of the elemental oxygen to flow through. This has elevated the oxygen levels in your brain, and damage is occurring.

"I see them showing Bob his eyes, the baby's eyes. Bob's spirit, while attached to the baby's body, is out of the body. As they speak to him through telepathic thought, his mind's eye sees those eyes. They show him the damage and how the eyes will look as he proceeds through childhood and into adulthood.

Spirit Guide: There is no damage to the brain; it is to the eyes. There is an increase in your intelligence. Though it is a minor increase, it will serve you well. You now have the option to reevaluate your plan for your life to see if these changes will serve your purposes. If you so desire, you may withdraw from this body, return to us, reevaluate a new host family, and draw up new plans.

"Bob fires off a lot of questions rapidly to his guides. He asks about his ability to walk. He wants to be reassured that his body will still be able to function as he expects. They assure him that it will. Then he asks:

Bob: What about my work?

Spirit Guide: This will be accomplished.

Bob: Will this handicap impede my evolutionary process in this lifetime?

Second Guide: Let's see.

"Between the guides and Bob, in the middle of the air, is the planning board for his old life on the bottom, a transitional planning board above that, and above that the board for Bob's life as it will be after this change. These boards are like a hologram—filmy in appearance, not solid. Their thoughts create these boards and draw lines on them. Lines represent the process of growth.

"A diagram forms. There are little branches along the way. Some of them are houses. For example, the home his family occupies at the time of his birth, the home they move to, and the places he occupies in adulthood, even college, are mapped out on this board. It all happens very quickly.

"With their thoughts, they move elements from one board to another. The first thing they take from the original planning board to the transitional board is his mother.

Spirit Guide: Let's begin with your mother. She will remain in this life with you and will continue to be your mother.

Bob: That's good.

"Bob looks reassured. He takes a deep breath and lets out a sigh [of relief].

Spirit Guide: Your father ...

"They move him from the original board to the middle board.

Spirit Guide: He will still be with you.

"Very quickly other elements are moved—family pets, relatives, things like that. They all go to the transitional board. As the guides move these elements to the transitional board, they also appear on the top board.

Spirit Guide: These elements are unchanging and will remain a steady influence, focus, and force in your life. But your teachers will change. This school [*points to a school element on the lower board*] is no longer relevant because of your condition. You will now be going to this school [*points to a school element that suddenly appears on the transitional board*]. This school will serve your needs best and will give you the guidance you need to live in the world under these conditions. Next, let's take your friends.

"They move into high school. These friends move from the original to the transitional board. There are friends who are important to Bob at that time in his life. Bob is shaking his head in agreement. He's holding the fingers of one hand up to his mouth, and he is holding that arm's elbow with his other hand.

"The conversation speeds up very rapidly at this point as the guide moves elements from the original plan into the transitional plan. I'm told that these are elemental pieces—nothing we need to include for the purposes of the book. Now, I ask them to slow down as we get to the more important part.

Spirit Guide: The woman who agreed to be your wife may opt out of this agreement. You will still be served challenges to your self-acceptance, but without her. You will experience a stronger challenge because of the absence of a supportive partner in your life at that time.

"Bob says nothing. He is listening and thinking this over. Now, he asks about the woman. He's calling her Maureen.

Bob: Will I at least have Maureen's friendship?
Spirit Guide: That is her choice. Let us bring her in.

"At the speed of thought, she is brought in. She hadn't yet been born. From the middle of the ribcage up, I see a physical form. It's not solid — you can see through it — but it is the same shape as a female human body, the body she will take in this life-to-be. She appears to be between twenty-five and forty-five years of age. Below that is the lightbody, the spirit body. My guide is saying 'the cloak of the body.' She is wearing part of the cloak. It's an instantaneous thing that happens as she recalls her plan for her life and how it intersects with Bob's. I'm told that only part of her is in the cloak because already she is changing her mind about taking part.

"She is shown the new diagram of Bob's life. For a long time, she says nothing. She finally says:

Maureen: I'd rather not.

"I see her left hand come up; her right hand touches the fingers on the left as she counts the reasons why.

Maureen: The school in which we were originally planning to meet will be irrelevant. Bob will not go there because of this.
Spirit Guide: No matter, we can still arrange for you to meet.
Maureen: No, no, I don't want that.

| Spirit Guide: | We can even arrange for you to meet at the same age you would have met previously. |
| Maureen: | No. It's very important we share a history that begins in school. It's not just my comfort with Bob; it's Bob's comfort with me. It's more important for him. |

"They turn to Bob and ask his opinion. He says he understands and agrees with her, though it is obvious he is also disappointed.

| Bob: | I release you from your agreement with me. There will be another time and place when we can come together again and share our lives as one. |

"She takes his hand.

| Maureen: | Thank you. Yes, there will be. In three lives from this, we can be together again. |

"He nods his head in agreement, and there is an embrace. Instead of walking out of this room, her spirit form disappears. I hear an audible sigh from Bob as he releases her and his expectations. I was told to tell you [Rob] that he releases his expectations, because even on the soul level we wrestle with that. We have an easier time of it, but it is still an issue for many of us *not to place expectations and assumptions on other individuals who are important to us.*

"Maureen could see very clearly that the direction Bob's life would now go wouldn't necessarily serve her goals. It was both out of needing to serve her purposes and also through her unconditional love of Bob—through seeing that she was no longer the optimal choice for a life partner—that she bowed out of that agreement."

Staci paused, signaling to me that her guide was waiting for a question before he presented another part of Bob's planning. Staci had again demonstrated an extraordinary ability to see and hear a life planning session, though Bob's was actually a *post-birth* planning session. In viewing this rare event, we were peering behind the veil to witness a soul forging a new design for an incarnation already begun.

Spirit had presented Staci with exactly the information we sought. We discovered that certain elements of Bob's original blueprint had been preserved though others had been altered. I was eager to see what else we might learn. The outcome of the impromptu planning—Bob's decision to continue living as a blind person—was already known. Given that Maureen had bowed out of his life, why and how had he reached that decision?

"In this lifetime," I said to Staci, "Bob wanted to work on self-acceptance and self-esteem. Is there any other talk about how blindness will further those goals?"

"The [new] life is through being plotted," Staci announced as she jumped ahead in the planning session. Her spirit guide was now taking her to a different portion of the conversation.

"Bob has absorbed all the changes.

Bob: I understand the unique needs I will have if I choose to accept this body and life. Tell me how this will help or hinder my progress as I strive to reach the goals I originally set for myself.

"The reply comes from both spirit guides as if they were speaking in one voice.

Spirit Guides: You will come to know yourself at a much earlier age now. You will skip almost two decades of the development process because of the lack of visual stimulation that would have disoriented you from your past and from knowing who you are and who you chose to be.

Bob: I like the sound of that. That means I get to skip a lot of wasted time and difficulty.

Spirit Guides: Yes, that is correct. But there will be new difficulties appropriate to the uniqueness of the blindness.

Bob: I understand.

Spirit Guides: Though you will still be challenged to love yourself, you will know yourself better at an earlier age, and this will bring you halfway there. By the time you start elementary school in this life, you will be at the same state of evolvement as you would have been in high school.

Bob: That eliminates a lot of stress that was built into my life as we had planned it originally.

Spirit Guides: Yes. There will still be times when you will question yourself, when you will wonder if you are good enough or if there is something wrong with you. But your intelligence will be increased, and your ability to reason will be enhanced. You will make sense of the strings of your life better and earlier, and you will cause less hurt to those who love you.

"When I say *strings,*" Staci explained, "they are showing me an image of a higher self [soul] and lower self [personality]. The strings run between the higher self and lower self. Bob will be able to gather all of that together and make sense of it at an earlier age.

"Evidently, Bob's marriage was supposed to lead him to fully understand himself as a homosexual. There is no question here about Bob trying to live a heterosexual lifestyle. That step will be skipped. His growth will be more directly related to homosexuality and the lifestyle that comes with it. Bob nods in agreement, still taking it all in.

Bob: How will I know about being homosexual?

Spirit Guides: Your experience of yourself will be uniquely different from the way you would have experienced yourself without the accident and the accompanying physical challenge. Without the visual distractions, you will have insights and awareness about yourself and be in constant or near-constant contact with your inner being.

"I'm told that 'inner being' is the term for the intelligent interface between the soul and the living [physical] being. There is an enhancement of Bob's creative ability because of this. When there is an enhanced connection to one's creative energy, there is always an enhancement to one's spiritual growth, whether it is conscious or unconscious.

Spirit Guides: You will develop an appreciation for kindness—the gift of temperament—that you would not have had. That will remind you that you are good and worthwhile, and although human, full of love and capable and worthy of being loved and giving love. While it is not without work, it is less challenging than if you were a fully sighted human being subject to the distractions that might hinder you.

"They point to that element that represents the different school he goes to.

Spirit Guides: You will know while you are still in that school that you are different. You will know that you are attracted to the sound of a man's voice, to the smell of a man, to all things unique to the male of the species.

Bob: I see.

"That's true," Bob said later. "I knew it from an early age. Even when I was eight or nine, I always enjoyed being hugged by men more than women. By thirteen or fourteen, I would have more of a reaction when I was with boys. Voice attracts me. Smell attracts me."

With that, Staci and her guide concluded their fascinating presentation. It was now time for questions.

From my earlier conversation with Bob, I was aware that blindness had led to experiences that tested his self-esteem and provided him with both the motivation and the opportunity to look within himself for love. Yet we had been told that one of his goals for this lifetime was to be more among people.

"Staci, please ask your spirit guide why Bob accepted the challenge of blindness when he knew that it would cause some measure of isolation."

Staci's speech slowed as her spirit guide began to talk directly through her.

"In your time frame, this soul was informed of this new challenge two days after birth. The blindness was not in place completely, but it was developing. The precedent was being set. This soul, like all souls, spent a great deal of time in and out of the body in the first few weeks of life.

"The soul saw a way to work with this challenge and still maintain a high degree of comfort." (I took *comfort* as a reference to the previous lives in which Bob had grown accustomed to isolation.) "A goal for this lifetime is to learn emotional independence."

"How does Spirit define emotional independence?" I inquired.

"The realization and recognition that one is responsible for creating one's own sense of happiness and well-being."

"Did Bob feel that he didn't create his own happiness and well-being in the lifetime as a monk in Spain?"

"We would not put it in those words. We would say that he still suffered from acute emotional sensitivity. He found it easier to deal with the world by closing himself off from it, by limiting his interactions with others and his involvement in day-to-day life."

"Why was it felt that blindness would further the goal of emotional independence?" I wanted Staci's spirit guide to offer as much explanation as possible for anyone wanting to understand why a soul would choose to experience blindness.

"Because it presented an even stronger and greater challenge to the soul. The only way the soul would survive as a person in this lifetime—at its happiest and best—would be to recognize and learn the lesson that it is its own source of well-being. In learning that lesson, one must gain self-esteem. The soul was given the choice of opting out of life. The soul chose to stay. This soul likes tough challenges."

"Why did Bob choose to experience homosexuality?"

"Prior to the conditional changes in this soul's lifetime, there was an agreement with one woman to share a marriage experience. It was not supposed to last lifelong. There was the struggle within this soul's person to recognize the underlying homosexuality, face it, and become okay with it. It was going to happen later in life. That experience would have served the same purpose that the homosexuality has already served in this lifetime. It has presented a challenge and a focus for the self-worth issue.

"Blindness and homosexuality are not well accepted, recognized, and dealt with in Western culture. They are challenges. To be okay as a homosexual man is part of learning self-worth. Sometimes you need greater challenges in order to learn a lesson. This soul has always been up to hard work."

I then asked how a blind person would know if the blindness had been planned before birth or if it had occurred unexpectedly. He said that if someone is born blind or with a genetic predisposition toward blindness, that would indicate pre-birth planning. When I wondered what other motivations a soul might have for making such plans, he explained that many composers incarnate blind so they can continue to hear the music easily; that even when souls have not been composers in past lives, they often have a desire to increase their hearing or other senses (which may happen as a consequence of blindness); and that artistic souls frequently choose to inhabit bodies with nonfunctional eyes.

"What else would you like people to know about the challenge of blindness?" I asked in conclusion.

"Blind people sometimes see things they would not see if they were sighted."

⌒

Bob embodies courage. Originally, he planned a difficult journey to self-discovery, self-acceptance, and, ultimately, self-love. When he realized his plan was no longer possible, he devised another in which he kept the original challenge of homosexuality and added to it the new challenge of blindness. To choose an "alternative" sexuality in a world that still struggles with tolerance is a bold act in its own right. To then add the unplanned challenge of blindness is remarkable. Rather than sidestep this new challenge by returning to spirit—an understandable decision and one to be respected—Bob chose to embrace it.

In Bob's first blueprint, he and a soul with whom he shares much love designed a lifetime in which they were to marry. The marriage was not intended to endure. In the course of my research, I have found that we generally know before birth whether a marriage will last. Divorce is not failure; rather, it is part of our plan. We intend to come together in marriage to teach and learn from each other and to balance karma. When this growth is accomplished, the marriage has served its divine purpose. I do not suggest that divorce or lifelong marriage is predestined; we always have free will. We can choose to leave someone with whom we had planned to spend a lifetime, and we can opt to remain when we had intended to have a temporary union. The choice is ours.

Initially, Bob choreographed a life in which he was to realize and accept his homosexuality while married. Imagine the degree of self-love he would need to fulfill his plan. He would first have to acknowledge his homosexuality to himself. He would then need to summon the courage to tell his wife. Ultimately, he would have to love himself and his spouse enough to leave a marriage that no longer reflected who he knew himself to be. Whether or not he would have developed such self-love is unknown; it would have hinged on the freewill decisions of his personality and on the ways in which he rose to his self-created challenge. Clearly, however, he designed a life in which this kind of blossoming could occur.

When blindness unexpectedly entered the picture, Bob created a new plan that would foster the same unfolding. As Staci's spirit guide told us, neither blindness nor homosexuality is well accepted in Western culture. When Bob chose to incarnate in the West at this period in history, he knew he would be shunned at times, that isolation and loneliness were likely—a prolonged rendering of the same lack of acceptance Bob's wife would have shown when he announced his homosexuality.

Bob created a learning-through-opposites life plan. Knowing how society would sometimes respond to his blindness and homosexuality, and determined to grow in self-acceptance and self-love, Bob planned circumstances that would drive him to discover within what was not offered without. Though a greater challenge than he had originally sought, blindness in some ways increased the likelihood of Bob attaining his goals because, as his spirit guides pointed out, it freed him from external distractions.

The guides knew that blindness would make it easier for Bob—and to some extent force him—to hear and heed inner wisdom.

Imagine a room at the Louvre in which a great landscape hangs on the wall. One person may walk through the room without ever seeing it; perhaps other paintings divert this person's attention. A second individual may walk through the gallery and notice the landscape from a distance. He or she may admire the work of art in passing but never stop to see it truly. A third person may sit in front of the landscape for hours, savoring every nuance—the brushstrokes, the texture of the oil, the interplay of color, the use of light. This person recognizes the painting as a masterpiece.

Bob chose blindness because it presented an opportunity to rediscover his magnificence. The destination—self-love—remained the same, but the route to that endpoint changed dramatically. Bob does not need eyesight to observe the beauty of his internal landscape. He is, however, free to look away from it, notice it in passing, or appreciate each contour and facet.

Bob has accomplished much. He has developed a heightened empathy, particularly in regard to, as he said, the "underdog," and a keen intuition that allows him to sense the essence of a person. Though blind, Bob sees what is important: relationships with people, kindness, and compassion. He has learned to trust both the animals and the people who guide him. Though he has at times been ostracized because of his blindness, he continues to reach out to others. He is sweet and gentle, a deeply sensitive soul. Such is the inner beauty to which he reawakens in this lifetime.

When Bob notices a quality like kindness in himself or others, he is seeing with the heart, not the head. It is a heart-knowing that makes Bob a "barometer of kindness." Beauty and love in any form are truly understood only in this way. When we look upon a flower in full bloom, we do not reason that its colors are appealing, that the petals are attractively shaped, that the fragrance is pleasant and therefore deserving of enjoyment. When we see a newborn baby, we do not analyze the shape of the face or the dimensions of the body to conclude that the child is worthy of appreciation. These experiences speak instantly and directly to the heart, just as kindness does. The mind is bypassed; no interpretation is necessary. Understanding is immediate and natural.

When we are Home in spirit and thus unencumbered by the hazy, distorting filters of a physical brain, this kind of heartfelt knowing is our very nature. If we choose to incarnate in the current epoch—one that nonphysical beings sometimes refer to as the Age of Reason because of its emphasis on mental processes—we may lose touch temporarily with our hearts as we immerse ourselves in our intellect. In short, we explore who we are not. Because painful life challenges can be genuinely understood—and healed—only by the heart, they force us to shift from analyzing to feeling. No longer exalted on a throne, the mind now serves the heart that was once subservient to it. As we return to a heart-centered way of being, we remember who we really are. This experience results in a more profound self-knowing, one that would not be possible without the contrast provided by the physical realm.

Bob's guides knew that blindness would give him "an appreciation for kindness—the gift of temperament" and that this heartfelt appreciation would remind him that he is "full of love and capable and worthy of being loved and giving love." They also knew that his previously planned life contained "visual stimulation that would have disoriented you … from knowing who you are and who you chose to be." As a soul, Bob *is* kindness, sweetness, and gentleness. These qualities, so easily and often obscured by the loud crush of the physical, are prized in spirit. Bob's blindness has kept him closer to these aspects of his inner being. They are the doorway to the self-acceptance and self-love he sought to experience in this lifetime. Without eyesight he does not see his physical form, but through kindness he glimpses his eternal identity.

Bob's life plan, like that of so many who choose to incarnate in a period when love of self is lacking, was designed to give him a deeper understanding of self-love through both its lack and the *experience* of its subsequent creation. When we are in spirit, we know love of self as easily and as naturally as we know love of others. We know, too, that these are one and the same. Only in the physical can we courageously forget and then remember the feeling of self-love. Life challenges bring us to that love, showing us that it lives within, reflecting to us that *we* are the great love of our lives.

CHAPTER 5

⌒⌒⌒

Drug Addiction and Alcoholism

TO MAKE THIS BOOK AS helpful as possible, I have
focused on some of the most common life challenges.
Certainly, substance addiction is among these. This
chapter explores drug and alcohol addiction from two perspectives: from a parent whose child has an addiction and
from a person experiencing the addiction. In the former
category is Sharon Dembinski, whose son, Tony, has battled
an addiction to heroin.

Like Sharon, millions of parents around the world struggle
to understand why their children choose to use drugs. They
feel tremendous guilt and blame themselves for somehow
failing their children. Many view the addiction as meaningless suffering for both the children and their families. I
wondered if the concept of pre-birth planning could in any
way ease these parents' pain, perhaps helping them to see a
deeper purpose for the experience.

When I began to research this life challenge, I did not
know whether such challenges were planned before birth.
I had already spoken with Jennifer (chapter 3), whose two
sons were born with multiple handicaps. That Jennifer
and her sons had planned these handicaps made it seem

probable that a parent and child might also plan the child's addiction. But Jennifer's sons had been *born* with those challenges, whereas Sharon's son had become addicted to heroin in his teens. If Sharon and Tony had, in fact, planned his addiction, how could they have known that it would develop later in life? Moreover, why would two people, one of them a loving parent, plan incarnations in which the child would have a drug addiction? What spiritual purposes would this challenge serve for the parent? for the child? And how would parent and child coordinate their life plans so that each experienced the desired growth?

Sharon's Story

Sharon, a pediatric nurse practitioner in newborn intensive care, was at work when she received the call from her daughter, Sarah. Sarah and Sharon's husband, John, had found Tony unconscious on the floor of their bathroom, a bloody syringe next to him, a belt wrapped around his arm, his skin blue.

"I was crying hysterically," Sharon recalled. "I ran out the door and got in my car. The doctor I work with chased after me. She said, 'Calm down! You can't drive like this.' She was holding on to my window. I kept saying, 'Please let go of my car!' Finally, she let go. I drove as fast as I could, all the way praying, *Please let him be alive when I get there! Please don't let him die!*"

Sharon met Sarah and John at the hospital. Tony had overdosed on heroin; he was semicomatose and in great pain from what was later determined to be a heart attack. When physicians decided to transfer him to a larger hospital, Sharon jumped in the back of the ambulance.

"The EMTs [emergency medical technicians] both said, 'Ma'am, you have to get out,'" Sharon recalled. "I said,

'I'm not getting out of this rig! If your baby's ever in my unit, I will give you professional courtesy. Now let me stay here!'"

The technicians agreed, and Sharon rode at her son's side. When they arrived, Tony was placed in special pulmonary intensive care. Doctors told Sharon he probably would not live through the night.

"I promised—begged—God to save him, and I would do everything I could to help him and anyone else who needed help," Sharon said softly. "He looked so beautiful lying there. He had a head full of curls, medium dark brown, as he did when he was a baby. I spent a lot of time putting my fingers through his hair, playing with his curls, thinking about how beautiful he was, thinking through his whole life, how much I loved him. I lost three babies between Sarah and Tony. I wanted Tony so badly. I wanted a son so badly. I'm one of six daughters. I was never close with another man, besides my own father and husband. Never had a brother or good male friend, so I really wanted a son. And everyone who came in the room, every nurse, every doctor, commented on what a good-looking boy he was."

Tony made it to morning, at which time doctors told Sharon he might survive but that brain damage was likely. After all, they said, he had probably been unconscious in the bathroom for ninety minutes.

Tony remained unconscious for the next five days, Sharon at his bedside throughout. Finally, "he opened his eyes and looked at me. I knew his brain was fine," Sharon said tearfully. "He said, 'I'm sorry' and cried. I said, 'Please don't say you're sorry, Tony. It's all right now. You're going to be okay.'

"After we held each other, I asked him if he had wanted to take his life. He told me no, it was an accident. He didn't want to die. That was so much of a relief to me! That meant there was still hope that he would beat his heroin addiction." Sharon was sobbing now. "I'll always wonder what I did wrong when I was raising him," she said sadly.

After the hospital stay, Tony went to a rehab program and then to a halfway house. There he accepted heroin from one of the other residents and overdosed again. After he received medical care, Sharon brought him home.

"I didn't know if I should feel hopeful or scared," she remembered. "I went from one feeling to the next within minutes. One minute I would be desperate. The next minute I'd think, Everything's going to be okay."

Despite those swings, Sharon focused on the positive in her talks with Tony, pointing out that on almost every day during rehab he had chosen *not* to use drugs. "How many days did you make the right decision?" she asked him encouragingly.

In her quest to help her son, Sharon began to participate on Internet message boards, including one for methadone advocates. Chemically similar to but less addictive than heroin, methadone is often used in treatment programs to wean people from heroin. "The people I met—some were addicts and some were involved in advocacy—were caring, open, and loving," Sharon told me. She formed a particularly strong bond with Eddie, a man who was struggling to overcome his own addiction.

Sharon relied on Eddie for insight into Tony's feelings. Tony was now isolating himself in his bedroom, on some days coming out only for food. Eddie assured Sharon that her son's behavior was normal, that Tony was avoiding the world because he wanted to recover but feared that something might trigger a relapse. "Eddie would say profound things that really opened my eyes," Sharon said. Some of Eddie's messages were so inspiring that she printed them out and taped them to the mirror in Tony's bathroom. Eventually, Tony grew to be as fond of Eddie as Sharon was.

Three months after Tony left rehab, Eddie died from a drug overdose. Sharon learned of his death in a message on the Internet board.

"Tony came into my room and sat down on the end of my bed," Sharon recalled. "I said, 'Eddie's dead.' He said, *'What?'* I said, 'Eddie is dead. Overdose.' He got off the bed. I stood up. We walked to each other, and he held me. We didn't say anything—just cried."

Eddie died fifteen months before I spoke with Sharon. Since then Tony has been doing well; he has a new girlfriend and is looking for a job. I asked Sharon how she has changed in those fifteen months.

"I've become more compassionate, more understanding," she replied. "I have a lot of perspective now. The big thing I've learned is that I can't control Tony's behavior. I can support the positive. I can not enable him. I can't control him. I can only control how I respond to him."

Sharon's professional life has changed as well. Motivated by both Eddie's death and the promises she made to God when she prayed for her son's life, Sharon launched an innovative program at her hospital. Mothers on Methadone (MOM) provides medical care and emotional support to pregnant women who have been receiving methadone treatment and to their children. In MOM Sharon combined her love of babies with her newfound passion to help people who have experienced heroin addiction.

"We interact with the parents to make them feel accepted and trusted," Sharon said happily. "If they're not supported, they're going to relapse, and then that baby has no mother. That baby goes to foster care, and its whole life is changed dramatically and not for the better. Think about the impact. If those mothers go on to not relapse and be able to kiss their child, that is *huge*!"

Before she started MOM, Sharon sometimes judged such women. "I felt, How could you do this? That's changed."

Sharon has also seen changes in her colleagues at the hospital. "To see my family go through this, it hits close to home for them. If it could happen to my son, then it could happen to their kids. That really changed how they respond to the patients."

"Sharon," I asked, "what would you like to say to parents who have a child addicted to drugs?"

"Don't keep it a secret. If you share what's happened, people are going to help you."

Sharon's Session with Glenna Dietrich

In the days since my conversation with Sharon, some of her words had weighed heavily on me. I did not want Sharon to feel that she had somehow failed Tony. I had seen people shed remorse and sadness and adopt a completely new perspective on their life challenges when they learned they had planned them. I hoped Sharon's session with Glenna would provide her with peace of mind.

Glenna started by sharing information she had already received from Spirit. "I was told a few things about your son. He experienced other lifetimes where he was in an occupation that was very magical to him. He experienced situations where things just happened for him. Maybe he was even a magician or a shaman. He's looking to re-experience that kind of magic. That's part of the reason he was drawn into that [drug] lifestyle. There is a magical kind of chemical reaction within the body when he takes those drugs.

"His life is all about creating nonordinary things. He came in with a lot of talent. He's very gifted. When you look at Einstein and people who brought in some tremendous information, musical ability, or creative process, their young adulthood is fraught with problems because it is very difficult to bring that vibration fully into the body. Once they mature enough, then you see that flowing."

"Before he got involved in drugs, his artistic ability was astounding," Sharon confirmed. "He doesn't do that anymore, and he hasn't in years, but he has that ability. His IQ is 140."

Glenna shifted the focus. "When I tune into him, I see fear. That's what it feels like to me."

"That's what I feel, too," Sharon acknowledged.

"When we have a great gift to use and there are no outlets for it," Glenna continued, "that creates an energetic block in the body. Blocked energy creates disease. So guide him toward expressing his creativity again. And love him, love him, love him. He's feeling like he's done something wrong and has lost respect and worthiness in your eyes."

Glenna's compassion was palpable. I relaxed, knowing that Sharon was in good hands.

"Did we plan this ahead of time for the greater good?" Sharon asked.

"For the greater good, and also because it was what your soul needed to experience," answered Glenna. "We come here to experience everything. We've all been murderers, rapists, saints. We've experienced it all, or we're going to experience it all. And we set those things up ahead of time so that we have the perfect scenario for whatever we need to learn this time around.

"For you personally, you didn't need to come back again. You have completed your learning cycle, but you came back to assist him. I'm not saying that's your only purpose, but that was the main thing that made you decide to come back. He knows that on some level. That can be both wonderful and very, very difficult, because it makes him feel guilty."

I was surprised by this information; it was the first time I heard that a soul had not needed to reincarnate. Thoughts of Sharon's MOM program flashed through my mind — the way she had taken her pain and used it to help others. It occurred to me that Glenna and I were speaking with a highly evolved soul.

"He doesn't know how to nurture himself," Glenna told Sharon. "Those are the lessons he came here to get. You have incredible nurturing ability. That's where your gifts lie. He not only receives it from you, but he's also watching you, and he's going to emulate you."

"He said something to me the other day that completely blew me away," Sharon replied. "He said, 'Mom, you inspire me every day by everything you do for everybody.'"

Sharon, Glenna, and I chatted for several more minutes. Then a few moments of silence elapsed as Glenna's consciousness departed and another consciousness joined us.

"It is with great joy that we accept your invitation," came the warm greeting from the entities that were now using Glenna's body. Evidently, more than one being had joined us, but they were speaking as one. There was indeed a joyful tone to the voice. They spoke softly and gently.

"We welcome you with love to this edge between our world and yours. We live in dimensions that are as close to you as the width of a hair on your head. We are two that are guides. One of us has worked with you, Sharon, since the moment of your conception and actually before that time in planning all things that your soul decided to make known to you in this incarnation. We live in the angelic realm, and so you might call us your guardian angels. Do you have questions for us?"

Sharon had agreed to let me to take the lead in our inquiry. I began by asking the channeled beings for their names.

"It is that our names are vibrations, and so it is unclear to us how to formulate sounds through the medium's lips," they replied.

"Thank you for speaking with us today. Did Sharon and her son, Tony, plan before birth for him to experience a drug addiction, and if so, why?"

"The answer to your question is yes," the angels said. "All experiences are contemplated before the incarnation has been chosen. The exact time, those situations and energies available for other people, all must be perfect in order for the soul to experience those gifts of knowing and wisdom that are available through your realm."

"What did Sharon hope to learn or how did she hope to grow as the result of being the parent of a child with a drug addiction?"

"It was essential for her to experience these things in a space of humility. Her soul and her personality in this incarnation have an abundance of the qualities that create abilities and energy and give in a bountiful manner. So, there is a need to create limitation, as the soul uses limitation in your realm for growth. As you experience limitedness, there is a need to overcome frustration, work within one's own parameters, and focus energy — an energy that cuts through the density in your realm and creates spaces of light and a higher vibration."

The angels had just provided us with a succinct explanation of why the physical realm is so appealing to eternal, nonphysical souls. As they spoke of limitation, I remembered that Doris's soul (chapter 2) had told me that souls see themselves as unlimited. Because contrast leads to greater self-knowing, souls incarnate on the physical plane to experience the *perception* of limitation. That perception, which is itself an illusion, contrasts dramatically with the great power we know ourselves to have when we are in spirit. On the physical plane, we challenge ourselves to work within — and, at this time in humanity's evolution, move beyond — the illusion of limitation.

I decided to explore this concept with Sharon's angelic guides. "What specifically is Sharon experiencing that would be classified as limitation?"

"In her experiences with her son, she has been allowed to believe that she must be perfect. She experienced situations in which her abilities and wisdom were at times not enough to control all aspects of her environment, including the actions of her son. She was also to honor and respect the path of those people around her, even if different from her own path. She has learned this lesson quite well, and has tested and expanded her compassion, and also expanded her belief in the goodness of humans. These are no small things."

The angels had beautifully summarized Sharon's life blueprint. Apparently, she and Tony had planned his drug addiction in part so that she might know herself as respect and compassion. Rather than adopt a belief in the "badness" of people who choose drugs — a false belief that might then need to be healed in subsequent incarnations — Sharon had used the experience to rely on others and thus see their goodness. She had willingly received love from others, and in so doing had given those people a great gift — the opportunity to express love. Because our true nature as souls *is* love, we consider our physical lives well spent to the extent that we give and receive love.

Still, there were many ways in which Sharon could have planned before birth to gain such self-knowing. "The things you mentioned could be accomplished with other life challenges. Why did Sharon choose specifically to be the parent of a son with a drug addiction?"

"Her son's request," they said simply.

A moment ago the angels had referred to frustration. From my conversation with Sharon, I knew she had felt great frustration with the limits of her ability to control Tony's behavior. I also knew she had moved beyond frustration to acceptance of the fact that she cannot control him. "How has the experience of being a parent of a child with a drug addiction allowed her to overcome frustration?" I asked the angels.

"It has shown her avenues of reaching out to those around her," they said quietly. "It also allowed her to reach into her own essence and strength in ways that, had she not had this experience and this intense love for her son, would not have been to the same depths. She explores now the continuum between the dark side—the fear of loss of the life of her beloved son—and the light side—an avenue of compassion and caring that offers her love to the world."

"As I understand it," I said, "when we are in spirit, we are able to do or create what we like without resistance. If there is no resistance, then there is no frustration. If that's true, why would a soul care about learning to overcome frustration?"

"It is simply the feeling that is derived. Growth comes through emotions in your realm."

"You mentioned Sharon is also learning to work within her own parameters. What do you mean, and how has her experience taught her that?"

"Her soul has experienced much over many incarnations. She is genuinely complete and whole in her experiences.

And so reincarnating into this body, holding that level of wisdom and understanding, she brought in with her much knowing and awareness. There is that sense of being not like others around you, that sense of arrogance, that need for humility. Until the human experiences those situations of desperation, those situations of feeling out of control of the outcome, there cannot be the understanding, there cannot be the compassion. Compassion is created by experience only, not by watching others go through the experience, nor by reading about it, or being told about it. Only by walking through it does the human acquire that understanding."

Earlier, the angels had mentioned another purpose for Tony's drug addiction: helping Sharon to focus her energy. I asked the angels what they had meant.

"She now has the ability to take the compassion and love that she has clarified through this experience and use them in a very highly focused way. She has a very clear purpose and goal in mind. The clarity of that goal has come through the process of getting rid of that which no longer fits."

"You mentioned she also wanted to honor the paths of others. How has this experience helped her to do that?"

"She has created a place for herself wherein she has an understanding and a compassion for those who are experiencing their lives by choice in a different fashion than she. It is the choice that becomes honored. She now has the ability to acknowledge and recognize that all paths bring awareness. Those lessons are what is important, not the path that is chosen. This is a great level of wisdom."

The angels' words made me think of people in my life whom I had judged. How often had I wondered why someone chose a particular path, one that to my way of thinking was clearly a mistake? Like Tony, those people had selected paths that brought the awareness they needed.

"You said the experience has expanded Sharon's belief in the goodness of people. How did the experience do that?" I was particularly interested in this answer. Sharon had taken experiences that often produce bitterness, anger, self-pity, and feelings of defeat and somehow used them to see *more* good in others. I wanted to learn from Sharon's example.

"There have been events small and large in which she has felt desperately out of control. Her quest saved her son's life and rescued him from an obsession which she believed to be life-threatening. At those times she reached out, and others responded to her in kindness and support. This builds the foundation of trust for the self not only to go deep into that well of strength, but also to know that there will be those around—even complete strangers—who will support and acknowledge and provide information and guidance. She has now chosen to be among them." I recalled Sharon's advice to people: Reach out to others.

Despite the love she had received from others, Sharon's path had still been one of great pain. What else had inspired her to plan this experience? Had her primary motivation been the deepening of lessons previously learned? What about her love for Tony and her desire to assist with his life plan? I asked the angels to explain further.

"When the soul incarnates into a human body, there is memory lapse involved," they explained. "And so there are those things [lessons] which are recognizable but not stored in the conscious mind. So, these [experiences] are reminders for her. There is a belief on the part of her soul that limitation through these experiences would solidify any understanding or wisdom she already possesses."

"But is her motivation primarily to be of service to her son?"

"It is out of the love for her son that she has chosen this path."

"Was part of her motivation for planning this experience to do something that would be of benefit to the world?"

"All things that are situations of learning, all emotions, all wisdom that one individual creates for themselves [on Earth] is brought to others in your realm and also moves throughout the dimensions. Nothing is done, nothing is said, nothing is thought that does not create a ripple effect outward from the being itself through emotional vibration that moves through all of the dimensions. This is not clearly understood in the human brain and is information that may not be taken in on some levels. We, however, choose to share it with you."

In all the sessions, nonphysical beings offer much important information. Yet certain moments stand out to me as the dispensing of particularly vital wisdom. This was one such moment. The angels had just described the awesome responsibility — and opportunity — borne by each human being. We are responsible for everything we do, say, and think. That responsibility becomes infinitely more profound when we realize that every action, word, and thought affects every other being — not only on Earth, *but also throughout the entire cosmos.* How often, I thought, do we feel insignificant or powerless? If this truth were understood, no one would feel that way ever again. And we would strive to express love and only love in every moment, including in our "private" thoughts.

Sharon, it seemed, was already aware of this wisdom on some level. I recalled the passion with which she had described the impact of her MOM program. As a soul she would have designed her life with full awareness of the phenomenon the angels had just described.

"As a result of the experiences Sharon has had," I said, "she started a new program at her hospital to help pregnant women who have an addiction to heroin. Was doing that work part of the reason she planned the experience with Tony?"

"Yes," was the angels' simple reply.

Now, the full beauty of Sharon's life plan was becoming clear. Given the comprehensiveness of the plan, I wondered if Eddie had also been part of the blueprint.

"There is an individual Sharon met who is now back in spirit—his name here was Eddie—who provided much support to her. Is Eddie part of Sharon's soul group, and was he part of the plan with Tony?"

"He is part of Tony's soul group," the angels corrected, "and yes, he participated in the planning."

"When they were planning, how did Sharon and Eddie know they would eventually find each other?"

"It is planned," they said matter-of-factly. "All things are synchronous." Here, the angels were referring to the truth that there are no coincidences. People like Sharon and Eddie who meet by "happenstance" on an Internet site are actually drawn together by their similar frequencies: Like attracts like. Had they not met on the Internet, they would have met another way.

I asked the angels if Tony's near-fatal overdose had been planned.

"Yes," they said again.

"Why did Sharon and Tony want the experience of the overdose in addition to the drug addiction?"

"It brought energies to a culminating point and a crescendo of emotion that helped to bring about a transmutation and a place of decision making."

"Tony had two other drug overdoses. Were those planned as well?"

"Yes."

"Why did they feel it would be beneficial to plan three overdoses?"

"Each event created a separate explosion of emotional energy which then created a transmutation of those energies." I was not sure what the angels meant, but felt it might be related to Sharon's MOM program.

"Sharon could have planned before birth to start a program to help pregnant women with a drug addiction without herself having a child with a drug addiction," I pointed out. "What is the connection between the experience with Tony and the program she started? Why did she plan both?"

"There is a certain amount of passion — transmuted emotional energy — that was created through the events of the drug addiction and the sense of helplessness and hopelessness in Sharon's life. This transferred, then, to the making of this program, which is helpful in bringing a higher level of awareness to those individuals involved. Clients of this program have chosen their paths and these experiences for themselves. In so doing they allow individuals such as Sharon to create compassion and trust in the world. They allow Sharon to experience compassion over and over in many different ways. They also allow her to view their past with honor and respect instead of anger and pity. There is much to be learned in your realm about sadness and the use of pity, which is very disrespectful. These lessons are being taught to bring awareness and high wisdom into your realm."

I asked the angels if there were any reasons why Sharon had chosen to be the mother, rather than the father.

"In your realm," they answered, "the biological connection between mother and child is much stronger. Culturally, this is important, as the male of the species is not required to have, nor is it honored for him to have, extremely close emotional connections with the child. In this case there needed to be an extremely close connection in order for the support to be offered, needed, and wanted. This level of nurturing comes through the female of your species in a much clearer and more articulated way. We see this as changing and becoming more balanced, but this does not come fully into your realm as we speak."

"Are there any reasons why Sharon chose to have a son rather than a daughter with a drug addiction?"

"The gender choice was inconsequential."

"When Sharon and Tony were planning the drug addiction, did they specifically choose heroin and, if so, why?"

"Yes," stated the angels. "Chemical makeup. There was a need for a very strong addiction. This particular drug suited that need." Although I already knew that pre-birth planning was quite intricate, I was nevertheless amazed by the degree of detail in Sharon and Tony's blueprint: They had planned not only the addiction, but also the specific addictive substance.

"What kind of influence does the soul exert over the mind or body that results in drug addiction?" I inquired. I was trying to determine how Sharon and Tony could have known that a drug addiction would actually occur.

"There are influences from many areas. Many of them are very well known to your scientists and to your past. One is astrology, where plans influence personality traits, abilities, and physical attributes. Another that you recognize is the transfer of DNA, cellular information, from one person to the next generation."

"When Sharon and Tony were planning this experience, did they consider the possibility of Tony having an addiction to alcohol? If so, why did they not choose that?"

"The chemistry was not appropriate."

"When Sharon was planning her life, did she consider having more than one child with a drug addiction?"

"No."

"Why did she want specifically one child with a drug addiction?"

"Her level of wisdom and knowledge is such that these events would be enough to propel and inspire her in the directions she needed to go."

"Did they discuss the possibility of his actually dying from a drug overdose?"

"Yes."

"Why did they not choose that?"

"There are more opportunities in this combined lifetime that will create spaces of healing and also more awareness between the two of them," replied the angels. It occurred to me that had Tony's death offered a more meaningful experience for Sharon and Tony, it would have been in their pre-birth plan.

"I understand that souls can choose to incarnate in any location at any time. Why did Sharon and Tony choose to incarnate in the United States at this time in history?"

"There are many opportunities for them to experience their own limitations, as well as to expand awareness, both for themselves and others around them. This is a time for exponential growth in your realm. Many who have chosen to incarnate at this time are finishing the reincarnation cycles and becoming ready to move on to other realms."

"Why are there more opportunities to experience limitation now than at other times, either in the past or in the future?"

"The planet is experiencing a systems breakdown. At those points in time when old systems break down, chaos is created. Chaos is a component—a very necessary component—of limitation and growth. It is perhaps the most fertile space in which to learn."

"What would you like to say to a reader who is addicted to drugs and is struggling to understand the deeper spiritual purpose?"

"It is essential to honor your past, know yourself, learn about who you are, and then love yourself," the angels said.

"What would you like to say to a reader who is the parent of a child addicted to drugs?"

"Very much the same."

"What is important or helpful for readers to know that I have not asked about?"

"It would be helpful to be aware of the possibilities for the expansion of awareness. Expansion can be accomplished without destroying the body or causing the body harm. Techniques are available to all who are in your realm. It is now time to reconsider those cultures and populations that have lived before you and begin to understand and perhaps incorporate the abilities the ancients held dear."

I asked the angels what they would like to say to young people who have an addiction to drugs and who feel that they've let their parents down, or who perhaps feel other forms of guilt or self-judgment.

"They have chosen their paths with a true purpose in mind," the angels responded. "There are times in life in your realm that true purpose becomes clouded with values and judgments thrust upon you from those around you. The pressures of the culture and family contribute to that. There is movement now in the lives of young people to move beyond the generational values and allow those old systems of religion, education, science, politics—those things that are rulers in your realm—to either expand or collapse completely to be rebuilt anew."

"For readers who are judgmental of those with drug addictions and who might like to give up those judgments, what can you say to help them?"

"In very many instances, the judgment of people around them helps those who are experiencing addiction with drugs to experience the full gamut of emotions they realized would be a part of this choice, part of this path. And so all things are useful. Nothing that is created in your realm is without worth. All things must be honored. Whether you are in agreement with them or have an understanding of them, they must be honored."

"How does someone with a drug addiction grow as a result of being judged by others?" I wondered.

"This creates limitations for them which they must overcome by deciding that they are worthy of love from themselves and others, despite the fact that there are those who place judgment on their action."

Sharon now posed a question to the angels.

"Can you tell me how successful the program I developed at my hospital will be? Will it grow?"

"We would say to you truly that any effort you have put into the creation of such an organization that supports those around you has tremendous success. Only thought, only experience, only energy—these are the things that successfully impact others in your realm. And so we invite you to view your program and your efforts as successful despite any observation of any other party. Hold these things in a place of honor in your heart."

"Thank you," said Sharon.

"Thank you very much for speaking with us," I echoed.

"You are greatly blessed," said the angels. "It is truly a pleasure, always, to be invited amongst you."

With that farewell, the session came to an end. There was a period of silence as Sharon and I took in everything that had been shared with us. I sat quietly, savoring the warmth and affection I had felt from the angels.

"There were a couple of times where I was crying," said Sharon, filling the silence.

I asked which moments had touched her.

"The two that touched me the most," Sharon replied, "were when the spirit was discussing the limitations and the loss of control and how this experience basically humbled me. I mentioned before how it changed me so dramatically to a much more compassionate person. Had you asked me five years ago if I was a compassionate person, I would have said, 'Of course I am!' I didn't know what that was until now. And when you asked about Eddie, my friend that's no longer here with us, just mentioning his name was emotional for me, but knowing that he is part of Tony's soul group—it makes so much more sense to me now."

❧

Like so many of us, Sharon and Tony designed lives of learning through opposites: they scripted temporary, physical roles that contrasted markedly with their eternal, nonphysical identities. Tony is not the heroin addict; rather, he is a courageous soul who undertook the life challenge of drug addiction to learn self-nurturing. Sharon is neither the frustrated mother nor the nurse who looked at drug-addicted pregnant women and wondered, How could you? Instead, she is a deeply loving soul who planned moments of frustration and judgment so that she might eventually experience and thus know herself as respect, tolerance, and compassion.

Beyond the personal experiences and wisdom they sought, Sharon and Tony planned his drug addiction as a form of service to humanity. Such is the life plan of lightworkers, whose blueprints entail the sharing of inner light for wide-spread upliftment. Before she was born, Sharon expected she would respond to her son's addiction by starting a program to help drug-addicted pregnant women. After her birth Sharon could have exercised her free will by hardening her heart and not reaching out to others. Through previous lives, however, she had evolved to a point at which compassion was the most probable response. One can well envision Tony planning the challenge of drug addiction and Sharon saying, "I will be the mother who loves you through this, and I will build upon this experience to help others."

Sharon and Tony's story reminds us that the physical plane is one of illusion in which nothing is as it appears. Sometimes, service takes the form of large-scale, public programs. More commonly, it takes the form of opportunities for us to move beyond judgment. Judgment separates us from those we judge. Separation, in turn, creates fear and prevents us from awakening to a truth we knew before we were born: that we are all one. Each of us is a spark of consciousness in a larger, unified Consciousness, a cell in the heart of one Divine Being. To judge is to separate ourselves from our divinity; to release judgment is to remember it.

It is important to ask what aspects of self are called forth by our judgments. If, for example, we judge someone with a drug addiction as weak, then there is a part of ourselves we judge as weak. If we did not see ourselves as weak at certain times or under certain circumstances, then it would be impossible to hold that judgment of someone else. Instead, either we would not notice the behavior or traits that we view as weakness, or we would not see those behaviors and traits as weakness. All judgment of others is cloaked self-judgment. It is necessarily so. Profound spiritual growth occurs when we bravely pull that cloak away and acknowledge how we feel about ourselves. This process is difficult and requires unflinching self-candor, but its rewards are great.

Sharon now personifies nonjudgment of others. Rather than condemn her son for his relapses, she instead reminds him of the many times he chose not to use heroin during his recovery process. She provides unconditional warmth and love to pregnant women who have a heroin addiction. She sees beyond the troubles of the addicts she met online, peering into their souls to find compassion and caring. She does not pity them. As Glenna later said to Sharon and me, "Pity divides us, compassion unites us." To pity someone is to see the person as a victim and thus overlook the great courage demonstrated in living the planned challenge.

Indeed, the only person Sharon still judges is herself. That self-judgment derives in part from her belief that she was not perfect. Our beliefs, particularly those we have about ourselves, constitute much of the limitation of which the angels spoke. The journey to self-love and self-acceptance requires that we recognize and challenge such beliefs. It is my sincere wish that the session with the angels helped Sharon—and will help other parents of children with drug addictions—to see that there is no blame.

Judgments are thoughts, and thoughts are living, moving energy. Because energy attracts like energy, judgment attracts judgmental people. The world is a mirror in which we glimpse ourselves. If there are judgmental people around us, it may be that life is asking us to examine our own willingness or tendency to judge.

In addition to giving us opportunities to move beyond judgment, people with drug and alcohol addictions gift us with the chance to offer compassion. Truly, their desire to offer such a gift is part of their motivation for planning the addiction. As the angels told us, the heroin-addicted mothers in Sharon's program allow her to experience her own compassion over and over. Who is serving whom? If we care for someone who has a chemical dependence and wonder why that person is causing emotional agony for us, we might consider the possibility that we sought in this lifetime to show and thus know ourselves as compassion. The one we love is expressing love for us by providing the experience we desired. We can choose to feel angry, hurt, and burdened, or we can recognize that the experience, though painful, is a magnificent opportunity for enhanced self-understanding.

Sharon's experiences with her son have been a gift in yet another way: they have deepened her belief in the goodness of people. Consider the choice Sharon made. She could have chosen to believe that life is little more than pain and struggle. She could have chosen to believe that people will judge and hurt her. She could have decided that the best approach to life is to numb her feelings and keep an emotional distance from others. Instead, she chose to tell others about her struggle and accept their love. By being strong enough to be vulnerable, and by rejecting bitterness and cynicism, she acquires an expanded appreciation of love, one that would not be possible without Tony's addiction. As the angels said, "Growth comes through emotions in your realm." In choosing to feel love on the physical plane, where contrast allows choices that do not exist in spirit, Sharon instills within herself a deeper knowing of love.

The love Sharon gives and receives in this lifetime has an impact that extends far beyond her immediate sphere. "Nothing is done, nothing is said, nothing is thought that does not create a ripple effect." The importance of this truth cannot be overstated. Like stones dropped into a still pond, our lives have effects that radiate infinitely outward. Though our eyes cannot see these ripples, they reverberate throughout the universe. In this way self-transformation can change others—if they are ready to receive the energetic effects. In developing respect and tolerance for different paths, Sharon makes it easier for all of us to respect and accept the choices made by those in our lives. By expressing compassion for Tony, she paves the way for us to offer our own compassion. Through her love for the women in MOM, she fosters the giving of love by people she will never meet. As she discovers self-forgiveness, she engenders it in those who will never hear of her. And as Tony learns self-nurturing, he helps you, the reader, to nurture yourself. Whenever one person heals one aspect of self, all humanity heals through the increase in vibration. Such is the extent of our power. At times the effects are immediate and measurable. At other times they are indirect and imperceptible, though no less profound. The world follows in our energetic wake.

Before we are born, we know our power. In full awareness of theirs, Sharon and Tony planned his drug addiction to show the world what love looks like.

And they have.

HAVING EXPLORED THE PRE-BIRTH PLANNING of substance addiction from the perspective of the parent, I sought next to understand it from the perspective of the soul who would have the addiction. I spoke with Pat, who had experienced more than four decades of alcoholism. The length of Pat's addiction suggested that it was part of his life blueprint. Though a relatively brief use of alcohol might be a person's freewill decision—that is, an unanticipated path—it seemed unlikely that Pat's pre-incarnation planning would not have included such a significant aspect of his life.

Pat's Story

"I was born at a very early age," Pat began, prompting both of us to laugh. Though we were going to talk about a serious subject, Pat's sense of humor was nonetheless at the forefront. "June 7, 1933." Pat grew up in Amarillo, Texas, which explained the slight drawl I was hearing. His voice radiated warmth and friendliness.

Pat said he had stopped drinking at the age of fifty-eight. He had started at fourteen, when he and a friend attended a teen dance at Amarillo's new community center.

"Both of us were so bashful and shy," Pat recalled. "My friend and I got some beer and drank it—got beyond the terrible taste—and its effects immediately let me feel like, 'Man, I can dance, and those ladies in there love me!' And by golly, I went in and danced and had a good time. Alcohol brought out the Fred Astaire in me, my super-good looks, and my wonderful mentality—all of this crap I knew I wasn't, but alcohol gave me the false sense I was."

Pat's strongest desire at that time was to escape Amarillo. At sixteen he quit high school and, with his mother's permission, joined the navy. "When we went over into Japan and Hong Kong, I was able to play [drink] with the big boys—seventeen, eighteen years old. I was a hard-core alcoholic when I got out."

After the navy Pat drank almost daily. He often went to work drunk, sobered up on the job, and then resumed drinking at home. He would not go to a restaurant unless it served liquor or to a movie theater unless he could smuggle in alcohol. "It controlled me as if I were a puppet," Pat acknowledged.

Over the years Pat held a variety of jobs, including lifeguard, teacher, manager of a church camp, and, most emotionally rewarding, executive director of an outdoor education center for inner-city children. "Everything I did, I could go to the top immediately," Pat said matter-of-factly. "Every time I would rapidly escalate in my position, I would be freer to drink, and at about that time I would run. Looking back, I was afraid I had been promoted beyond my abilities." Pat's brief reference to fear did not stand out at that moment, but it would eventually acquire greater significance.

Pat is married to his second wife, Shirley. He has three children—Kathy, Donna, and Andrew—by his first wife, Carole. Pat left Carole, their children, and his position with the education center to be with Shirley. At that time he took a job rebuilding automobile alternators. During their marriage Shirley had her own battles with alcoholism.

As Pat described his family history, I wondered if his wives and children had known before birth that he would drink. If so, how did his alcoholism serve their goals for this lifetime? There was also the question of whether Shirley had planned to experience her own addiction to alcohol. I made a note to address these questions in Pat's upcoming session with the medium.

"The more I drank, the more I wanted to drink," Pat continued. "And when I drank, I would think, 'I don't need to quit. Everything's perfect.' Even the night I realized I was an alcoholic, I was congratulating myself for not being an alcoholic."

"Pat, what happened that night?" I asked with great interest. It seemed we had come to a pivotal moment.

"I was fifty-eight. After work I went on home, and there was one beer there, and I drank it." There was now a palpable tension in Pat's voice. "Then I started talking to myself. I was sitting in the middle of the floor. I said, '*You know, Pat, there's absolutely no way you could be an alcoholic. Last night you only had one. Tonight you only had one.*' I can hear myself talking to me, just sitting there. '*There's vodka and wine. There's everything in this house, and you didn't even touch it. That pretty well proves you're not an alcoholic.*' So, I congratulated myself and had a party." Pat started to cry. "I drank everything in the house, everything I could get my hands on. My mind was relatively clear, but my body was completely helpless. I was totally paralyzed with alcohol.

"That's the night I asked God to help me." Pat was straining to hold back his sobs. "You see, I had denounced God for years. I had taught my kids that there might be a God, but if there is, he's a sorry S.O.B. I didn't believe there could be a living, loving, personal God. It was impossible.

"'*God, please help me!*' I said. I meant it with all of my heart and soul. I was defeated—absolutely, totally, flat-footed defeated. I couldn't go any further. It was then the miracle started happening. There was no bright light and burning bush, but I knew God was there." There was utter conviction in Pat's voice.

Pat's life did not turn around immediately. In fact, he continued drinking for the next three weeks. During that time the power of that night stayed with him, eventually prompting him to check into a treatment center. Four days later, "all of my desire to drink had passed," Pat said. "Before that, I didn't have any concept of not drinking."

I wondered if Pat had inherited his near-lifelong impulse to drink. My research on pre-birth planning had clearly indicated we choose our parents before we are born. If Pat had wanted to experience alcoholism in this lifetime, he might have selected alcoholic parents.

"Pat, were your parents drinkers?" I asked.

"My father probably was an alcoholic, but he was a closet drinker. He had a little flask he carried. My mother was a teetotaler."

"How did drinking affect your first marriage and children?"

"I drank to the point where I didn't know I was married," Pat admitted. "I literally ran away from my children. When I left them, I didn't even say goodbye. It was very destructive."

In the years that followed, all three children had difficulties. As a child, Andrew was a disciplinary problem; he later became involved in drugs and alcohol. Kathy, too, turned to drugs. Pat told me that each of his children has turned things around, but he still regrets the pain he had caused them.

"I look back at leaving them at such a vulnerable..." Pat's voice trailed off as he began to cry. He paused to compose himself. "They needed a papa. They needed a father's image. I didn't have one evidently."

I asked Pat how drinking had affected his relationship with Shirley.

He told me that Shirley never judged him for his drinking, nor did they argue about it. But "I blamed her for all of my problems, which is a real typical thing for alcoholics," Pat said. "I thought Shirley was my albatross and the reason I came down from an executive position to rebuilding alternators for a living. The fact is, I quit that job."

Pat hesitated for a moment. I waited quietly, sensing that he was trying to decide whether or not to say something.

"I tried to commit suicide off and on, several times," he said suddenly. "I had a van, a little mobile shop [for alternator repair]. I had my van booby-trapped. I had a big toolbox sitting right behind my driver's seat. I had heavy alternators sitting on top of that toolbox aimed right at my head. My plan was to run into a tree, the biggest sassafras tree I've ever seen, on a twisty, turny Missouri road. There's no way I could have lived through that; the alternators would have knocked my head off.

"I tried that two or three times. Every time something happened. One time there were lights from oncoming traffic, and I couldn't take a chance on anybody else being hurt. One time a rabbit intervened."

"A rabbit intervened?" I asked, surprised.

"It ran in front of my van," Pat laughed, "and I wouldn't—I couldn't—hit a rabbit. I followed the highway instead of straying off and hitting the tree."

"Do you think the rabbit may have been more than coincidence?"

"Oh, you bet. I think the headlights coming was more than a coincidence." Pat sensed intuitively something I had learned in my research—that there is no such thing as coincidence. Synchronous events, which are often arranged by angels or spirit guides, keep us on the path we had planned. They bring to us—and keep us alive for—the experiences we need for our spiritual evolution.

"Pat," I asked, "what role did anger play in your drinking?"

"Liquor brought my anger down," he explained. "I can be triggered—boom!—at the least little things. I can drop a saltshaker and become infuriated. The difference is that now I don't drown myself with alcohol. I immediately make conscious contact with the God of my understanding."

"Pat, for a long time you thought there couldn't be a personal, loving God. Then you arrived at a place where you know God is loving. How did you go from where you were to where you are now?"

Pat mentioned again the night on the floor when he knew God was with him. He also credited the love and tolerance parts of Alcoholics Anonymous with helping him to know God.

"Now," he added, "if life becomes real threatening, which is rare, I check and see which of my character defects are involved, turn it over to God, and then have peace. I've discovered that we're all children of God. And he ain't no bad dude. He won't strike you down. Fact is, the only thing God does is lift us up."

Pat said he has made amends to all his loved ones, who, in turn, have forgiven him.

"My baby daughter [Kathy] said, 'Dad, I'm thankful for everything you did while you were drinking. I had to go through everything you allowed me to go through to be the person I am.' This astounded me!" In a letter of amends to Carole, Pat closed by saying that he loved her. "I love you, too," Carole wrote back. "That just melted me!" Pat said. "It was unbelievable that she could love an old boy that had left her!"

"Pat, what would you like to say to a reader who loves someone who is struggling with alcohol?"

"We don't know we're sick," Pat replied, suddenly tearing up again. "We're the last ones to know. If somebody don't tell us, we're liable to kill ourselves and others."

"What would you like to say to people who struggle with drinking?"

"Hang around 'til the miracle happens. The day will come. It's just that simple."

Pat's Sessions with Staci Wells

In talking with Pat, I sensed just how much he had suffered—and healed. The contrast was striking. It seemed that Pat's loved ones had also suffered and healed greatly. Neither Pat nor I knew just how much of this experience had been planned or why, but we were eager to find out. I felt confident that Staci and her spirit guide would provide much insight into Pat and his family's pre-birth planning.

Staci conducted both a primary and a supplemental reading, which have been combined in the narrative that follows. Each family member who appears in Pat's pre-birth planning session agreed to be included in Staci's readings. As usual, I provided Staci with names and birthdates so her spirit guide could access their Akashic Records, and I told her how each person was related to Pat.

"Pat, as I tune into you," Staci said, "I see that relationship issues are a huge challenge for you for this lifetime. I also see that working out your karmic learning experiences through your relationships is what you've chosen to do. The other karmic theme I see is you evolving spiritually. You might say, 'Aren't we all doing that?' Well some of us choose—*really* choose, at the soul level—to make that a primary focus in our lives. Some of us choose not to make it a focus at all. You'd be surprised how common it is that people have to go all the way to the negative side of that challenge in order to be motivated enough to become more spiritually evolved.

"As I focus on why at the soul level this alcoholism came into being, I keep sensing some connection with your father. Do you know what that is?"

"I wouldn't have any idea," Pat answered. "He passed away when I was about nine. Didn't know him well, and was very afraid of him."

"We'll find out more about that as we go deeper," Staci replied. "There is one other area of karmic challenge I want to mention, and that is responsibility to family—the family you were born into, the family you went on to create, and whoever you think of as family.

"The most important karmic challenge in Shirley's life was to overcome too much impulsiveness. I am seeing several lifetimes with lots and lots of babies. There was a sexually compulsive side to her that she'd been working on. And even though working on her spirituality was not of karmic importance in this lifetime, she recognized on the soul level that this [alcoholism] would help her to overcome impulsiveness."

We now had the first reason why a soul might choose before birth to experience alcoholism. I was not sure, however, just how such an addiction might help a soul cope with impulsiveness. "Is it that through overuse of alcohol Shirley would act impulsively, suffer negative consequences, and learn, or that alcohol would prevent her from acting impulsively?" I asked.

"The former," said Staci. "And it was the impulsiveness that caused her to use the alcohol. I often see misuse of mood-altering substances or addictions when I see this karmic lesson in somebody. And I am being told by my spirit guide that she did choose alcoholism in her pre-birth planning.

"Now I am going to close my eyes and focus more deeply on you, Pat, and see what I can pick up in the pre-birth planning session." There was a brief silence as Staci deepened her trance.

"The first thing I am seeing is you sitting on the floor, Pat. I see others around you, but right now they are not clearly in my focus. It's like you are sitting with a checkerboard, but it's much larger. The squares are about four inches and are black and white. I am told these are the periods of time when you will be working on certain themes.

"You are sitting on the floor with a male spirit guide and a man who says he is your uncle. Together, the three of you are plotting the diagram of your life. You are being given either/or choices. Either you do this at this age—seems age ten is the first one—or you do that, and if you do that, then this is going to happen down the road. It is that sort of talk.

"I am also seeing another spirit guide here. Rob, as an aside to you, it seems in every session we do there are one or more spirit guides, but there is also somebody much larger in stature serving in the capacity of supervisor. Pat, the one I see you working with on the floor is your main spirit guide who has been with you your whole life, especially, I am told, when you were struggling with the drinking addiction.

"There was some talk in this planning session of your genetic lineage predisposing you toward alcoholism. I am seeing ancestors of yours, farm people, who had a taste for homemade liquor. I don't see that anybody is recognized as an alcoholic. They were functional and able to carry on their work, but they drank every day. There was definitely a dependence on it. So, there was some talk about a genetic predisposition, and you were okay with that.

"There was definitely an agreement between you and Shirley to walk this journey together. There seems to be a great deal of love between you two at the soul level, a kindred spirit kind of friendship. You have been friends between lives and have been in past lives several times. There was some discussion that since both of you were going to be working on the same issue, you would come together hand-in-hand."

"Did they specifically plan to experience alcoholism together?" I asked Staci.

"Yes," she replied.

"That rings a bell," said Pat. Pat's intuitive remembrance was meaningful to me. I had come to understand that all our memories, including past lives and the time between incarnations, are stored in our DNA. I viewed Pat's "bell ringing" as a resonance with the information contained in his genes.

"I see them holding hands as they talk about this," Staci told us. "I have the feeling it is the last thing they talked about before one of them was born.

Shirley: I will join you.

Uncle (to Pat): Are you sure you want to do this?

Pat: Yes, it's the only way I am ever going to learn to be unafraid.

"Pat, you drank to cover up anger and fear. Being afraid of your father served to consciously remind you that you were working on letting go of fear. I am seeing that this fear stemmed from being a soldier [in a past life]. You died in war quite young, around the age of nineteen. I see you walking alone through a battlefield of fallen soldiers. You eventually—I don't even want to describe it—got killed. Your fear was like bile rising in your throat. You were the last of the survivors.

"Fear seems to be a theme through other lifetimes as well. I am being shown another where you were among the earlier settlers in the United States. You were in a covered wagon. Your wagon train was attacked, and everyone was killed. So there is fear there, too.

"The fear [in your current lifetime] is not a fear of dying. It is a fear of being alone and of not being able to handle life on your own."

Now the picture was coming into focus. Evidently, Pat had carried into this life the energy of fear. Souls seek to heal in subsequent lifetimes those aspects of the personality that were left unhealed in previous lives. Pat had known before birth that he would drink in part to cope with his fear. Depending upon how he eventually responded to his drinking, the fear might be transmuted. His plan was bold and ingenious: fear would cause alcoholism, which, in turn, could lead to a healing of fear.

"That is one of the reasons why Shirley chose to share this journey with you," Staci said to Pat. "She is very much there to console you and give love along the way. Her intent was to always be by your side."

I asked Staci if there were other reasons why Pat had planned to have an alcoholic partner instead of going through the experience of alcoholism on his own.

"There is somebody who understood it rather than judged it," Staci explained. "Somebody who would allow him to go through his natural course of development rather than forcing him to change." From the perspective of pre-incarnation planning, Shirley was, therefore, a wise choice as a partner. Had Pat been forced to change, he would have been pulled out of his pre-birth plan and denied the healing experience he had sought.

"Pat, do you feel that's the way it has been with Shirley?" I inquired.

"Absolutely," he said firmly.

"She never did demand that you stop drinking?" Staci asked.

"No. Never threatened to leave me," Pat replied.

As I listened to Pat speak, I thought of the many people who are criticized by their friends and family either for choosing an alcoholic partner or for remaining with that person over a long period of time. Such decisions are often viewed as unwise, indicative of a lack of self-esteem, perhaps even self-punishing. And yet Shirley, out of her affection for Pat—an affection that existed before they were born—was lovingly granting both him and herself the experiences they needed for their spiritual growth. What was really transpiring between these two souls was something far more beautiful than most would ever imagine.

I asked Staci if she could learn more about how alcoholism would serve Pat's purposes. There was a long pause as she listened to that part of the conversation.

"There is a warning here about how rough life was going to be, especially childhood, and that you, Pat, wouldn't be given a chance to 'shake loose from the tree'—the tree being your father. You wouldn't be given a normal process of development that a boy goes through. In this case the tree was taken from you, and you were left as a limb on the ground.

"This sets up the predisposition to fill the void with alcohol. You would never be given a transitional process of making that leap from being your father's son to being a man. The alcohol was going to come into your life early, because you would not know how to feel your way through that process. There was anger as an adolescent. The anger covered up fear, and the alcohol dulled the anger and anesthetized the fear. This was all plotted out for you. You agreed to every step."

I was astonished by just how much Pat had known before birth about his upcoming lifetime. He had been aware not only of the life challenge but also of the anger and fear that would underlie it and the time at which it would begin.

I wondered if perhaps Pat's father had agreed to die at a young age in part to further Pat's life plan. I asked Staci.

"I am told his father didn't agree to that," she informed us. "His father was alive already during this pre-birth planning session. His father's death was already planned. Patrick's choice of this man for his father was—I am getting the words from my guide—'in alignment for Patrick to experience what he needed to experience in order to overcome alcoholism.'"

This was a significant revelation. We were just told that Pat had planned not only his alcoholism but the *surmounting* of that addiction. Having seen this pattern in many life plans, I understood that Pat had yearned for both the contrast between being and not being an alcoholic and the experience of making that shift. As souls, we value both the contrast and the process of creating it, and neither would be possible without the duality provided by a physical lifetime.

I was still curious about why Pat had selected that soul as a parent. "He chose his father in part because he knew his father would die when he was young?" I asked

"Yes," said Staci.

"And he wanted that experience because it would then lead to alcoholism?"

"He knew that would set him up for the alcoholism, along with the genetic factor."

"Did he know before incarnation that he was going to be an alcoholic for several decades?"

"Yes."

"Why did he want to experience alcoholism?" The healing of fear was one motive, but I wanted to see if there was more to Pat's pre-birth plan.

"Because he had lost his connection with All That Is, with God, with his own divine nature and spirituality. This was the road to rediscover it. He was unable to find it otherwise. You know how we learn the hard way? This is one of those examples of learning the hard way."

This was the insight I had hoped Staci and her guide would be able to provide. Staci mentioned earlier that Pat had wanted to focus on spirituality in this lifetime. Now we knew why. Apparently, in some of his previous incarnations Pat had lost his perception of God. Having thus had the experience of losing his spirituality, he now wanted to have the experience of recreating it. And Pat had wanted to do more than simply experience spirituality. Were that his sole desire, he could have planned an entire lifetime of spiritual pursuits. Instead, Pat had wanted to have a feeling of profound disconnection so that he could then have the experience of building—and therefore more deeply knowing—his connection with God.

I felt we had reached the core of Pat's life blueprint. Now that we knew Pat's objective, I was eager to understand why he had felt his plan would work.

"How does the experience of alcoholism bring him back in connection with himself and God?" I asked Staci. Perhaps

Pat's roadmap could show the way for others struggling with either alcoholism or their spirituality.

"The return to seeking and achieving spiritual connection is motivated by the total lack of it, which the alcoholism causes," Staci pointed out. In other words, Pat had designed a classic learning-through-opposites life plan. He had wanted to heal unresolved fear from previous lives and experience—while in body—a strong connection with God. Prior to birth he had identified alcoholism as the catalyst that would drive him toward those goals.

But what if Pat "bottomed out" with alcohol and stayed there? There was risk in his plan. I asked Staci if Pat knew before birth that he would be able to turn things around.

"I am told this has to do with cyclical timing in his life," she replied as she listened to her spirit guide. "He knew that by a certain age—at the end of a certain cycle—he would have the wherewithal to overcome the addiction and meet his goals."

At the beginning of the session, Staci had mentioned that Pat has been balancing karma through his relationships—a common purpose of a physical lifetime. "Staci," I asked, "what does alcoholism allow Pat to accomplish in regard to relationships?"

"The relationship with the substance becomes primary over the emotional relationships with others. After so many decades, you realize that this bottle does not take the place of true, unconditional love. Your longing for unconditional love supercedes the longing for anesthesia, and the anesthetic effect lessens with long-term use. In general, I am being told that because of alcoholism, you experience the lack of relationships, and that motivates you to want relationships."

"Very true," Pat agreed.

Yet any number of life challenges could have driven Pat to reach his goals. I asked Staci if he had considered other challenges, like having a handicapped child.

"I am told that being a handicapped child's parent was not in his experiential awareness," Staci answered. "He had just come from a lifetime where he had seen the other soldiers around him using alcohol not just for their wounds, but for their psyche. That is what he was familiar with." Staci's response confirmed what I had seen in others' prebirth planning: that souls often select challenges to which they have some previous exposure.

"Staci," I said, "as you know, we always have free will. What would have happened with Pat's goals if he had chosen never to drink?"

There was a long pause as Staci listened to her guide.

"The experience would not have been as intense," she said. "It might have taken an additional lifetime or two to rise to this challenge. He would have married. He would have had several children. But the anger would have stayed with him, and he likely would not have been an emotionally available parent. He probably would have chosen an addiction to work instead. Being emotionally intimate, nurturing, and available still would have been a challenge, and he would not have learned that in his lifetime. He's learning it now."

As Staci relayed this vital information, it occurred to me that there were probably many times when Pat would have happily traded an addiction to alcohol for an addiction to work. And yet that exchange, though it would have resulted in a less painful life, would also have produced less growth. How many recovered alcoholics, I wondered, viewed their drinking with regret, perhaps believing they had wasted years of their lives? How many judged themselves for what they perceived as weakness? What if they knew this was exactly the experience they had desired? How would their feelings change if they realized that alcoholism had accelerated their growth—in some instances by so much that an additional one or two incarnations would not be needed?

We had just heard why both Pat and Shirley had planned the experience of alcoholism. Now I wanted to see if the other significant people in Pat's life—his first wife and children—had chosen before birth to have an alcoholic husband and father. I asked Staci to listen to their pre-birth conversations.

"I'm closing my eyes now and seeing that room I always see in the planning sessions," said Staci. "I'm seeing Pat's daughter Kathy in her lightbody, not in her two-legged, humanoid form. And she is radiant! There are sparkles of light that shimmer all over her. I see her float over and come down to the ground. I hear her ask Pat, 'How can *I* help you?' With the emphasis on *I*. I get the feeling that this is an extremely caring, nurturing, empathic soul with a great deal of inner strength. I am told by my guide that she is a teacher and, as such, has been a teacher to Pat in previous lifetimes. She has already agreed to play a part in Pat's life, although when she agreed her role was not quite determined. Now, she is sitting down with Pat to determine what he needs from her. Pat talks about how his life will be rudderless at times. And I hear that word *rudderless* very strongly.

Pat: I will need you to show me direction and give me strength from time to time. Though you will be a child, I will always know who you are. Although I will feel the responsibility of a father toward you, my child, some part of me will see a brightness in you, and I will know on an inner level that I must follow the direction you lead me.

"Kathy smiles and nods her head in agreement.

Kathy: But I will need you, too, to show me the way, because I will be your child. Because I will be dealing with issues of self-esteem, I will feel lonely at times, and I will need comfort. I will reach out to you, too.

"Pat puts both hands on her lightbody, as if he were putting them on her shoulders.

Pat: I know, and I agree to be there with you.

"Kathy talks to him about how one of her purposes in this life-to-be is to find balance in regard to individuality, meaning where she ends and someone else begins. She talks about how she will have the strong tendency to take on another person's pain and feel another person's problems.

Kathy: I will use you as part of this purpose—to help me find my balance and learn how to delineate between myself and my own circumstances and feelings and those that belong to another. Because I will be your daughter and love you so deeply, I will have a tendency to take on your pain and feel your emotions, though I may not understand them.

Pat: Yes, yes, I know.

Kathy: I will look to you for guidance and to mirror me, to show and remind me who I am, but it is up to me to learn. I do not demand that you take on the responsibility of ensuring that I learn this lesson. That is mine and mine alone. You are going to act as a guide for me in your own way, and I expect nothing more from you.

Pat (relieved): I love you, and I will welcome you as my daughter when the time comes.

Kathy: I will stay here until that time. When you need me, you can call me in your sleep, and I will be one of many in your dreams.

"Their conversation ends. Let's see who or what comes next." Staci was silent for a moment as she tuned in to another portion of the planning session. "It is Pat's other daughter, Donna. She appears in a humanoid representation, two legs, a little girl of maybe nine or ten with her hair in pigtails."

This was a surprising development. Why had Donna assumed the form of a young girl? I asked Staci's spirit guide to explain.

"It is a precursor of the attitude she is adopting for this lifetime, the attitude of the younger child," Staci responded, relaying the words of her guide.

"Is that how Pat would have seen her in the conversation?"

"Yes. My guide says it is the soul wearing the cloak of the personality and the physicality it will take on in that lifetime. Part of the pre-birth planning is learning to recognize certain physical identifying markers. Ninety-eight percent of the time there are markers embedded into the unconscious of a person that help them to recognize soulmates in their lives." By *soulmates* I knew Staci and her guide meant important people, not just romantic partners.

"She skips over to him. She seems very happy. She sits down in front of Pat.

Pat: I want you to be in my life so I can hold you, cherish you, and give you guidance, and so you can show me the path before me and lead me where I need to go.

Donna: Daddy, I need for you to be mean sometimes. I will be forced by your meanness and what seems like your rejection of me to look within myself. Though I will know it is because of the bottle, it will force me to go within, to measure my own feelings and my own sense of reality. I need this, because it reminds me in a very strong way to be who I am. Though at first it will look like it makes me self-conscious and full of doubt, it is part of my growth. This is part of the path I need to walk in this lifetime. This is what I need you to do for me.

"Pat pats his daughter-to-be on the head and agrees.

Pat: I'm sorry for what will happen. I love you. As much as I know this needs to be, I am sorry I will cause you to feel pain.

"Donna takes his hand, the hand that was patting her on her head, and holds it to her heart.

Donna: No, you will not be causing the pain. It is my choice. I am responsible for it.

"And then she leaves. Now I'm asking my guide to show me more.

"I see Carole, Pat's first wife, coming in. She is dressed in what I can only call prairie clothes. She looks like she did in a previous lifetime as a woman on the United States prairie, probably early to mid-1800s. She is wearing a simple dress of cotton calico cloth; her hair is pulled back very simply. My guide tells me that the clothing shows both how she is still clinging to that past life and also how practical her nature is.

"Carole and Pat are fulfilling a life cut short in a previous lifetime. I am being shown that life in the prairie in Missouri." (This was the same state in which Pat had planned to commit suicide in his current lifetime.) "They had one child. They and two other families were attacked by Indians. We used to say 'scalped,' but they look beheaded to me. Carole agrees to be with Pat in this lifetime so she can have all she was supposed to have in the previous life. A hard life is one of those things; children are the other part."

"Staci," I asked, "does she say why she wanted to marry someone who experiences alcoholism?"

"I ask my guide to show me that.

Pat: I will likely have problems with drink and emotional unavailability.

Carole: If you will do it my way, you will not have this problem. [*Shakes her finger at him.*]

"At first, he feels sad about that, as if he's not living up to her expectations. But then I see him sit up straight and say,

Pat: Then I need to be in your life to show you that life is not just one way, that life cannot be made of just black and white. I must be there to show you shades of gray.

"She's not happy about this. She pinches her face together in an upset look. Then she releases that resistance.

Carole: I suppose you're right. Then I will open myself to you. I will take you into my heart in the hope that you can break the block, the impenetrable wall, around my heart and emotions. I have only let my children in, but I will let you in, also. I am afraid this will mean that I will be hurt. But I will let you in, because I know you love me and because I care for and love you, too.

"Pat takes her hands in his and holds them for a few moments. She nods and gets up and leaves.

"I see Pat's son, Andrew, coming over. He calls Pat 'Papa.' He talks about energy. He talks about hyperactivity. And he talks about perfectionism.

Andrew: I will always want more than I have. I will always strive for something more for myself and my life.

Pat: Yes, yes.

Andrew: Sometimes I will lack balance, and I will forget those around me who depend on and love me. Inasmuch as I agree to be your son and do the things you need me to do, I need you to pull me back during those times when I am so filled with my own relentless energy that I forget my family and where my feet are and that they need to be on the ground.

I need you to be the grounding point in my life, even when you yourself are not grounded. If you don't remind me where the ground is, I will know by watching you where the ground is not. Your example serves me. It's there to teach me the importance of not letting myself go too far out and of staying focused.

"They talk about the extreme intelligence Andrew possesses. Andrew has spent lifetimes working on mechanical things, inventions. He was an assistant in Einstein's lab. But he's never gotten to the place where he could see a project through from start to finish. He'd always lose focus, go on to something else, and wind up not being productive. Andrew is taking this lifetime out from his scientific studies so he can work more on being focused, but achievement is still part of his nature. That incessant drive to do and *be* something will remain. He looks to his father to remind him to stay focused and grounded."

Staci fell silent. She and her guide had finished their remarkable glimpse into the nonphysical realm.

Evidently, Pat's loved ones had been an integral part of the planning of his life challenge. Moreover, they had not simply acquiesced to his blueprint; they had seen it as a means to foster their own personal growth.

I was waiting to talk with Staci's spirit guide about the information he had presented. He was always a source of great wisdom, and I had many questions for him.

"Staci," I said, "please ask your guide what other reasons souls have for planning alcoholism."

"There are *many*," she responded, echoing her guide's words. "Some of the souls who choose this are not comfortable in a physical body, and the alcohol becomes a means for them to live between two worlds. Others have made choices in past lives where they have abused others, and they balance that behavior by choosing to abuse their own body. My spirit guide is unfolding an accordion, a very long list of reasons."

By *choices*, Staci's guide was referring to freewill decisions made by the personality after birth, not to roles that had been scripted with other souls prior to incarnation. Had the abuse been agreed upon before birth by all involved, such karmic balancing would not be necessary.

I was intrigued by the idea that a soul might be uncomfortable in a physical body. I asked Staci why that would be the case.

"I am told it can be the next stage of evolvement. They are not yet comfortable inhabiting the body at that new stage. Sometimes people who are born severely retarded or with severe body problems are at a new level of evolvement, so they get to live life more as an observer than a participant." I thought of Jennifer (chapter 3), whose sons, Ryan and Bradley, had planned physical handicaps so they could be more in the role of observer.

"Does 'next level of evolvement' mean that most of those souls are incarnating for the first time, or does it mean they're taking on new lessons?"

"More often than not it's their first physical incarnation at a new level of evolvement, not their first physical incarnation," Staci said, relaying what she was hearing from her guide. "There are cases, though, when it is somebody's first physical incarnation, specifically, people who have gone through other planetary schools and then come to Earth."

"What would motivate a soul to choose alcohol as opposed to any other drug addiction?" I wondered.

"Sometimes it's what is available [in the coming lifetime]. Other times it is the substance that would react best with the body. Many times it is just the familiarity of it."

"As I understand it, humans weren't designed to consume alcohol at all. What does your guide say about that?"

"My guide wholeheartedly agrees, except in those cases where fermented fruit has dropped to the ground. You will see animals eating that. Alcohol kills brain cells."

I was confused by this response. If God is omniscient, then God knew that humans would eventually use grapes and other plant products to create alcoholic beverages. I asked why those things were put on Earth if the human body were not designed for alcohol consumption.

"I am hearing," Staci said, "that grapes and grape juice don't need to be fermented to benefit the body, and that in the early uses of wine, it was not an intoxicating substance. The other thing is temptation. That's one of the things schoolhouse Earth gives us the opportunity to work with."

"Staci, your guide mentioned that some souls plan the experience of alcoholism because in past lives they abused someone else's body and now choose to abuse their own. I wonder if we can get more explanation, because I know karma is a form of learning, not punishment."

Staci's spirit guide replied that souls do sometimes design lives in which they treat themselves in the same way they once treated others. He went on to say that in the afterlife all souls are counseled on self-forgiveness. Some succeed in forgiving themselves without planning such an incarnation; others do not. Some seek to use what they learn in the time between lives to aid others in the next lifetime. These souls plan lives in which they will be counselors to addicts; some plan the experience of addiction into their life blueprints so they may be more effective counselors later in life.

"What," I asked, "is the difference between a soul who can forgive himself for abusing another person's body and one who can't?"

Staci's speech slowed as she began to channel her spirit guide word-for-word.

"Clarity, remorse, evolvement," he replied. He explained that souls who remain focused on the abuse lose clarity (and may therefore decide to punish themselves) and that self-forgiveness is a major step along the evolutionary path because it derives from unconditional love.

"Earth primarily serves the function of teaching you to let go of fear and love unconditionally," he added.

The reference to fear made me think of the way Pat had planned to heal his unresolved fear. "Staci," I said, "as I understand it, the soul takes energies and places them in the personality for the next lifetime so they can be healed. Is that a fair description?"

"My guide says yes."

"What does your guide say about the idea that negative emotions like fear cannot exist at the higher vibrations on the other side?"

"That's very true, but that doesn't mean every soul is at that level all the time."

"So, the souls with these emotions are at a lower vibration on the other side?"

"My guide says to be very careful how you describe that. 'Lower vibration' isn't accurate. Those souls who act as the 'higher' spirit guides—the ones who no longer are in need of physical embodiment—have achieved that. But that doesn't mean the rest of us are of any lesser value. He doesn't want this accidentally misinterpreted as a class system, because it's not."

"How does an emotion like fear survive physical death?"

"It depends on what the soul was experiencing and feeling as it left that lifetime," Staci replied. Her comment reminded me that Pat had died at least twice while experiencing great fear—once when attacked on the prairie by Indians, a second time as a soldier in battle. I thought, too, of Penelope (chapter 4), who sought healing in this lifetime for fear she had experienced at the moment of death in a previous incarnation.

"So, what people are feeling at the moment of death is crucial?"

"Yes. As they are dying, they are thinking over their lives, and the issues that are unresolved stick with them. Shortly after leaving the body, they usually make some decisions about that lifetime and what they do or don't want to repeat in a future lifetime."

"Then people should put themselves into the most joyful, loving space possible at the moment of death?"

"Yes," said Staci. "In my experience, the best crossings are when people are surrounded by their loved ones. It's the most peaceful kind of crossing."

∾

Like many who drink, Pat used alcohol to give himself a new identity. The alcohol did just that—only the identity it gave him was not the one he had expected.

Pat thought that alcohol made him a new man: a witty conversationalist, a brilliant dancer, a dashing figure of great appeal to the opposite sex. In truth, the man he became was actually a child—a child of God.

Alcohol literally brought Pat to his knees. At his darkest moment, he embraced his spirituality with a desperation that an easy life could never have engendered. With time, desperation turned into passion. It is with passion that he now embraces God and, in so doing, embraces himself.

When we incarnate—that is, when we place a portion of our consciousness in a body and focus our perceptions on the physical realm—we create an illusion in which we appear to be separate from one another and All That Is. In certain lifetimes this illusion seems more real to us than in others. In some of his previous lives, Pat believed in the reality of that illusion and so lost his perception of both God and his own divine nature.

In planning to experience alcoholism from a young age, Pat had desired to begin his current lifetime in that state of perceived disconnection. From that starting point, he had intended to reach a place where he would be "absolutely, totally, flat-footed defeated." The night on the floor when Pat cried out for God, a night of stark loneliness and apparent isolation, was precisely the experience he had sought. In that painful abyss, Pat had hoped to find the spark that would rekindle his spirituality. As Staci and her spirit guide pointed out, "The return to seeking and achieving spiritual connection is motivated by the total lack of it."

Alcoholism is sometimes chosen as a life challenge because it gives us as eternal souls the experience of *creating* the *feeling* of connection to the Divine. Through its creation we come to know that feeling more deeply. With more than two million members worldwide, Alcoholics Anonymous uses the well-known Twelve Steps as part of its recovery program. Like Pat, each person who participates in this program agrees in the third step to "turn our will and our lives over to the care of God." That alcoholism leads so many to the same experience of divine connection is more than coincidental.

When we are Home in the nonphysical, we cannot create anew this feeling of connection because we are never without it. In spirit, we are ever aware of our oneness with all creation. We know that we are part of the Divine and that we *are* divine. Though we can never lose our divinity, we can while in body forget our awareness of it. Having had that experience, Pat longed to renew his feeling of union with God. When he returns to spirit, Pat will carry with him a profound feeling-knowing of connection that would not have been possible without the contrast created by alcoholism during a physical lifetime.

With much strength, Pat lived forty-four painful years of perceived disconnection. Who but the bravest of souls would cast himself from the Love that is his birthright so that he might know Love better? As Pat shows us, the experiences of the physical plane are not what they seem. What some would brand as weakness or retreat is actually a full, unflinching embrace of one of the greatest challenges a soul can plan. Society's condemnations belie the grandeur of those who live this plan; they are so much more than they may appear to be. Their role may include alcoholism, but the actors in that role are courage incarnate.

It is here that illusion layers itself, often in polar opposites. Ostensibly, the world may well have seen fear in Pat, just as he saw fear in himself: Fear of social situations. Fear of women. Fear of being promoted beyond his abilities in the jobs he held. Fear, as Staci mentioned, of being alone, of not being able to handle life on his own. These are but the current-life manifestations of fears unresolved in past lives. These layers of illusion conceal the bold soul who wanted to learn while in body to be unafraid, who chose before birth to fear his father as a conscious reminder of deeper fears, who planned to lose that father during his childhood in order to trigger the alcoholism that could eventually heal his fears. Only the courageous plan fear.

Our fears separate us from our real identities and are therefore to be sought, not shunned. In living them, we remember who we really are. Pat, for example, harbored a fear of being alone. Only when he felt utterly forsaken did he realize he was never and could never be truly alone. In seeming abandonment did he find connection; in surrender, sovereignty. By creating what he had most feared, Pat called himself into recollection of eternal truth. Thus able to peel away his self-created illusions, Pat demonstrated that fear is a master teacher who shows us to ourselves.

One might then ask: who is Pat really? Pat is love. Pat is the love that was expressed so readily, so freely, to the other souls in his pre-birth planning session. As love, Pat planned the life challenge of alcoholism to foster not only his own growth but that of his loved ones. Seen in this light, Pat's alcoholism is a form of service to those who chose to be in his life. Kathy learns about identity, boundaries, and balance. How better to understand balance than through the imbalances caused by a parent's alcoholism? Donna's experiences with Pat force her to look inward for self-love, a classic learning-through-opposites life plan. As Carl Jung said, "Who looks without, dreams. Who looks within, awakes." Meanness from Pat, something Donna herself requested, awakens her to her true nature as a loving soul. Andrew learns to stay focused and grounded. Carole comes to understand shades of gray, and Shirley has the opportunity to know herself as love and compassion. Through Pat's service, each of these souls expands, and each, in turn, expands Pat.

In Pat's pre-birth planning, the members of his family-to-be assumed personal responsibility for the lessons to be learned from his alcoholism. On the physical plane, where we lack memory of our pre-incarnation choices, we often believe that others inflict experiences upon us. We may respond with fear, anger, hatred, self-hatred, blame, feelings of victimization, or many other emotions that do not reflect our true nature as souls. When we awaken by turning within, we remember that we requested these experiences. We are then free to choose different responses, including gratitude toward those who have made our growth possible. To those we once blamed, we are now able to say thank you. Thank you for caring enough about me to play a role in which you bore the brunt of my anger for many years. Thank you for keeping your promise and honoring our pre-birth contract. Thank you, as Kathy said to Pat, for allowing me to go through what I had to go through to be the person I am today.

Thank you.

We live in a world in which millions of people think less of themselves as a result of their life challenges. Some are alcoholics. They may believe they have let down their loved ones. They may believe they have let themselves down. Yet perhaps they, like Pat, chose to play the temporary role of alcoholic as a form of service to others and as a path to personal expansion. That path appears to take us far, until, like Pat, we awaken to find what was there all along, hidden within as we looked without.

CHAPTER 6

∞∞

Death of a Loved One

O F THE MANY CHALLENGES PROVIDED by life
on Earth, death of a loved one is perhaps the most
universal. Unless we die at a young age, it is likely
we will lose someone we care about. The fact that virtually
all of us share this experience suggests it offers profound
opportunities for growth. Were it not so, we as souls would
be less likely to seek lives on the physical plane.

Yet, death is much more prominent in some lives than in
others. To understand why a soul might plan before birth
to lose loved ones, I talked with Valerie Villars. Forty-two
at the time of our conversation, Valerie had lost two people
whom she loved dearly, including her only child, Dustin,
who had passed away three months earlier. Valerie felt it
would be healing for her to talk about her experiences, and
she hoped to bring healing to others. I am grateful for her
willingness to speak with me at such a difficult time.

The loss of not one but two people in Valerie's life, both
unexpectedly and at relatively young ages, seemed to indicate that these deaths were part of her pre-birth plan. If so,
why had Valerie chosen to experience *two* such losses? And
why was one her only child?

Valerie's Story

"I did everything with him," Valerie said of Dustin, her son by her first husband. She had since divorced and remarried. "We did Indian Guides together, all the baseball and the basketball. I remember one time when he was little and was going to try out for baseball. We drove up to the field. As soon as we got out of the car, we saw these little Mickey Mantles whizzing and hitting balls like—wham! Everybody was really, really good. Dustin and I walked over to the fence. We were standing there, watching. Dustin had never even had a glove on his hand. He said, 'It's okay, Mom. I want to try.' He ran out there, not knowing anything, with all these kids who look like Mickey Mantle. I was never so proud of that child! He had guts. To me, that was quintessential Dustin."

To Valerie, two other outstanding traits were Dustin's intellect and nonconformity. His intelligence shone in his work with computers and cars; once he even assembled an entire automobile engine on his own. His nonconformity was evident in the way he constantly, restlessly questioned the world. "It's like he always knew a better way," Valerie observed. "Many things he had a hard time dealing with in society because of the lack of common sense in the way things are set up."

Valerie never knew just how many friends Dustin had until more than 250 of them came to his wake. "One by one they all started coming forward," she recalled. "Like Judah came up and said, 'Your son was one of the smartest people I've ever met.' They just kept coming and telling me the same thing. All of his peer group looked up to him."

One week before Dustin's death, Valerie was sitting quietly by her living room window, lights off, as a gentle rain fell outside. Dustin walked in and sat next to her. As he reached to turn on a lamp, Valerie told him, "No, Dust. I like natural light. Natural light is good." Together, silently, they watched the raindrops run down the windowpane.

Dustin was nineteen when he died. He had come home on a Friday night and walked into Valerie's bedroom, where they talked briefly and then hugged goodnight. "I love you," Valerie told him. "I love you, too," Dustin replied. To Valerie's surprise, Dustin let her kiss him; he wasn't usually a touchy-feely type of person.

In the morning Valerie drove across Lake Pontchartrain and into New Orleans. On her way home that evening, as the causeway once again lifted her above the water, "I looked to my left—pink clouds, a beautiful sunset," she remembered. "Sometimes, I wonder if that wasn't the exact moment Dustin died."

When Valerie arrived home, her dog, Tessie, came running to greet her, just as she always did. "Hey Tessie, how are you doing?" Valerie asked, patting her on the head. The house was quiet; Valerie assumed Dustin was out. Then "I opened the door to Dustin's room. He was lying on his bed with his feet on the floor, but like he had fallen back. He had both arms out to his sides, and his head was turned to the right. When you're a parent, from the time you have the little baby—I don't care how old they get—you're always going into their room and checking to make sure they're still breathing. It's a mother thing. I walked over to him, and I could see he wasn't breathing! I said, 'Hey, Dust.' No answer. I screamed it louder. '*Hey, Dust!*' No answer. I kept screaming it louder and louder until it was echoing in the room. I picked up the dog and threw her over by Dustin to see what she would do. She didn't even blink at him. He wasn't there for her.

"I ran into the living room, saying to myself, *God no! This can't be happening! This is a nightmare! This isn't true!* I thought, If I'm really emphatic about this and I say it emphatically ... "

Just then Valerie saw her husband's headlights in the driveway. "*Dustin's not breathing!*" she shouted from the door. Her husband rushed inside and administered CPR. "*Come on, Dustin! Come on, man!*" he yelled as he pounded Dustin's chest. Meanwhile, Valerie called 911, then ran outside to wait for the ambulance. When the paramedics arrived, they seemed to Valerie to be moving in slow motion. She pushed them into the house, yelling, "*Hurry! Hurry!*"

Not long thereafter the paramedics told Valerie that Dustin was dead. The cause of death, they said, had been an accidental drug overdose.

"Dustin had just taken his exams in college, and he was happy," Valerie said sadly. "He had gotten good grades. He had gone out to celebrate. He had just written me a beautiful letter for Mother's Day telling me how much he loved me. He'd never written one like that. You can't imagine what it's like to have your child there one day, and then all of a sudden they're gone."

On the day of Dustin's wake, Vicki, Valerie's sister, came to Valerie's home with something important to share. "Valerie, Dustin came to me last night. I never felt that much joy and happiness in my life. He was brilliant. He was light. And he said, 'Aunt Vicki, tell my mom I'm natural light.' I'm sorry, Valerie. I don't know what that means."

"I was so happy!" Valerie exclaimed. "It was Dustin's way of confirming through the person I trust more than anybody in the world that he was alive and well."

Two nights later, Valerie suddenly awoke from a sound sleep. "At the moment I woke up, I lifted," she said. "It wasn't my body that lifted; it was me. At the moment I lifted, I felt the essence of my child. There was no time to it. I knew everything all at once. There was an energy. It was the most powerful thing I have ever felt! I was him, and he was me, and I knew everything about him in those few seconds. He was happy. I knew that. I could feel it."

Dustin's death was the second devastating loss in Valerie's life.

Twelve years earlier, Valerie had been working as a waitress and attending college. As classes let out one day, she decided to visit to her cousin Lorraine's husband, Brad, who worked near the school. On that day, Brad's friend D.C. was also visiting. Brad introduced them; Valerie thought nothing of it.

Brad called Valerie later to say that he and D.C. had plans to go to a casino in a few days. Would she like to join them? "Sure, that would be great," she told Brad. When the appointed night came and her doorbell rang, Valerie opened the door to find only D.C standing there. Although D.C. denied it, Brad had — at D.C.'s request — bowed out so they might have their first date.

Valerie and D.C. began to fall in love that night. "It did seem that I'd known him before," Valerie said wistfully. Their affection for each other grew quickly. "Every minute we spent together was romantic. Our relationship was very much in the moment because we didn't know when he'd get called offshore."

D.C. was a commercial diver who maintained the pipelines to oilrigs. The work is dangerous and physically taxing, so much so that most divers don't continue that kind of work beyond their forties. Often, they don't know when they'll receive their next assignment. "You have to set up your whole life around the fact that these men could be gone a week or two months at a moment's notice," Valerie said.

"We started going out September 28," she recalled. "On February 17, D.C. proposed. We were in my condo, sitting on the bed, talking. There was a cardinal in the tree outside. D.C. said, 'They always travel in pairs. Just watch a minute, and you'll see the mate come.' And sure enough, we did. So, really quiet, he said, 'When are you going to marry me?' I said, 'As soon as you want me to marry you!' I was so excited!"

Less than an hour after he proposed, D.C. was called for a diving assignment. He and Valerie drove across the causeway to his apartment, where he packed his scuba gear. Johnny, D.C.'s friend and fellow diver, picked him up. "I can picture it like it was yesterday," said Valerie. "He got in the truck with Johnny. I stood in the street and waved. And that was the last time I ever saw him."

Two days later, as Valerie was waiting tables, she looked up and saw Brad and Lorraine. They pulled her into the restaurant's empty wine room. "Valerie, there's been a terrible accident," Brad told her. "D.C.'s dead."

"*No, he can't be dead!*" Valerie screamed. "*He just asked me to marry him!*"

Lorraine and Brad, who had not yet heard about the engagement, stared at each other in disbelief.

The next day Valerie received a letter from the diving company:

> At approximately 1400 hours, first diver Dave Copeland descended to a depth of 285 feet. Over the loudspeaker he voiced the desire to come above.

The letter stated that a series of grunts was then heard and that Johnny was sent to investigate. When he arrived D.C. looked into his eyes for an instant, then pushed him away. Johnny would later say that he knew in that moment D.C. was going to die. Then D.C. pulled his helmet off.

"He wasn't committing suicide," Valerie explained. "He had been diving for fifteen years, so he was a pro. He knew something was terribly wrong."

Valerie still isn't sure what happened. She does know that about a week earlier, D.C. and Johnny had been watching a football game at Brad's house. "When D.C. came over later that night," Valerie remembered, "he had a huge knot on his forehead. I said, 'What happened to you?' He said, 'I'm just so happy I met you. I was thanking Brad, and we were cutting up and butting heads.' I suspect that when he butted his head—which ironically he did because he was so much in love with me—he had a hairline fracture or concussion that gave him incredible pressure when he went down there."

The pain from D.C.'s death was so overwhelming that, for a short time, Valerie turned to alcohol to anesthetize herself. It took two years, she said, until she felt normal again.

"Before he died," Valerie added, "we were sitting on the couch, and he looked at me and said, 'I'm sorry it took me so long to find you. I promise I won't take so long next time.' I didn't question it.

"He was my real love. They don't walk through your front door every day. I lost my future, or so it seemed to me."

Valerie's Session with Deb DeBari

I was deeply touched by my conversation with Valerie. She had faced two very painful deaths with grace and strength, and she was willing to speak freely about those deaths in hope they would bring comfort and meaning to others in their grief.

In that search for meaning, and because the loss of a loved one is such a universal experience, I asked Valerie, and she kindly agreed, to allow me to explore her pre-birth plan with three mediums. One was Deb DeBari. Deb had already provided readings for several people who had shared their stories with me. They had found her to be sensitive, insightful, and remarkably accurate. I knew from those sessions that she is able to speak readily with "deceased" loved ones. She also hears her own spirit guides quite clearly. They work closely with Deb to provide her clients with wisdom and information about both the physical and nonphysical realms.

As the session began, D.C. immediately made contact with Deb. Though I had heard Deb speak with people in spirit, I again marveled at her ability to do so.

"I'm not the ex," D.C. said to Deb, who repeated his words to us. "I still consider her my fiancée." It was a sweet note on which to begin.

"I knew my life wasn't going to be long," D.C. continued. "I knew I wasn't going to live to old age. I had some close calls [before the diving accident]."

"He's showing me he had a contract," Deb explained, referring to D.C.'s pre-birth agreements with other souls. "This accident was planned on the other side. He's showing me a motorcycle. Did he ride a motorcycle?"

"Yes," Valerie confirmed.

"He had a few close calls with that," said Deb. "If that didn't take him, something else was going to."

"What actually happened?" Valerie asked with some urgency. She had wondered about D.C.'s death for a long time.

"I felt like my brain was going to explode," D.C. replied. "This is the worst type of death. I had to stop this." D.C. was confirming what his friend Johnny had told Valerie: he knew he was going to die and had taken action to end his life quickly.

"What was your lesson from this?" Valerie asked him.

"There are so many," D.C. answered. "I was a daredevil. In some ways I did not have respect for life. I put my life on the line needlessly. A lot was carried over from past lives. I had lives as a soldier. So many times I had to put my life on the line for causes I didn't believe in. There is also a lesson to appreciate love. I learned a lot and am still around you. I'm not going back [incarnating again] right away. There are certain lessons I want to learn before I go back. I want to be better equipped. I want to know my purpose. This [last] time, I didn't know my purpose."

D.C. was referring to the forgetfulness each of us experiences when we enter the Earth plane. As eternal beings, we are well aware of the purposes of our lives before we incarnate. When we are born and cross the veil between the physical and nonphysical, we forget—in some instances permanently, in some temporarily—the reasons why we came here. Life challenges often serve to remind us of our purpose.

"I want you to know that I still love you," D.C. said to Valerie.

"I love you, too," Valerie told him.

"I don't want you ever to believe that I left because I didn't love you," D.C. added. "I left because I do love you. I don't want to use the past tense. It always continues."

"Why is it so difficult?" Valerie asked softly. "Why can't we just do all that on the other side?"

"On the other side," Deb explained, "we don't experience negative emotions like we do here. The negative emotions are—I don't want to say not 'allowed'—but we don't feel them the way we do here."

Deb was speaking of the absence of duality or opposites in the spiritual realm. We can experience ourselves as peace, joy, and love in spirit and on Earth, but only through an incarnation can we truly understand "lower vibration" feelings like anger and hatred. In that experience, however painful it might be, we birth the knowing of our true selves.

At that point D.C. stepped back, and Dustin appeared to Deb.

"D.C. fades, but he stays nearby," Deb told us. "He wants to give energy to Dustin."

"I wasn't happy," Dustin said to Valerie. "I couldn't figure out what I wanted to do. I made a mess of things and couldn't get it fixed. This wasn't suicide. It was an accident. I was on a path to have this happen. I was addicted to drugs. Some people can take drugs once in a while and be fine. I wasn't one of those. I tried to hide it from you. I tried to maintain some type of normalcy, but I was raging inside. I struggled with this rage. I wasn't thinking clearly. I went through life with a blindfold on. I couldn't trust. I made decisions out of lack of trust. I'm sorry. I didn't want to disappoint you."

"I know," Valerie said gently. "I'm not disappointed in you."

"This was the second opportunity," Dustin explained. "A few months before, I came close to overdosing."

I asked Dustin if he and Valerie had agreed before birth on the timing of his death.

"I would die before twenty-five," Dustin replied. "I had from fifteen — those ten years — [in which] to choose to die. My contract said that if I lived beyond age twenty-five, I would stay. I had the choice."

"But that choice is made at the soul level, not at the level of the personality, isn't it?" I asked.

"It's at the soul level," Dustin confirmed.

"What were we trying to even out?" Valerie asked. "Is this my lesson?"

"It was a mutual lesson," Deb told her. An image of one of Valerie's past lives now came into Deb's mind. "In a past life, Valerie was the [Dustin's] child. Valerie died first. This was an injury, falling off a horse. Valerie, you were clearing the land, farming. It was pioneering days. I'm seeing clothing that looks like the pioneering type. Dustin was very brokenhearted."

I asked Deb how Valerie had benefited by reversing that experience in her current lifetime.

"I'm hearing [from my spirit guides], 'She's in a state of grace,'" said Deb, "which means she moved up spiritually. Often, that mitigates many lessons that were set up, or it makes the lessons a lot easier. There was huge growth there."

The explanation of grace mirrored my own comprehension. In the course of exploring many life plans, I had come to understand one definition of grace as a putting aside of karma or planned "lessons." In Valerie's case, the sudden and unexpected death of her only child had such a profound impact on her that other lessons in her life blueprint may have been rendered unnecessary. I thought of the if-then points that medium Staci Wells sees in people's life charts in their pre-birth planning sessions. No doubt Valerie's life chart had its own key if-then points: if Valerie learns from her son's death, then X happens. If she does not, then Y.

But what was the "huge growth" that had resulted in Valerie's state of grace?

"Empathy, as well as compassion," Deb replied.

"That's what's happened," said Valerie. "This is a knowing that becomes part of who you are, and it never goes away—ever."

"She used it and transformed it for good," Deb added. At the time, Deb had no idea just how prophetic her words would prove to be. After Hurricane Katrina struck New Orleans, Valerie was shopping in a convenience store and happened upon a woman standing alone in an aisle. Traumatized by the hurricane, the woman was sobbing, her body racked with convulsions. "I just hugged her and hugged her," Valerie later told me. As their embrace ended, the woman said gratefully, "You have a lot of strength." In that moment Valerie was the living embodiment of empathy and compassion. The physical expression of such divinity is a driving force behind the soul's decision to enter the Earth plane. As Valerie concretized those traits in the physical realm, she knew them in ways and to a degree that would not have been possible without her own experiences of physical loss. In that instant Valerie turned her pain into love. She triumphed.

"Deb," I asked, "what would your guides say to people who are tempted to push away the pain?"

"They say, 'Embrace it. Embrace the pain and say, "I'm going to cry until I have no more tears." Then cry some more to release the pain,'" said Deb.

Then Dustin began to speak again. "I wasted the talents I had. Next time I have to utilize them. And I have to be a little tougher next time so I will be able to take it when people don't agree with my truth. I will need to trust myself. I feel bad that my death made you so sad."

"But that was something we decided together," Valerie said.

"I know," Dustin replied, "but we're not doing that again. We will not do anything to make each other sad again. That chapter is closed. Now, we go to something higher. I'm very proud of you. I will try to make the phone ring once. I'm learning how to play with electricity. Look for a message. Sometimes when you dream, that's when I can talk to you. When you wake up, try right away to remember your dream. I try to give you messages. I love you so much."

"I love you, too," Valerie said.

"I know," Dustin told her. "We feel love here. We feel it differently. It's more overpowering."

"He's showing me a wave of energy," Deb explained. "When they feel love, their whole being resonates to that feeling."

"You see how much good you did in people's lives, don't you?" Valerie asked Dustin.

"Yes," said Dustin. "I didn't realize how much I was doing. Next time it's going to be even better."

"Deb," I asked, "would your guides like to say anything else to people who are dealing with the loss of a loved one?"

"They're saying it's not personal," replied Deb. "It's not God sending a lightening bolt just to them. When we realize it's not personal and that it's something we've chosen, then it changes our perspective."

Speaking with Valerie's Soul

Through Deb, both Dustin and D.C had confirmed that they were well and that their early physical deaths had been planned before they were born. I sensed that the experience of talking with them was healing for Valerie. She learned more about why their deaths had occurred and, more important, was able to convey her love to them. And they, in turn, conveyed their love to her.

To understand better why a soul would choose prior to incarnation to lose both a fiancé and a son, I asked medium Corbie Mitleid to channel Valerie's soul. I sought to learn more about Valerie's life blueprint and the deeper purpose of her life challenge. In addition, I was eager to hear the wisdom Valerie's soul would offer in regard to how and why souls plan incarnations in general.

Because our souls contain the consciousness of every personality they have ever incarnated, they sometimes express themselves as "we" when channeled, just as Valerie's soul does in the conversation that follows.

The channeling began with a few moments of silence as Corbie entered a trance. When I felt she was ready, I began with the fundamental question.

"Why did Valerie experience the loss of a fiancé and a child?" I asked.

"She has been through both before, handled badly. Both have to do with the world war," announced Valerie's soul.

Just as every person has a unique energy, so, too, do nonphysical beings. As Valerie's soul began to speak through Corbie, I felt a sudden change in energy. In a way that was beyond the conventional five senses, I felt the presence, the life force, of Valerie's higher self. And having spoken at length with Corbie on several occasions, it was clear that the tone, pacing, and inflection of her voice were now entirely different.

"She lost her fiancé in 1916," continued Valerie's soul. "There was a superstition that when you went back to the front [in World War I], you were not supposed to get engaged, because that was like putting a bull's eye on your back. She and her fiancé thought they would be the exception. When the fiancé was killed, she lost her mind. She tried to throw herself out windows, refused to eat, and frankly became something of pity and scandal with her family, which, while not noble in the southern part of England, was certainly well connected. She succeeded in killing herself in 1920.

"She was born very shortly after, as many suicides are. She was born in the western area of the United States. She was of foreign extraction. She was married at eighteen and had a son shortly after. She was put into the internment camps in the United States [during World War II] because she was not sufficiently American. She lost track of her child, who had been taken from her. There was the constant, desolate hope that the child would be found alive. The child was killed before age twenty in an automobile accident, crossing the road while drunk.

"The fiancé, the son, and she have been playing out love and loss for some time. It is to be hoped and prayed that the personality [Valerie] understands now the transience of loss and that it is possible to go on with one's life having loved, but then having put that aside until meeting [again] out of the body."

I paused for a moment to take in everything that had been said. This wealth of information had been presented in a factual yet compassionate tone. There was no hint of judgment, simply the recognition that Valerie had been overwhelmed

by her losses in two past lives. Interestingly, her child in the
World War II lifetime had died at approximately the same
age as Dustin had in this lifetime. I wondered what might
come next.

"Are you Valerie's higher self?" I asked with great
interest.

"Yes."

"I want to clarify the previous lives. Was D.C. the fiancé
who was killed in the war in 1916, and was Dustin the son
who died when Valerie was interned?"

"Yes."

"You mentioned that you want Valerie to understand the
transience of loss. Why is it important for a personality to
understand that?" Deliberately, I had inquired in a non-
challenging tone. I wanted Valerie's soul to know that my
questions were intended to uncover meaning, not to suggest
any perceived faultiness in the life plan.

"Consider misunderstood loss as a derailment. When
you understand impermanence, when you understand that
change is truly the only constant in a space-time continuum,
then you understand that such losses come and go. These
souls have been with her time and again. They are truly
soulmates. She can extract from the experience the blessings
given by both and take them with her to improve her life
instead of derailing her positive direction with recrimina-
tions toward herself or God or the faith.

"The personality is created by the soul, the higher self,"
Valerie's soul added. "The personality is the illusion that is
required on Earth in this space-time to learn the lessons.
For without a body and without time, there are lessons that
cannot be learned."

Now that the subject was raised, it seemed a good time to
explore the distinction between personality and soul.

"My understanding of the personality," I said, "is that it consists of a permanent, eternal core that survives death and reunites with the soul after death, as well as certain temporary traits that exist only during the lifetime."

"That is accurate."

"So, when a personality dies in a particular lifetime — say, when Valerie dies in this lifetime — then her permanent core will be reunited with you?"

"At this point it is not separate. Do not consider reuniting, for that betokens a separation. There is never any separation. What the personality feels [after death], when it feels as one with God and higher self, is simply the brushing away of cobwebs that obscure its view, but it does not mean that it has not been connected."

This idea, which I had heard in other conversations with Spirit, was reassuring to me. Nevertheless, I still felt some discomfort over the depth of Valerie's suffering. It was difficult for me to comprehend its necessity, even after what Valerie's soul just said. In truth, I had felt this way about each person with whom I had spoken. I wanted to know why each had suffered, and I wanted to offer some understanding that might lessen the suffering.

"How does the soul grow as a result of physical incarnations?" I asked.

"Earth or other physical places can sometimes give lessons that cannot be done without a body, without physical needs, and without a physical interaction. Let us go to the example of hunger and thirst in two personalities. If the emotions of greed and fear are uppermost, then the one who has food and drink prevents the other from getting, or steals the little that they have. When the emotion is that of generosity, of service, of universal love and the understanding that the situation is transient, then benevolent emotions can reach out and assist the other personality, and the soul is advanced.

"All discuss before incarnation what is to be done. Is it too much? Things are altered, decisions are changed, until an imprint is decided on and published in the Akashic Record. [In this instance] the deaths were looked at as one more try in an experiment. The guides discussed that if there were enough advancement [by Valerie], then this opportunity might be taken in a more productive way, rather than the way it had been."

"Why did the life plan call for two deaths instead of one?" It seemed to me the transience of loss could be grasped from one death, and even multiple deaths could still fail to instill this understanding.

"Often," replied Valerie's soul, "when this personality has experienced death, she did not do well. We felt that given where and when the personality would be first schooled [on Earth] and the information with which she would surround herself, she would stand a better chance of being able to handle these [deaths]. While this time on Earth is fraught with difficulty and in many ways dark, the ability to take in spirituality, which has normally been hidden, is all-pervasive. It is easier, much easier, for the personality to learn spiritual truths this time because they are more widely spread."

"Do you feel that Valerie is accomplishing what you would like her to accomplish?"

"She is brave. Her ability to see transcends most personalities we have incarnated in the past two hundred years. We believe that these lessons can be dispensed with after this lifetime, should she take those deaths, make them meaningful, allow for their transience, and complete her life with their input as part of what makes her whole, not what makes her broken.

"She can take her pain, learn from it objectively, then take her newfound strength and reach out to those who have lost their children or a fiancé. She can give them the same ease and the understanding that the loss is transient and that they can extract the good things from the life and incorporate them into the years left on Earth.

"With any lesson, it is one thing for you to learn, but it is like reading a book and keeping the information to yourself. Along with the book, the information is lost, and it dies. What we souls learn, we teach others by being guardian angels and spirit guides for them. In the personality, what is learned must be left to others, be it one person or a book that reaches the whole world."

Here, Valerie's soul was echoing an idea I had heard in a different form: that we do not and indeed cannot complete our cycle of physical lifetimes until we have left our accumulated wisdom on the Earth plane.

"You said earlier that these three personalities have been repeatedly playing out love and loss. Can you tell me about other incarnations they shared in which they worked on these things?"

"There has been a husband-wife pairing with the two adults often. This stemmed from a life some fifteen hundred years ago, when the decision was made which set the lesson requirements in motion. The child sometimes comes in as a child, sometimes as a friend, sometimes as a sibling. He does not always have to come through the [Valerie's] body."

"What happened in that life?"

"Fifteen hundred years ago, they were part of a raiding party ... "

"You are referring to Valerie and D.C.?"

"Yes. They were particularly assigned to kill the women and children, which they did with great dispatch and some relish. Such trauma creates the need to feel the loss that one inflicted. Since these two at that time were as close as brothers, the bond was forged time and again [in subsequent lives]. The lessons continue."

"And in this raiding party they were both incarnate as males?"

"Yes."

Feeling that I now knew why the two deaths had been planned, I decided to expand the focus of the conversation.

"Valerie's story will be read by people who have lost a loved one," I said. "We've talked about understanding the transient nature of loss. What else would you say to help someone who is grieving?"

"Learn to pierce the veil. None are ever truly lost. If you knew that by stretching your faculties you could reach the souls of those who loved you, would you feel the loss as much? They are no longer with you to go on picnics or do the dishes or attend your child's graduation in form [body], but they can still see. Affection for souls does not die. How many people see their parents or grandparents dead for what they consider many, many years, and yet the love is still strong and vibrant? When one is lost, be assured all that needed to be gained has been gained from that personality. If one is lost, if a personality discorporates, take those treasures and move forward with them in your own life. Whether one dies at forty or eighty, the life has been lived as it was meant to be lived."

"For what other reasons do souls plan before birth to experience the loss of a loved one, particularly at a young age, perhaps from what we might consider to be unnatural causes?" I asked. I wanted to provide as much consolation as possible to parents like Valerie who had lost children.

"You are assuming that we are the only one that made this decision. Think of the boy, the child. What if he decided that he was going to have an abbreviated life, wanted the benefits of having Valerie as the mother-personality for the time he was on Earth, and she agreed? Sometimes, short lives are chosen when a soul wishes to accelerate its growth. We ask you to know that there are no simple answers. All lives are interconnected. This is a basic spiritual tenant. So, to ask did A happen simply because of B — no, it happened because of B, B prime, C, and many other reasons. This is why planning is required before incarnation — to make sure that the life weavings benefit all for the lessons they wish to learn."

"Are there things you can do to encourage the personality to learn?"

"This is always done on a subconscious level. But when a personality stops running asleep, centers, stills itself, and reaches in time to touch the eternal core, all approbation, all encouragement, all belief in what can be accomplished is there. As someone is sleeping soundly, you cannot put in front of them a book and say, 'Read this.' They are asleep. Yet if they wake and look at you, the book can be handed over."

"In many instances," I said, "I've seen a pattern in which the personality is asleep and there is some small crisis. If the personality doesn't wake up, there's a slightly larger one. If the personality still doesn't wake up, there's a larger one yet. It seems to accelerate like that."

"That is not encouragement, that is a wake-up call. What you asked about were encouragement, love, kind touches, so that pain can be avoided and difficulties surmounted. What you are talking about now happens when [the personality is] asleep. It is easier when someone goes inside to look for that core. Then most pain can be dispensed with, and much understanding can be exchanged."

"It sounds as though Valerie is learning what you would like her to learn. But if she were not, and if she were also not responding to love and encouragement, could you or would you engineer some kind of life crises to bring about the awakening you want?"

"There might be a loss around her," answered Valerie's soul. "She might look at film footage of widows and orphans in Iraq and be moved to examine her own loss in context. But we do not intentionally see having her lose people one by one in her life until she wakes up. Not in this incarnation."

"Are there some lives in which that is the life plan?"

"It is hypothetically possible, but this is not something we have chosen."

"What else is important for people to understand about the life challenge of losing a loved one?" I inquired.

"It has not happened because they are bad. Even looking at the life fifteen hundred years ago, that is judged neither bad nor good. You cannot kill a soul. This is perhaps a concept that is difficult for people to understand. This is not to say that we condone or shrug off one personality killing another; otherwise, karma would not exist."

"When you plan a lifetime, do you talk to ascended masters or God as part of the planning?"

"Of course. But just as there are certain ways that we can guide the personality and not other ways, there are certain ways that the ascended masters work with us, but they are not willing necessarily to plan point by point, for then how does the soul learn? The ascended masters are souls of finer vibrations. Part of our growth as souls is to reach that kind of understanding and ability to assist others. Life is based on love and service. There is nothing else."

"When Valerie's lifetime was planned with Dustin and D.C., did you plan specifically when and how they would die?"

"There are always three or four or five possibilities. No one has just one exit door."

"What other possibilities were discussed for D.C. and Dustin?"

"With D.C., a mugging, stroke, failed brakes, cancer." When Valerie's soul mentioned failed brakes, I thought immediately of the way in which D.C. had created the image of a motorcycle in Valerie's session with Deb. Apparently, D.C. had come close to dying in a motorcycle "accident," and that, too, had been planned as a possibility before his birth. "With the child, we had to leave open a point of conscious suicide; there was an opportunity for the child to die saving another child. There was also an opportunity for the child to die later in a suicide bombing."

"Did some of the alternative exit points come before their actual deaths in this lifetime?"

"Yes."

"Why did the deaths occur specifically when they did and the way they did?"

"It was agreed among all three souls that this appeared to be the time when the most growth could be triggered in all involved."

"That makes it sound like the souls caused the deaths of the personalities. Is that an accurate understanding?"

"It is not that we caused the deaths," Valerie's soul explained. "As an example, someone is in an accident where beyond all reasonable doubt they have survived. While in that accident, the personality could not make a decision to live or die. The soul looked and decided now is not the time. Remember, the soul and the personality, while they may feel separate, one does not fight the other. The soul does not argue with the personality, 'It's time to go,' 'No, it isn't.' You must understand that the personality is a construct."

"In Dustin's case," I pointed out, "there was an accidental drug overdose. He wasn't trying to kill himself. So how is the soul's decision translated into an action on his part that leads to his death?"

"As you say, it was accidental. The dose could have killed him or could have been just under what would have."

"But his soul decided at that time to end the incarnation?"

"You would have to ask that soul. From our vantage point, we would agree."

"Then Dustin's death wasn't caused by the absolute quantity of drugs he took, but rather his soul's decision to allow that quantity to end his life?"

"That is correct."

"So his soul's decision was translated into a biochemical response in his body?"

"That is correct."

"And had his soul not wanted the incarnation to end, that same quantity of drugs wouldn't have caused his death?"

"Or the soul would have arranged outside circumstances so that a fatal dose of drugs was not available."

"How would a soul do that?" I wondered.

"How would a soul get a car to go left instead of right?" replied Valerie's soul.

"That's a good question. How *would* a soul get a car to go left instead of right?"

"Impulses. Let us take another child that is deciding to commit suicide by taking drugs. Somehow, in the middle of it, the personality is touched by the soul. The personality wakes up. In the hands is enough to kill, but the personality does not take the rest. There was no [such] wake-up call for Dustin."

"You mentioned earlier," I said, "that a physical incarnation provides a way to learn that cannot be accomplished otherwise. As I understand it, there are many beings who choose never to incarnate. If incarnation is the only way to learn certain things, why do some beings choose not to have physical lifetimes?"

"The human experience does not encompass every experience that is important for a being's growth. There are no words to explain some of the concepts that can be learned when a soul never incarnates on Earth or in a human personality."

This struck me as a natural point in the conversation to raise the topic of learning-through-opposites life plans. I explained that from my research, it seemed many souls had planned lives in which the personality experiences the opposite of what the soul wants to learn.

"If one wants to learn unconditional love and comes down where one is judged, that is a motivational life," answered Valerie's soul. "The difference is between motivation and inspiration. Most personalities learn by motivation. From the way the Earth is constructed, negatives for millennia have been most of the way personalities learn. Now that you are moving forward, time is speeding up, and vibrations are higher, inspirational conduct may be of more service."

"In some instances, I've heard references to specific energies being placed by the soul in the personality. Is this part of the way in which personalities are constructed?"

"Yes."

"In Valerie's case, what were these?"

"Given to her were particular intelligence, curiosity, fortitude, and the willingness to move beyond pain."

"How does the soul create a quality like fortitude?"

"Ask God how He creates a flower. There is no quantitative or qualitative that can be explained."

I then asked how much of what happens in a person's life is planned before birth.

"There is not just one way to do it. Certain souls at their level of growth need things completely planned. As a soul is older, it is more willing to leave many doors open for choice. You would not expect a soul going through its first incarnation on Earth to be able to leave as much to chance as a soul who has done this many, many times. Not all souls are equal in advancement. Not all methodologies for creating personalities and karma are the same."

"What else would you like to say to Valerie that might be helpful to her?"

"That her heart is both bigger and less wounded than expected. That there has definitely been soul growth through her effort. That we wish her to look in the mirror and be at peace."

"Why did you expect her heart to be smaller or more wounded than it is?"

"This has been a difficult lesson for the personality. She has made great strides this time. This is something for which we are pleased and grateful."

"Why didn't Valerie and D.C. have more time together?"

"Because what needed to happen was the engagement, the agreeing to spend life together," Valerie's soul replied. "The life itself was not the object."

"You've touched on this somewhat, but I want to make sure I understand clearly. Why was the engagement itself so important?"

"When two personalities become engaged, it is the matching of emotions. It is the lowering of boundaries. It is the mark of trust. In the archetype of marriage, each of those involved says, 'I am you.' Often, people say the words but do not mean them in the marriage ceremony. Valerie and D.C. had no untruths to untie. Therefore, the one part of the relationship, the binding, was completed. Then the second part, the loss, could occur."

"Valerie lives in New Orleans, which experienced a severe hurricane. Was the hurricane also part of her pre-birth plan?"

"The experience of the hurricane sets her up uniquely in a place where there have been many who lost loved ones. If she can indeed take the lesson of that transience and reach out [to others], there is no better place than New Orleans for her."

"And is that why you planned for her to live in New Orleans?"

"Yes."

"Were there souls in her pre-birth planning who said to you, 'I am creating an incarnation in which the personality will experience great loss of loved ones through a hurricane. Could we coordinate our life plans so that Valerie can provide assistance to the personality I am creating?'"

"This could have happened, but it did not."

"Valerie is interested in spiritual growth. What would you encourage her to work on or look at?"

"We would encourage her to bring her emotions to a central point. When one swings a wide arc, there is a long way to come back. When one is still and at a central point, then one has abilities to reach any area and not have to come back so far through difficulty or time."

"What would be the best ways for her to accomplish that?"

"She will know. The soul does not give a syllabus. If we were to say, 'Do A, B, C,' she would not look. She would not experiment. She would not taste. Personalities often want too much detail because they are afraid of doing something wrong or missing something, but that is incorrect. There are many opportunities that she will have placed in front of her. They are hers to pick and choose. Otherwise, the personality is truly an automaton."

"What else is important for me to understand that I have not asked about?"

"Your questions have been more than sufficient."

"Is there anything else you would like to say?"

"We have given you everything needful at this time."

"Thank you for speaking with me," I said.

"You are welcome," said Valerie's soul.

Staci's Supplemental Reading for Valerie

To offer as complete a picture as possible of the design for Valerie's life, I asked medium Staci Wells to access the prebirth planning session in which D.C.'s and Dustin's early deaths had been discussed. Prior to the reading, I informed Staci that Dustin had died of an accidental drug overdose. As we began, I waited expectantly, quietly, as Staci's spirit guide opened the Akashic Records and presented her with the information we sought.

"She is doing the initial conversation with her spirit guide," Staci announced, "who I'm told has been her teacher and mentor on the spiritual plane for three lifetimes. He was husband and father to her in previous lifetimes. I hear them talking about themes Valerie has experienced. She has many interests on the soul level. She's very serious. She likes to take things systematically and orderly, but when she gets into physical embodiment, that's a big challenge to her.

Valerie:	I have experienced many challenges staying focused. I often get pulled off balance by something that catches my attention. I focus on a particular issue, and then my life goes in a negative direction.
Spirit Guide:	There shall be imbalances from time to time to cause you to shift your focus, yet also serving to lead you back to your center.

"The scene is changing now. I see her in discussion with D.C." Staci paused to listen to their conversation. "There's a strong desire on Valerie's part to link up with him again romantically in physical life. I hear him saying,

D.C.:	I'm not good for you. My plans are to be in physical embodiment for a short time. I would leave you.

"She was willing to have him in her life for whatever time they had together. She wanted him that much. There is also discussion here about how it will serve her purpose to experience this. They discuss that they will make plans [together after incarnating], even to the point of discussing children.

D.C.:	But you're going to be so disappointed.
Valerie:	If it means having you in my life for a short time, that's all right. It will serve my challenge to find myself again, the challenge to find inner harmony and balance after all of that. Your presence in my life would be a gift to me.

"He agrees to do this, even knowing that eventually his life will bring her sorrow because of his passing. I see him reaching out to her and stroking her face with one of his hands. He is so full of love for her, but also full of compassion for what she will go through. But he understands the role he will serve for her. His agreement about passing on early was already made with somebody else before he sat down with Valerie to be part of planning her life.

"I will go on to Dustin now."

Again, there was a pause as Staci's guide took her to that part of the planning.

"I'm being let in on the middle of their conversation," Staci explained. "He's already calling her Mom. It was established that, for his own purposes, he was going to leave this life early. I hear the words, 'It will be one way or another.'

"This is balancing karma. In a previous life, the roles were reversed. In that lifetime, she died much younger than he died in this life. He was her mother. They lived a difficult life, a farm life. Very poor, very hard working, very dull. Dustin craved more excitement, so his plans for this lifetime included possibilities that would give him what he felt was more aliveness. I get the feeling that it was hard for him to keep his mind focused [in his incarnation as Valerie's son]. Dustin agrees to help Valerie gain balance through her need to pay him back for the care, love, and energy he gave her in that previous lifetime.

Valerie: [to Dustin]	I want to take care of you. I just want to give birth to you and care for you for as long as I'm able. These kinds of responsibilities are very easy for me to take on. I will continue to grow through the responsibilities of

caring for home and family. It is a source of my identity.

Spirit Guide: You need to develop a stronger sense of self-worth, not just self-discipline. Even when you come back [to spirit after a lifetime], you still carry with you confusion about who you are. You tend to identify yourself as someone's wife, mother, or girlfriend. It has been a long-term challenge for you to discover fully who you are and allow that to be enough. This lifetime will help you find balance within yourself.

"Dustin says he loves both worlds — physical existence and spirit — equally. He has a lot of energy from the previous six lifetimes. They moved very slowly and were mundane. He wants to expel and express this energy during the lifetime-to-be. I hear him say, 'That's it. I come. I get it done.' There were things he wanted to do. He wanted to get right to it, do them all, and get back home.

"There are things he does on the other side, many souls he interacts with who have been relatives in several past lifetimes and in this lifetime. He works with children. He feels that is at least one-third of his work on the other side. He thrives on it. These are children who cross over between the ages of five and fifteen. Dustin helps them, especially when these are sudden crossings, to feel comfortable, play, and reorient themselves. Also, he loves and is very involved in music. He wanted to get things done in physical life — and get them done quick — so he could get back.

"There is someone involved with his death who he had an agreement with [before birth]. This is the person he got the drugs from, his primary contact. This guy was his closest friend, especially once his life turned toward drugs. I hear Dustin use the words 'Take me out,' as in 'be the cause of my death.'

"And there's more. I see the two of them in a past life in medieval times. I see knights with armor—pieces of chain mail and armor headpieces—on horseback. They were soldiers who fought together in a king's army. When Dustin's friend lay dying after being wounded in battle, he asked Dustin to run him through with his sword so he would not have an agonizing death. Dustin understood and obliged his friend.

"Dustin has no negative energy at all in regard to the experience of drugs or death or dying. He doesn't see it as a negative. He sees it as serving his purpose. What is his purpose? To leave early. This was not supposed to be a life of burden for him. He was supposed to get in, get things done, enjoy along the way, and leave. The drugs were simply an experience. Dustin had the assurance that he would be cared for throughout his life, that whatever happened to him before and after his involvement with drugs he would be okay because he has that agreement with his mother. He knew she would always be there for him. The drugs were part of his expression of personal freedom and a way to end the life.

"I want to get back to Valerie," Staci added. "In each of these discussions, there was acknowledgment that she would experience quite a lot of sadness as a result of other people's choices. She felt she was able to handle this. She understood that by experiencing such emotional extremes there would be a pendulum effect that would eventually lead her to a place of balance within herself."

∾

We who are immortal cannot know death, but we can create the illusion of it on the physical plane. This illusion is not part of our lives in the nonphysical realm, where we are ever aware of both our eternality and our unity with all souls. When in spirit, Valerie knows always that Dustin and D.C. are one with her, as she is one with them. She could not perceive herself as truly separate from them. As souls who have shared other incarnations, their love is deep, the bonds of their hearts inseverable. In spirit, Dustin and D.C. would forever be but a thought away.

And so they remain. As an angel in a previous story told us, the nonphysical dimensions are but a hair's breadth from us, overlapping and encompassing the physical. Valerie's perceived separation from Dustin and D.C., a seemingly immense gulf that she once felt powerless to bridge, is in truth her own creation as an infinite being. Who but the most powerful of souls could conjure an illusion that appears real to its very creator? By forgetting that she planned before birth to immerse herself in an illusion of her own design, Valerie may now recall—and thus know more profoundly—what it means to be limitless. As she reaches across the veil, whether through a medium or the "lifting" when her consciousness melded with her son's, she remembers that separation is illusory. Contained within that memory is yet another: the memory of self as an eternal, powerful soul. By remembering herself as such, Valerie comes to know deeply, experientially, who she really is.

While enveloped in perceived separation from her loved ones, Valerie also experiences and thus comes to know herself as trust and faith. In the preceding story, Pat planned before incarnation to live decades of alcoholism in order to feel the complete separation from God that would ultimately recreate his spiritual connection. Like Pat, Valerie now touches other dimensions through an inner knowing, a knowing birthed and deepened by pain. If Dustin and D.C. did not appear to be absent, what would it mean for Valerie to trust that they are ever present? If they did not seem to be deceased, what would it mean for Valerie to have faith that their lives are endless? Of doubt is truly meaningful trust born; in uncertainty is real faith created. Only in these circumstances are contrast stark and choice significant. Each time she chooses to pierce the veil and feel the love that Dustin and D.C. continue to send to her, Valerie takes another step toward understanding the illusion, the transience, of physical death. To understand the illusion of loss while in body is to understand in an expanded way the impossibility of loss in spirit. We are never without our loved ones, and they are never without us. When her lifetime is complete, Valerie, having felt apparent loss and seeming impermanence to her very core, will return to spirit and share with Dustin and D.C. a new and more profound appreciation for the permanence of their lives and love.

Just as the circumstances of this incarnation engender a feeling-knowing of trust and faith in Valerie, so do they allow her to experience herself as empathy and compassion. As Valerie would later say, "I have an absolutely magnificent understanding of human suffering." And so she does. Yet it is more than an understanding; it is now a way of being. When Valerie embraced the woman whose life had been devastated by Hurricane Katrina, she felt — truly felt — her despair. The depth of Valerie's empathy and the intensity of her compassion had been forged by her own dark night of the soul. In that moment in the convenience store, Valerie's anguish allowed her genuinely to understand someone else's.

Valerie could have planned a carefree existence for herself, but such a life would never have created the pathos, the heartfelt resonance, that was sparked in the coming together during the hurricane. As Valerie hugged her, the woman felt the empathy and compassion of someone who *knows*. She felt understood, and because she felt understood, she was no longer alone in her pain. Valerie, who had felt so utterly alone after Dustin's and D.C.'s deaths, was able to ease that pain only because she herself was living it. The energetic impact of such an intimate connection is immeasurable and far exceeds that which could be offered by someone with only a conceptual understanding of suffering. And in that spontaneous expression of love, Valerie created a new awareness of herself as empathy and compassion. After she leaves the physical plane, she will carry that heightened self-knowing into spirit, where it will remain part of her soul long after the pain that made it possible has faded into the recesses of time.

As Valerie heals and helps others to heal, she will forge within herself a feeling of centeredness and balance, an inner stillness that contrasts markedly with the raw, intense emotions that accompany death. This, too, is part of her life plan. As Valerie said in her pre-birth planning session, she has experienced other lifetimes of being pulled off balance. The soul seeks to balance in subsequent incarnations what has been left unbalanced. That D.C. and Dustin would decide before birth to leave Valerie is difficult to comprehend from the level of the personality, but at the level of the soul these plans were made in love. D.C. and Dustin scripted lives that would foster their growth and that of everyone with whom they shared their lives, including Valerie. As Valerie's spirit guide observed, it is the imbalances caused by their deaths that will actually lead her back to her center. Valerie will find that center and experience the pendulum effect Staci mentioned as she shifts to a soul-level perspective in which the transience of loss becomes more recognizable.

Over the course of her incarnation, Valerie's brave surrender to her life plan will give rise to the feelings of self-worth of which her spirit guide spoke. As she sees the courage she shows daily in living without Dustin and D.C.; as she comes to know herself as the powerful creator of all she experiences; and as she expresses herself on the physical plane as trust, faith, empathy, compassion, and balance, Valerie will come to know feelings of self-love that are not dependent upon the role she plays in a particular lifetime. Valerie's current life is one in which loss, by her own design, motivates her to shift gradually from personality to soul consciousness. As her spirit guide told her, she has defined herself in past lives as someone's wife, mother, or girlfriend. Those self-definitions are part of this lifetime as well, but the loss of the people for whom she played those roles calls Valerie into recollection of herself as something more. Valerie's life blueprint asks her to know herself in the same way she now knows D.C. and Dustin — as eternal souls.

Valerie's story also shows us that because we do not know another person's pre-birth plan, we cannot render judgment against the way in which that plan is lived. For example, many would be inclined to judge the drug dealer quite harshly, and yet on the soul level there was such love between Dustin and him that they planned another incarnation together, one in which Dustin entrusted him with a vital role. Like Valerie, the drug dealer allowed Dustin to have the life — and the death — he needed for his growth. When the drug dealer eventually returns to spirit, Dustin will greet him with love and thank him for playing his part to perfection. By the same token, Valerie will express gratitude to

D.C. and Dustin for making possible the learning she had planned. Importantly, there will be no blame. All will know that they were not victims and that, in fact, there are no victims. Guilt will be absent and forgiveness unnecessary, for what is there to forgive when all performed the plan well and lovingly?

Though these roles were chosen and agreed upon before birth, the enactment of the plan still creates painful feelings of loss. Valerie has learned and has much to teach about living with such feelings. Following her son's death, she knew from experience that she would have to embrace the pain. As the spirit guides advised in Valerie's session with Deb, "say 'I'm going to cry until I have no more tears.' Then cry some more." The guides know that pain suppressed is pain unhealed.

To heal pain, it may be helpful to consider that we have relationships with ourselves in the same way we have relationships with others. If a dear friend comes to us for support after losing a loved one, we do not fold our arms across our chests and turn the other way, nor do we tell our friend that we have no time for her or that he needs to put the pain aside and go on. Why then do we sometimes treat ourselves in this manner? Valerie turned away from herself after D.C.'s death when she sought solace in alcohol, but after Dustin's passing she loved herself enough to feel the loss. When we are grieving, we need more than ever to extend the same love to ourselves that we would offer so freely and generously to a friend in mourning.

Because grieving is painful, there is at times a desire or temptation to rush the process or even push it aside altogether. For the soul, grief is an expression of love, and every expression of love is healing. If we resist grief, we literally wrap energy around our pain and lock it into place. Crying is the body's natural means for clearing such energetic density; tears keep energy flowing and so allow for further healing.

When we understand the value of grieving, we may be inclined to think that we *should* cry. On a nonphysical level, the energy of *should* is incompatible with true healing. *Should* is the intellectual construct of a mind trying to control a process of the heart. When we tell ourselves that we "should," "must," or "have to" do something, we are allowing the mind to set the vibration at which we act. Yet far more important than what we do is the frequency at which we do it. Mourning is most healing when it is a natural, spontaneous expression of emotion. To cry because we "should" is to mourn through and with the ego. To cry because we want to is a gentle and loving way to nurture ourselves.

Spirit never abandons us in our grief, and no one mourns alone. The "solitary" mourner is surrounded and embraced by a caring family of spirit guides, angels, and the departed, whose love for us is transcendent. Bodies die; love does not. As we think of those who have returned to spirit, the energy of our thoughts calls them to us. Often, they attempt to speak with us, just as Dustin sent a message to Valerie through her sister. They are able to place ideas in our minds—both when we are awake and even more so when we dream—and feelings in our intuition. Because they are now energy unencumbered by physical restrictions, they can, as Dustin said, communicate through devices like telephones. Like spirit guides and angels, they can arrange for "coincidences" that guide, heal, or otherwise benefit us. It is not uncommon, for example, for a grieving person to be guided to (and then adopt) a stray animal shortly after losing someone. Then, too, loved ones in spirit are able to create familiar scents, such as the cologne or perfume they used, to signal that they are still with us. Our grief sometimes interferes with our ability to perceive their messages, but our openness to the presence of deceased loved ones is an invitation to them to work healing miracles in our lives.

Ultimately, the death of the physical body is a decision made by souls after their life plans have been fulfilled. "When one is lost, be assured all that needed to be gained has been gained," Valerie's soul told us. This assurance brings with it the understanding that we are not to blame for a loved one's death. Fatal accidents or circumstances for which we may feel responsible are simply some of the exit points planned by our loved ones before birth. For you who feel you caused or should have prevented another's death, know this: no one dies without consent. Therein rests your self-forgiveness. Therein lies your peace.

Faith and trust in the wisdom of our pre-birth plans allow us to know that those we love extracted from their lives all the growth, beauty, and richness they originally sought. They are at peace in the knowledge that they lived their lives just as they had planned, and they would share that knowing, and the peace it brings, with us.

CHAPTER 7

⬦

Accidents

O N THE EARTH PLANE, PHYSICAL accidents appear to be random events. When they are minor, we label them unfortunate; when they are severe, we call them tragic. The recipients seem to suffer at the hands of an uncaring universe that dispenses good fortune or unhappy fate arbitrarily, in cold disregard and unequal measure. In response, we often fear accidents and so tint our lives with a darker hue. But as I have suggested in previous chapters, little in the physical realm is as it appears.

This chapter explores a seemingly paradoxical notion: the planned accident. Many accidents are planned before birth for the purposes of spiritual growth, service to others, awakening, and deeper self-knowing. Profound growth is possible not only for the person who experiences the accident but also for everyone that person touches. Ultimately, because all lives are interconnected, *everyone* is touched.

In this chapter you will meet two people who experienced catastrophic accidents: Jason Thurston and Christina. Christina's occurred many years ago; Jason's is much more recent. Before they were born, both chose to face an extraordinary challenge.

Jason's Story

"It doesn't get any better than this," Jason thought as he surveyed the scene in his backyard on a warm, sunny August afternoon in 2004. His friends were milling about and chatting happily as they awaited the barbeque dinner Jason and his wife, Davina, were going to prepare. Later, after sunset, they would gather around a roaring bonfire. Jason and Davina's sons, Jaron and Garrett Fox, affectionately called "Fox" for short, were splashing in the swimming pool while other children were running across the grass, laughing and playing games. Jason had recently completed his final interview for a chef instructor position, a job that would be the fulfillment of a lifelong dream. Earlier in the day, he had push-mowed his acre lot in one quick swoop. "I was Superman," he said wistfully.

Moments later the course of his life was altered forever.

Davina called to Jason and asked him to begin cooking dinner. Playfully, he ran away from her and jumped into the pool to splash Jaron. "I jumped like I normally would, only this time it was different," Jason recalled. "This time I hit my head on the bottom. It was like a lightning bolt shot through my spine. I wanted to move my arms to swim to the top, but I couldn't. I was drifting down into the water, completely helpless. I surrendered to the water.

"The next thing I know, I saw vivid pictures of all the people I love. I was being shown all the things I didn't want to leave behind. I can't stress enough the amount of peace and tranquility and serenity I felt. I wanted to embrace that feeling and stay with it, but I was a thirty-two-year-old male with a wife and kids and career. It wasn't time. The message I received from a Higher Power was, 'You're going to get through this. You don't have any room for guilt, regret, or negative thoughts of any kind.'"

Jaron was the first to realize that something was wrong. When he tried to lift his father, there was no response. Then he looked into his father's eyes—and saw that he wasn't there. Friends pulled Jason from the pool; Davina pounded on his chest, screaming, "*You're not gonna die! You can't go like this!*"

Jason had crushed two cervical vertebrae. He was air lifted to a hospital where doctors performed emergency surgery. As Jason and his family would soon learn, he was now paralyzed from the chest down, though he could still move some muscles in his arms.

"When I woke up, I had a hard plastic tube down my throat," Jason said. "I was connected to all kinds of tubes and wires. I didn't have a whole lot of feeling from my shoulders down; however, there was more excruciating pain than I had ever imagined. It was in my bones, deep inside. My first instinct was to rip out the tube so I could speak because my mind was racing. That was the longest day of my life, an entire day of not being able to speak. I just wanted to tell people, 'I'm still here. Everything's gonna be okay.' When they went for a deep vein for the IV, my father saw a tear run down my cheek, and that's how he knew I was still in there."

In the days that followed, and despite his condition, Jason focused on how others were feeling.

"I took it upon myself to make people feel as good as possible," he said. When the respiratory therapists placed a vibrating vest on him to loosen fluid that had collected in his lungs, Jason saw an opportunity. "I sang for them. I did Elmer Fudd's version of Bruce Springsteen's "Fire." I was like, 'I'm dwiving in my caw...' It drew a crowd outside my room. People were laughing. I was so glad to be alive and so empowered by my experience with God! I wanted to make everybody around me happy even though I was going through one of the most difficult things I could imagine."

Jason was in intensive care for two weeks and rehabilitation for more than three months. The rehab process was slow; at first his muscles did not respond. He needed others to feed him and to change his clothes.

As Jason progressed through rehab, he was confronted with the realization that his life would never be the same. A particularly difficult moment occurred during occupational therapy, when he was asked to cut a sandwich in half.

"My therapist took a small French knife and put it in my hand," Jason remembered. "I had been a chef for many years and was able to do a lot of things with a French knife. I was staring at it, thinking about how I used to start my day at work by getting six big onions and a bunch of carrots and a head of celery diced up and sizzling in a pot within fifteen minutes. Now, I could barely even hold it, let alone cut the sandwich. I broke down and cried."

Jason made it through rehab by repeating the motto "I will until," meaning "I will try until I can." He also imposed a rule upon himself: never use the word *can't* without the word *yet*.

Although he was happy to leave rehab, his return home was difficult.

"People didn't know, didn't understand, and were confused and worried they were going to hurt me," Jason explained. "Every single day, I had to come to grips with the amount of help I need, the amount of stress I put on people."

For Davina, whom Jason describes as empathetic by nature, the experience has been intensely difficult. "She has been overwhelmed by seeing her husband not be able to move from the chest down," Jason told me. "She holds her feelings in to prevent me from thinking that she sees me as less of a person." They have struggled with the impact on their sex life. "A lot of sadness, a sense of loss," Jason said quietly. "We're working at it."

"Jason," I asked, "how have you talked to your sons about the accident?"

"Fox will say things like, 'Daddy, remember when you used to move your legs? Remember when we used to go fishing?' I say, 'Daddy will still be able to go fishing. It'll just be a little different.' Jaron has an enormous amount of compassion for my situation. He doesn't see it as a tragedy. He's had to be there for his mother and brother a lot more. He has stepped into that role."

Jason's mother has also assumed a caretaking role, though their relationship has been strained at times. "She is very meticulous about my care and doesn't ever go as fast as I want," Jason explained. "So, I'll suggest steps ahead, and she'll get real frustrated. She's actually cried and left the room. 'Oh, this isn't fast enough? See you later!' But she's shown that unconditional motherly love. She would do anything for me."

There has been an outpouring of love from the community as well. A benefit dinner and silent auction raised money for ramps and wider doors for Jason's home. Friends split and stacked firewood; on one occasion they carved "JT" into one of the logs and presented it as a gift. A local church donated a new shower unit. So many people have contributed in so many ways that Davina published a letter in the newspaper to thank all of them.

"There are, however, a few friends who don't come around anymore," said Jason. "A friend from college came to see me in the ICU and said, 'Honestly, I didn't want to see you, because I want to remember you the way you were.' He came by one more time while I was in rehab, but I haven't seen him since. There are some people who still see me and not the accident, and some people who see the accident and not me."

Gradually, Jason is adapting to his new life. After much practice, he is now able to feed himself. He can wash himself as long as he's placed in the shower. The daily process of bathing and dressing sometimes takes up to four hours. It's difficult for Jason to hold a pen, but he can write by moving his entire arm. "The patience lesson comes on many levels," he observed.

"I can't regret the split second I dove into the pool," he added, "especially in light of my understanding that it happened for a reason."

"Jason, what would you like to say to someone who just had an accident or is caring for someone who had one?" I asked.

"I think about what I still have," he replied. "I am still able to remember things, problem solve, do crossword puzzles, and be sharp. And a lot of people who never would have met have bonded over my experience. I'm grateful for that."

"What else would you like people to know?"

"Crying helps to heal. And there's still that person inside. Just because they don't look or move the way they did before doesn't mean that they're not still in there and that you can't still love them. I believe that we are adaptable creatures. We adapt and overcome."

Jason's Session with Staci Wells

In talking with Jason, I was struck by his determination to maintain a positive attitude. Over the course of many interviews with people, I have concluded that we are given the gifts—personal qualities, people, and synchronicities—we need in order to accept and then use our life challenges for our personal growth. Whether or not we do so is a matter of free will. Jason, I sensed, had been gifted with an unusually strong will, one that was propelling him forward despite, or perhaps because of, the difficulty of his challenge. Inspired by his near-death experience, he had chosen not to focus on negative thoughts. He knew intuitively that the accident had occurred for a reason, and he was searching for that meaning. I felt that he would never give up that search.

To see what insight Spirit might offer regarding the purposes of Jason's accident, I asked Staci to listen to his pre-birth conversation. Prior to the reading, I gave her the names and birthdates of his family members and informed her that he was now a quadriplegic as the result of a diving accident. (Quadriplegia is defined as some paralysis of all four limbs.)

"I see him speaking to three guides," Staci announced as she began to hear and visualize Jason's pre-birth planning session. "I see three-quarters of the room taken up with Jason and the other souls in his soul group, both those who he will interact with [on Earth] and those who will be staying behind in spirit. The three spirit guides take up the other quarter of that room. Jason is talking very passionately to these guides.

Jason: I want this challenge.

Spirit Guide: Do you realize that after this everything changes?

Jason: Yes. I have too long been in distress, captured by the sense of the immediate when I have been in physical body. When I get into physical life, and as I grow into adulthood, I forget that there is more than what I can see. I have a habit in life after life of focusing on the immediate — social structures, what is popular during the time, social recognition, status, and achievement — and denying any spiritual focus that I wanted before entering into life.

I want to be selfless, not just for my family, but for a larger group of people. I want to show them the way by my spirit and what I inspire them to do or feel. I want to be of service to others in a way that will help me see my own spirituality once again.

Spirit Guide: Your greatest spiritual growth and leap *in* faith — not leap *of* faith — will occur three to fours year following your accident. This will be a time of accelerated growth. You will hear ringing and other noises in your ears as a manifestation of clairaudience. Your sense of hearing, both physical and spiritual, will increase during this time.

Jason: Wonderful! I welcome that.

"I am told that Jason is 'perfecting this level of evolvement,'" Staci added, quoting her spirit guide. "He wants to work on this lesson for the last time. He's doing exactly what he intended to do in order to achieve that."

Given that this life challenge would have a great impact on those who love him, I knew that Jason must have discussed his plans with the other souls with whom he would incarnate. I asked Staci if she could hear Jason's conversations with some of those souls, beginning with his mother.

"He talked to her about this [accident] happening around the time he was ten," Staci said. "This would have been a different kind of accident. I see her bursting into tears. Her hands come up between them and wave in a gesture of no.

Mother: No, no, no! I can't agree to that! It would be like losing you. I lost you before. There have been other lifetimes in which you left before me. I do not want that to happen again. Even if you were still there but trapped in your own body, it would be too much like losing you again.

"Was Jason her son in those lifetimes?" I inquired.

"Son, brother, and mate," Staci answered. "In the lifetime where they were mates, she was the husband, and he was the wife."

"How does he explain why he wants to do this?"

Jason: My goal is to experience something that will force me to realize on the conscious personality level that I am more than my body and more than these petty structures by which we judge ourselves. I am the biggest judge of all.

"As I hear this," Staci said, "I get an image from the 1700s. He was a member of high society. Looks, social functions, and social standing were everything. This lifetime is his attempt to get beyond that and balance it at the same time.

Mother:	I wish that this would not occur in your childhood.
Jason:	I agree to delay this. I will work it out with my wife.

"Now I'm seeing Jason's wife, Davina. This is a very serious conversation. There is talk about their first getting together. There is talk about their love growing, getting married, having children, and the relationship becoming more serious as Jason's life takes a left turn. There is talk about this so-called accident, which we know is not an accident.

"I see Jason putting his hand to his neck. I hear the word *drastic* as he talks to this woman who will be his wife.

Jason:	The results of the accident will be catastrophic. It will change everything.
Davina:	It will enable you to expand on the spiritual level. It is like bread. Once in the oven, it rises.

"Davina has come to an understanding of why he makes this choice: so that he can free his mind and grow beyond the self-limiting beliefs he has operated under in four different lifetimes. That's why the four limbs, the *quad*riplegia."

"Staci," I asked, "what were the self-limiting beliefs?"

"The notion of there being only one right way," she replied. "In one lifetime, it was expressed religiously. In another lifetime, it was expressed as a rigid personality. I'm not told anything more specific than that."

This was an important revelation. In four past lives, Jason had experienced physical freedom and self-imposed limits in his thinking. For this lifetime, he had planned physical limits and freedom of thought. Indeed, the physical limits had been chosen *to create* freedom in his thinking. The symmetry was intentional, the cause-and-effect karma perfect.

"Staci, can you pick up any more of the conversation between Jason and Davina, particularly in regard to the accident's impact on their marriage?" I asked.

Staci then heard:

Davina: It will be very hard for me mentally, emotionally, and physically to care for you, let alone care for you *and* our family once this crisis has occurred. (*Sighs.*) It's not the first time I've had to work very hard in life. It fits with my goal to be of service to others, because I will be of service to you and others like you who you will come to know.

It's going to be quite a challenge for me. I don't know if I can love you enough to do this. I don't know if I can love you more than that.

"She means more than who you are as a quadriplegic," Staci explained. "I don't hear a decision about leaving him."

Staci's spirit guide then directed her focus to another portion of the planning.

"I see Jason talking with the soul who is his father in this lifetime," Staci announced. "As a soul, Jason's father looks self-aware and grounded. He and Jason have spent many lifetimes together in many kinds of relationships, usually familial.

| Jason: | I have looked to you for many lifetimes. I choose once again to be in a place where I can look up to you physically, even when I am fully grown. |

"It's a joke," observed Staci, referring to the lighthearted tone in which she heard Jason speak to his father. "Jason has humor when he says this."

At first I was startled that Jason had talked of his accident in this way. His tone was incomprehensible given the severity of his challenge. Yet in the next instant it occurred to me that Staci's spirit guide, a highly evolved being, had made a purposeful decision to present Jason's joke to us. Previously, each time Staci had accessed a pre-birth planning session, her guide had taken her to those parts of the conversation that were most important and potentially most helpful. His choice to offer this piece of dialogue was no doubt equally meaningful.

As I thought more about Jason's joke and my initial reaction to it, I realized that I was seeing his injury from the vantage point of the personality. If we believe we can be permanently harmed, then a severe accident is indeed a grave matter. As eternal souls, however, we know we cannot truly be damaged. It was this soul-level perspective that allowed Jason to joke with his father and that Staci's spirit guide was now sharing with us.

Having reminded myself that Staci's guide selects each portion of the pre-birth conversation with good reason, I asked why he showed us Jason's mother objecting to Jason's initial plan to experience his injury during childhood.

"He says the conversation with Jason's mother demonstrates that we have free choice in these planning sessions," Staci replied. "It was her choice *not* to experience him having an accident when he was a child under her care. We decide what we want and don't want to handle. Jason's love for his mother motivated him to delay this accident. By the time Jason spoke with Davina, that decision had been made. He had decided to wait until he was an adult. When he turned to Davina, it was to see if she wanted to be part of that as his wife. She was given the choice to be part of his life or not."

"Do souls tend to have a preference regarding when accidents occur?" I inquired.

Staci's speech slowed; she was now channeling her guide verbatim. "It is a personal choice based on many things," he said. "Sometimes the soul is in a hurry [to complete the cycle of reincarnation]. Sometimes it is other elements, such as the energy available in or on the Earth at certain times in one's life. You use astrology and other numerical influences, such as numerology, to define and label these energies. The soul is well aware of these energies before being born."

"For what other reasons do souls plan to have accidents?"

"Balancing karma is a major factor. If someone has grievously injured somebody else in another lifetime, they will often make plans to be in the right place at the right time to suffer at the hands of that person. Many times there is a need for greater insight. The accident forces the person to change their viewpoint, thus enabling them to have insight that had eluded them on the physical level for many lifetimes."

"What would you like to say to someone who has had a life-altering accident?" I asked him.

"The spirit is more than enough. Always remember that you are more than your body."

"What would you like to say to someone whose loved one has been badly hurt in an accident?"

"There is great compassion for what you go through. This is a test of your ability to love unconditionally and to remember always that as you are of service, so might someone have been of service to you or *be* of service to you in the future in your time of need. And remember forgiveness, because great anger always forms at some point—anger at the accident, anger at the person who had the accident, anger that it had to be this way. Remember to practice forgiveness for all those times there is anger."

Jason's Session with Deb DeBari

In addition to Staci's reading, Jason had a session with medium Deb DeBari and her spirit guides. As we began, I told Deb only that Jason is a quadriplegic as the result of a diving accident in a swimming pool, that he has two sons, and that his wife's name is Davina. Deb then listened closely to her guides as they started to explain what Jason had sought to experience in his current lifetime.

"This is an agreement between the two of you [Jason and Davina]," Deb said to Jason. "Your older son—his coming to Earth was to help take care of you. This is a big learning lesson for him—compassion, empathy. But the main agreement was between you and your wife. I see that in several past lives you took care of her. One picture I'm getting is that there was an illness, something long term. It was during the Middle Ages. There was another lifetime; she was your brother and you were her sister. You wanted to take on a very big hardship to erase a lot of karma so you wouldn't have to come back again. You said to Davina, 'Let's do this [accident] so that it's not just in old age.' And she said, 'I want to be with you. I'm willing.'"

Like Staci, Deb had perceived Jason's desire to have the accident occur relatively early in his life. Evidently, she was accessing that portion of the pre-birth planning that occurred after Jason's mother had asked him not to have the injury in childhood. Although Jason had agreed to that request, he was still eager to take on a long-term challenge and therefore asked Davina if the injury could occur when they were young.

"The other thing," Deb continued, repeating what she was hearing from her guides, "is that you were actually given an opportunity to continue on or leave. Were you unconscious at any time?"

"I was completely unconscious, no pulse, no anything," Jason confirmed. "My wife gave me CPR."

"I was picking up that you had to decide whether you wanted to stay here on Earth and continue with your agreement or leave. You had your choice. During the time you were unconscious, you said, 'I'm staying. I want to follow through.'"

"I was shown a picture of everyone that's important to me," Jason told Deb, "as if to say, 'Do you want to stay with them, or do you want to go on?'"

"When we choose such a difficult task," Deb explained, "our guides give us a choice, an out. If you want to change your mind, you can do that, but you wanted to stick to your agreement. You wanted to say to the world, 'Just because I'm not whole in my body doesn't mean I'm not a whole person.' Everybody grows from it. It's not just you, your wife, and your children. You are giving others an opportunity to do good. When you need help, you're giving them a chance to open themselves up to something new."

As Deb discussed Jason's life plan, I wondered how he as a nonphysical soul could have been sure that the accident would actually occur on the physical plane.

"Deb," I asked, "how does a soul make or let an accident happen?"

"Usually, our guides protect us," Deb answered. "They give us warning signals all the time. Jason's guides would normally say [telepathically] to him, 'This pool is too shallow to dive into.' Instead, they backed up, because he was looking for an opportunity. He had this agreement ahead of time." Deb was verifying something I had seen in my exploration of pre-birth planning: our spirit guides place thoughts in our minds — thoughts that seem to be our own — to protect us from unwanted life challenges.

"My guides say that sometimes, when someone's getting ready to dive or do something they shouldn't, they will literally knock the person off balance. All of a sudden they 'trip' and fall the other way."

Once again I was struck by the wondrous ways in which Spirit works with each of us. Although I had not heard of spirit guides *physically* intervening in people's lives, this new information nevertheless confirmed my understanding that our guides do everything in their power to ensure our incarnations proceed as planned. In some circumstances that means taking action. In others it entails refraining from action, just as Jason's guides did when he was diving into the pool. In all instances our guides are motivated by their love for, and desire to be of service to, us.

I asked Deb if she could see more of Jason's pre-birth planning.

"The guides asked if this is what Jason really wants," Deb replied. "They also said it may happen one of several ways. Jason was firm about the age when it would happen, saying, 'This is not going to happen when I'm sixty years old.' Jason and Davina were shown what he would go through, how it would affect the children. The guides said to Davina, 'Do you really want to be a part of this? You will have to be wife, mother, nurse, and caretaker.' She agreed because there are certain lessons she has to learn, like how to deal with empathy. When you feel empathy for someone, it's a matter of transmuting that energy and literally sending it to the person as healing energy and love.

"Everybody had an exit point if they didn't want to participate," Deb added. "Even when Davina was giving CPR, she could have stopped, but her soul was saying that Jason needs to be here."

"As Davina was administering CPR, her soul was communicating with her to continue?" I asked with much surprise.

"Right," said Deb. "'*You have an agreement. Keep going.*'"

Deb then paused as she listened to something else her guides were saying. "I am told that Davina is learning patience."

"Davina *is* learning patience," Jason told us. "We were talking about this today. She said that if there's one thing she's learned out of all this, it's patience."

"There's also an issue of patience on your part," Deb said to him. "Maybe a little temper or a little too impulsive." As Deb made this observation, I thought of the difficult moments between Jason and his mother.

"Snappy, sarcastic," Jason agreed with a laugh.

"I'm being told," Deb continued, "that one of the big lessons for you is visualization. Visualizing your hands moving, visualizing reconnection in your spine. A lot has to do with mind over body. All this energy you were putting into your body, now it's going into your mind. It's up to you to work with that. Your path is to enlighten people, to let them know that the body might be injured, but the brain is still okay." Like Staci, Deb was seeing Jason's pre-birth desire to experience freedom of thought after—and as a result of—his accident.

"What I'm picking up is that sometimes people treat you almost like you're not there, like they're going to make decisions for you," Deb said. "Well, your brain isn't paralyzed. Part of their lesson is that they shouldn't overlook what you want."

"You're right," Jason told her. "There are a lot of decisions being made for me."

"Deb," I said, "you've mentioned that Jason wanted an experience in which he could balance karma and perhaps not have to return to Earth. Why would that be important to the soul?"

"Souls look through their Akashic Records, the book of past lives, and say, 'I was killed in war here. A horse trampled me there. I wasn't there long.' It's almost like, 'Well, here we go again.' There are other lessons they can learn in the other dimensions without the heaviness and physical pain they have here with the body." Evidently, Jason had wanted to move on to these higher dimensions and so had designed a life that would be the last in his cycle of reincarnation on the physical plane.

"Deb, can we get more information about the plan for Jason's children?" I inquired. "Why did they choose to have this experience?"

"Your older son, what is his name?" Deb asked Jason.

"Jaron," Jason said.

"I see him on the other side [before birth]. He was very connected with Davina. He wanted to live with her. She said to Jaron, 'Think about it. Is this too much for you?' He said, 'No, I will benefit from everything that will happen.' He also wanted to be supportive of Davina. He's learning unselfishness, is what I'm told. Your younger son, what is his name?

"Garrett," Jason replied. "We call him Fox."

"He wasn't sure where he was going to fit in. On the other side, they weren't sure if he was going to your family or another family. He's very connected to Jaron, and he came in mainly because of his connection with his brother."

"His brother asked for him," Jason laughed. "Jaron sat on Santa Claus's lap and said, 'I want a baby brother.'"

"And Garrett said, 'If he wants me, I'm coming!'" Deb said. "Those two have a very strong karmic connection from many lifetimes. They were brothers, father and son, and husband and wife. They're partners. They're a strength and support for each other."

I asked Deb if there were lessons for anyone we had not yet talked about.

"Yes, Jason's mother," Deb replied as she listened to her guides. "Again, it's empathy. She was begging Jason [before incarnation] not to do this." Deb was hearing the same pre-birth conversation Staci had heard. "She felt it was too hard. Jason said he had to. So, part of her was prepared. She knew something was going to happen.

"She's learning empathy. As much as she wants to rescue and do everything, she has to step back. One of her big lessons is to not take power away from people, because if there's a need, she wants to take care of it. Part of her lesson is to make it possible for others to learn from the situation. There's a lot of soul growth there."

"Deb," I said, "please ask your guides this: For someone who's just gone through a major accident and is trying to make sense of it, what else is important to know?"

"Let me see what they say," Deb said. She paused to listen. "There's hope. Too often, the doctors get too grim. People need to know that there is hope and life beyond a particular injury. You can will your body to heal. There is a possibility of more healing."

"Deb, please ask your guides what other reasons souls have for planning before birth to experience accidents."

"Sometimes, they only want to stay so many years," Deb repeated the words of her spirit guides. "An accident is planned so that they have an exit point. Sometimes, it's to shake people up. It's a way of saying, 'What's my purpose? Am I wasting my life or doing what I'm supposed to?' Many times after something like this people redirect their lives. And my guides just showed me that sometimes a soul will stage a walk-in. Sometimes, it is an opportunity for a different soul to walk in [to the body] and let the [original] soul walk out."

A detailed discussion of walk-ins is beyond the scope of this book, but it is indeed a real phenomenon. When a soul concludes either that it has learned or will never be able to learn all that had been sought in a particular lifetime, the soul can "walk out" of the body, meaning that it withdraws its energy from the physical form. Generally, withdrawal of energy results in the death of the body. If, however, another soul feels that its learning is best served by starting an incarnation later in life rather than as a newborn, it can choose to "walk into" that body. In this way, an exchange takes place. Afterward, the walk-in has all the memories of the original soul, just as if he or she had occupied the body since birth. Although the memories remain, there is sometimes a pronounced change in personality that may cause difficulties in relationships. Some walk-ins are consciously aware of what has taken place; others are not. Many who are aware choose not to share this information for fear of ridicule.

As Deb's guides said, accidents also redirect us. For this reason, potential accidents are planned for key junctures in our lives when we will need to remember our purpose. If we remember through intuition — impulses from our souls — the accidents need not occur. If, on the other hand, we ignore our inner promptings, then the message is delivered in increasingly stronger ways, including major accidents. I shared this understanding with Deb.

"Our souls keep trying to get our attention," Deb confirmed. "When they can't, they knock us over because we've agreed to certain things and we have to start doing them."

"Deb," I said, "when Jason had his near-death experience, he was told that it would be important not to have regrets or negative thoughts. What can your spirit guides say to help people with that?"

"People will wonder why this happened to them," Deb said. "They'll be angry. The guides are showing me that anger is energy. Don't direct that toward yourself. Take that energy to exercise, visualize, propel yourself forward. That's when you have real soul growth. And when you have a victory, even the tiniest victory, celebrate it. Be joyous. And every day bless your body. Don't say, 'This damn body.' Say, 'This wonderful body is going to serve me the best it can.' And the guides are telling me that when people feel sad, they can cry. If they push it within, it will come out as anger. Tears wash the soul."

"Deb, Jason has talked with me about how this accident has challenged his marriage. What would your guides say to readers whose relationship is challenged by an accident?"

"They're saying, 'communication, communication, communication.' They have to talk about everything. Jason, Davina doesn't want to tell you that she's worried or fearful.

But she has to say, 'I'm concerned about this.' Maybe give her a kind word so she can feel that she's leaning on your shoulder. She feels if she says something, it's going to hurt you. Then it gets to the point where it's overwhelming, so she thinks, 'If I take myself out of this, then he can heal better, and it will be better for both of us.'"

"I'm very curious," Jason said, "about the other people that are affected by this—friends, other family members, distant relatives."

"For them, it's soul growth, also," Deb told him. "You're giving them an opportunity to bring out the best in themselves. You touched their hearts, and they want to do something. It's that simple."

◡

A recognition of pre-birth planning can bring deep healing, but its place is to accompany or follow mourning, not substitute for it. Loss of any kind, including the loss of physical abilities, heals with mourning, and the mourning process is not to be abbreviated in a pained haste to move from personality to soul consciousness. Far better to sit with the pain and cry, should one so choose. Mourning is a gradual process of the heart, best lived softly and with grace, with kindness, gentleness, and compassion for self.

With time come shifts in perspective. One of the most healing shifts is to realize, as Staci's spirit guide said, that you are more than your body. This realization makes all the difference. Jason's near-death experience with God confirmed for him that there is something beyond the physical realm. How much greater his anguish if he believed there is nothing more, that he is his body, and that he ceases to exist at the end of his lifetime! Instead, he knows that he is spirit and that he comes from and will return to a place of, as he put it, "peace and tranquility and serenity."

When a recognition of pre-birth planning is added, perspective may shift even more. With such awareness, this lifetime becomes but one of many stretching into an infinite horizon. And it is not a random, haphazard occurrence filled with meaningless suffering, but rather a well-conceived plan rich with purpose. We who live such plans are more than a mere assemblage of minerals; we are our souls. And as souls, we are eternal.

In the realm of peace, tranquility, and serenity from which we came and to which we will return, we experience no opposites. There, peace is forever unshattered, tranquility always undisturbed, serenity constant. Lacking opposites, we could not truly know or appreciate these blessings. And so we decided to take form in a world of opposites, a place where these things are scarce *but can be created by us* as we live our life plans. As Jason said during his pre-birth planning, "I want to show them the way by my spirit and what I inspire them to do or feel. I want to be of service to others." Jason will fulfill his life plan by recreating *within himself* the peace, tranquility, and serenity of Home, and the anguish he now experiences will leave him with a profound understanding and appreciation of those feelings. And as Jason recreates within himself what Home *felt* like, those feelings will trigger a new and deeper remembrance of himself as an eternal soul whose nature and substance are love.

It is because he *is* love that Jason wanted to be of service. Indeed, it is because we *are* love that service is the basis for so many pre-birth plans. Love motivates service, and service gives form to love. One might then ask: Why would a soul like Jason, who is intent upon service, design a life in which his ability to serve is seemingly limited? The answer is that service can be energetic. In fact, all service *is* energetic, whether or not it entails action on the physical plane.

As Jason creates internal peace over the course of his lifetime, he carves a vibrational trail that is easier for others to walk as they build peace within themselves. Because this energetic pathway is not dependent upon physical action, Jason can have a profound effect upon the world—and the nonphysical dimensions—simply by creating peace within himself. A recurring message of this book is that our vibration affects the universe far more than our actions do, that who we are matters more than what our bodies do. The hermit who sits alone on a mountaintop radiating a vibration of peace does more to bring harmony to the world than the angry peace marcher, whose frequency serves only to create more of the very thing against which he rails so vehemently. For this reason, the limitations of Jason's body in no way restrict his energetic impact; to the contrary, they drive it. His healing will be our healing; his peace, the world's peace.

Though his energy alone can have a powerful effect, Jason's life blueprint calls for him to serve others through his relationships. In part, his service takes the form of teaching. As Deb pointed out, Jason planned a catastrophic accident to teach that a paralyzed body does not indicate a paralyzed mind, that a person remains whole even when the body does not. In part, Jason serves others by allowing others to serve him. Severe accidents are often planned because they provide opportunities for us to express and thus know ourselves more deeply as compassion, empathy, and forgiveness, including self-forgiveness for any anger felt toward the person who experienced the accident. All are virtues of our souls that cannot be expressed or known in the same way in the nonphysical realm, where physical disability does not exist. Too, Jason's service takes the form of direct action. Recently, he began a new career as an independent-living specialist, helping others who have been injured in accidents to adjust. Though the information he dispenses is valuable, his greatest impact is energetic. In his new life, he shows others the way by his spirit. He inspires them to do and to feel. He is of service. He is the soul who planned this life, and he is living it, bravely, just as he planned.

And as he lives it, Jason is inspired by a celestial chorus of loving beings, including the guides who helped him plan his life. At all times do they surround him with their love, serving him as he serves others, fulfilling their purpose by helping Jason fulfill his. Spirit stands in awe of Jason and all who transform personal suffering into world service. In gratitude do they applaud behind the veil, where Jason's every thought, emotion, and action are known, felt, and seen. Perhaps Jason's life plan calls for clairaudience so that he will someday hear the chorus that so esteems and honors his extraordinary courage and service.

Just as Jason's accident helps others remember themselves as compassion, empathy, and forgiveness, so, too, does it help Jason remember who he really is. In previous incarnations, Jason had not remembered his true self; in fact, he had lost sight of his identity as a soul. As he said, "I have a habit in life after life of focusing on the immediate." In some of those lives, he had focused on "social recognition, status, and achievement" and the "petty structures by which we judge ourselves." To balance karma and make the experience of remembering more likely, Jason designed a life in which such considerations would be rendered trivial. Importantly, he is not punishing himself for those past lives. Rather, he has provided himself with another opportunity to create and thus come to know his eternal, spiritual identity in temporary, physical form. The overarching challenge of his life is to express that identity — love — in matter; the accident he planned is but the catalyst of that alchemy.

Like Pat in the chapter on drug addiction and alcoholism, Jason desired a challenge that would "help me see my own spirituality once again." That spirituality, obscured in previous incarnations by his focus on what was popular during the time, is to be expressed in Jason's current lifetime as a "leap in faith." These words from Jason's spirit guide are highly meaningful. A "leap of faith" occurs when we take action without true faith. "Leap in faith," by contrast, denotes genuine growth in faith. Though it may be too soon after Jason's accident for that leap to occur, the seeds were planted. They were planted in his experience with God and in the message he received. They were planted when he felt the complete peace of the nonphysical. And they take shape even now in Jason's intuitive knowing that the accident happened for a reason. With a challenge so great, Jason's path may well be marked at times by painful losses of faith. Yet it is in the fallow periods that faith renews itself, growing silently and unseen, bringing ever closer the day when Jason will see himself once again.

Above all else, Jason's life is an expression of raw courage. His spirit guide understood the difficulty of this undertaking and questioned him accordingly. His mother knew its severity and so burst into tears, eventually persuading him to move the accident from childhood to adulthood. Jason realized that the accident would change everything, and this was his desire, for it presented an opportunity to perfect "this level of evolvement." These are plans of boldness, plans that few would dare undertake. They are the plans of a limitless soul who sought to know himself as such by courageously overcoming the very limitations he himself had created.

And yet courage is more in the living of the plan than in the creating of it. No soul who lives a plan like Jason's can fail to recognize the great courage it requires in every second of every day, and no soul who recognizes such courage can fail to grow in self-love. Ultimately, the creation and expression of love in all forms is the very purpose of physical life. Through courage does Jason now fulfill the purpose he chose before he was born, for it is the touchstone by which he shares his self, his love, with the world.

IN 1969 CHRISTINA EXPERIENCED A devastating accident. Though she survived, a death of sorts did occur—the death of her old way of life, the passing of former ways of thinking and being. In their place, a new spiritual awareness was born. Despite the extreme suffering she endured, Christina views the experience as a gift. Her journey to that perspective is as extraordinary as the perspective itself.

Christina's has been a voyage from anger and guilt to peace, forgiveness, and gratitude. That she has been able to transform her suffering so completely, and use it so positively, is due in part to her understanding of pre-birth planning. She realized long ago that she herself planned the accident that forever changed the course of her life, and she knows why she created that plan.

Christina's accident led her into a new career in which she has fulfilled her pre-birth desire to bring healing to many. Following the accident, she earned a Ph.D. in speech language pathology. In her practice today, she treats patients with neurological disorders, primarily brain injuries, tumors, strokes, and aneurysms. She also studied Reiki and ARCH, an ancient Hawaiian form of healing. She has helped thousands to heal. The recipient of many professional awards, she is considered a leader in her field.

In part, Christina's understanding of pre-birth planning and the spiritual purposes of her accident have come from conversations she has had with her spirit guides, Cassandra and Leona. Her story shows us the beautiful ways in which Spirit works with each of us so that we may not only live the plans we created before birth but also extract from them all the wisdom and growth they offer.

Unlike other stories in this book, Christina's is presented in two parts. Part I focuses on the accident and the near-term events that followed, including Christina's realization that she had planned it. To offer insight regarding how Christina arrived at this awareness, I then present my conversation with Cassandra. Part II of my talk with Christina, in which she shares additional insights about her journey and healing in general, follows that channeling.

Christina's Story—Part I

Seemingly, it was a day much like any other. Christina, a twenty-year-old administrative assistant in the department of political science at Pomona College, had just finished a routine day of work and was waiting for her husband to pick her up. He should have been there already; she wondered what had delayed him. Christina would later learn that he had lost track of time while reading. (In Christina's session with the medium, we would discover that he was not meant to be there.)

To pass the time, Christina decided to check her boss's mailbox in the basement of the building in which she worked. As she descended the stairs, she noticed a package in the mailbox. Fortunately, and without making a conscious decision to do so, Christina reached for the package from the bottom stair, never stepping directly in front of it.

"It was a time bomb," Christina explained. "It was wired around the edge so that when I touched it, it detonated. It blew me back against a solid, cement wall, and it blew six-foot wooden splinters into the walls. They stuck in the walls like big swords. It blew the skylights out four floors up.

"I was totally blind, because I had all these bomb-makings in my eyes. I had shrapnel throughout my entire body, my chest, my head, everywhere. It blew two fingers off and blew my eardrums out. *I was in so much pain!* One of the men I was working with at the college came to me and said, 'Who are you?' He couldn't recognize me."

People pulled Christina from the debris and carried her outside. "It was raining, this really beautiful, cool rain," she recalled. "I could feel the rain on my face." The man who had been unable to recognize her applied pressure to critical points on her body, in all likelihood saving her life. "Coincidentally," he had recently read his wife's nursing books and learned the location of the major pressure points. "I have no idea why I read them," he said to Christina. "I was just bored one day."

An ambulance rushed Christina to the emergency room. Just a few days earlier, the hospital had purchased a new magnetic device for debriding wounds. After sewing her eyelids open, doctors held the magnet above her eyes and extracted the shrapnel at the same angle at which it had entered so as not to cause more damage.

The days that followed were among the most difficult in Christina's life. "The headaches were horrible. I went from 120 pounds to 85 in six days. I couldn't eat because my lips were sewn up, and I couldn't open my eyes because they were swollen. My face was charred. The Los Angeles Bomb Squad came to the hospital. When they saw me, one of the men passed out."

In all, Christina underwent another ten operations, including plastic surgery on her face and several surgeries to her hand. In one procedure, physicians sanded off all but one layer of skin on her face and used wire brushes to remove the gunpowder.

"After a period of time, one day I opened my eyes and I could see color again!" Christina exclaimed. "I said to the nurse, 'That's a pretty red dress you have on.' Everybody was weeping and jumping up and down!"

Eventually, Christina decided to finish her college degree. Although her body had healed considerably, she was still in extreme pain and her vision remained poor. With a cast on her right arm, she had to use her left, nondominant hand to write. When she asked her professors for additional time in which to take written exams, they expressed concerns about cheating.

"It raised me to a level of anger that was quite profound," Christina acknowledged. Much of that anger, she knew, was not with her professors but rather with the accident itself and the person who had planted the bomb.

Then, just as her life had once before changed on a college campus, it did so again—this time through a nonphysical experience.

"One day I was walking across campus and feeling guilt, like I had created the accident," she said. "All of a sudden, a message was passed to me [from Spirit] that I was as good as everyone else and that just because I had physical disabilities, it didn't make any difference because I knew what I needed to know. *It was as though someone had picked the world off my shoulders!* The sense of forgiveness that overcame me was very profound. In fact, I could hardly move for a period of time. Then I started to feel elated. And I realized there wasn't any necessity for judgment of other people; a neutrality existed that I could live by. Forgiveness was the most critical piece to move forward from a victimization frame of mind."

As Christina described those pivotal moments, the emotion in her voice told me just how powerful they had been for her. Sometimes, the most extraordinary revelations occur under the most ordinary circumstances. And though there is a knowledge that comes in these moments, their power resides in feelings, feelings that bridge dimensions.

No words can convey these feelings, and anyone who has had such an experience is never again the same.

Spirit had gifted Christina with an understanding of neutrality—the pure nonjudgment with which wise, nonphysical beings view all experiences. From the perspective of the personality, life challenges are often "bad" because they appear to cause suffering. Yet from the viewpoint of the soul, challenges are neutral experiences; it is the judgment of them as "bad," rather than the challenges themselves, that creates suffering. As Christina walked across the campus, she felt and deeply understood neutrality. In that understanding, some of her guilt and anger dissolved.

I asked Christina to talk more about her emotional recovery from the explosion, including other messages from Spirit that had been healing for her.

"I went through the stages Elisabeth Kubler-Ross explains people go through toward the process of death. I went through anger and guilt. I tried to bargain. I tried all those things. Once it became clear to me that it was an agreement I had made [before birth], then everything calmed down. There wasn't any reason to struggle any longer."

"Christina, I gather you're in communication with spirit guides. Is that how you've pieced things together?"

"It is. That and through several other things. Sometimes, it comes to me through books. I'll go into a spiritual bookstore, pull a book off the shelf, open it to a particular page, and usually a message comes to me that way. I also have a guide named Cassandra and a guide named Leona, and they pass information on to me and protect me frequently in situations. I communicate with Michael the Archangel if I have to do something specific."

Of the many people with whom I had spoken, few had been familiar with the idea that we design our lives and challenges before we are born. Had they believed in pre-birth planning, they might have surrendered their struggles as Christina did. Society generally equates surrender with weakness and capitulation; we are often told that we should never give in. Yet in talking with people, time and again I noticed that resistance intensifies suffering and acceptance diffuses it. I therefore came to view surrender as a road to true power.

"I also received a message that suffering brings an energetic balance," continued Christina, "that as people suffer, it releases energy for other people to push forward with certain things. That made sense to me, so I just kept moving forward."

I asked Christina if she had ever learned the identity of the bomber.

"I never found out," she replied. "Years ago I thought, 'I wish I could contact the person who sent the bomb, because he needs to know that I forgave him a long time ago.' I made a contract with that person to have it occur.

"Once, when I was having eye surgery, I heard a voice. It said, 'Now you understand the theory of relativity. Everything happens at the same time and at different times.' So, I realized that if all events occur simultaneously, there is no reason not to forgive someone, because I've already lived through it."

"Christina, would it be accurate to say that the bombing was an act of service to you on the part of the other soul?"

"It was a gift," she said without hesitating.

"Would you say you're grateful for it?

"Yes, totally grateful."

Christina was now sharing one extraordinary feeling, insight, and experience after another. Yet what I found most remarkable were her forgiveness and gratitude. She had completely, unequivocally forgiven someone whose actions had resulted in years of intense physical and emotional anguish for her. Though many may have been consumed by rage and their lives destroyed by bitterness, Christina had found forgiveness and, with it, peace. Even more remarkably, she had forgiven the bomber *long ago*. Her forgiveness had not derived from the passage of decades and the healing of bodily wounds; in fact; she had made enormous strides in forgiveness while lying on an operating table during surgery to repair the physical harm this individual had caused. To forgive under such circumstances is rare; to eventually feel gratitude for the experience, even rarer.

To understand better how Christina was able to heal so deeply, I asked her to channel Cassandra. As you read Cassandra's words, bear in mind that you have enlightened spirit guides working with you in the same way Cassandra works with Christina. Christina's clairaudience does not grant her privileged access to Spirit. The same love and wisdom are showered upon all of us, whether or not our conscious minds can identify nonphysical beings as their source. Their guidance is offered to all in the form of feelings, intuition, impulses, images, and the yearnings of our hearts. It is up to us to listen. We can do that by quieting our minds and by choosing to believe we can hear Spirit. Otherwise, guidance may be obscured by mental frenzy or by disbelief in our ability to hear it.

As we began, I wondered if Cassandra's wisdom would allow me to look upon my own challenges, whether past or still to come, with greater forgiveness and gratitude. Perhaps, I hoped, it would allow others to do the same in their lives.

Christina Channels Cassandra

"Cassandra," I asked, "why did Christina plan before she was born to experience the explosion?"

"This one wanted to bring hope to the world," Cassandra answered. "It was her mission of importance. It brings a level of understanding that the human body is simply a shell, that you live many lifetimes, and that you have the opportunity to live those lifetimes with grace and peace."

With Cassandra's presence came a subtle shift in energy, a sense of a distinct consciousness. Christina's voice conveyed the words, but there was a different feeling to and behind those words.

"But there are certainly many life challenges Christina could have chosen to accomplish those goals. Why specifically did she plan a bomb explosion?"

"Simply, she could survive it. And it was intense enough that it would catch the attention of other people so they would listen."

"Why did the soul who created the bomb plan before birth to do that?" I inquired.

"It was a matter of freedom," replied Cassandra. "It does not have any negative connotation."

"Is it accurate to say that the planting of the bomb was an act of service on the part of this individual to Christina and the world?"

"Yes. The Divine One used that person as a vehicle to open the eyes of many people, throughout time, to see the truth."

"When the person who planted the bomb dies and crosses back into spirit, will he feel remorse or regret?"

"It will be part of the life review, but he will not have any sense of regret."

"Will this soul feel pride at having played his role well?"

"It will be neutral."

"Did the planting of this bomb fulfill any other objectives?"

"It did," said Cassandra. "It fulfilled an unconscious group thinking process. You [humans] are sometimes carried by the sea of thoughts that comes from the cosmic consciousness. You are sometimes carried by states of action. Those states of action can cause wars and harm to people. It [the explosion] causes many souls to think about what they are enacting while they live on the Earth."

Cassandra was now drawing an important distinction between individual and collective consciousness. On Earth, individuals are influenced by a group consciousness (energy). At this time in our evolution, that consciousness is based largely on fear: fear of death, fear of physical harm, and fear of economic reversal, for example. This energy affects our thoughts and feelings. Because the role and power of the collective consciousness is not well recognized, people tend to see all their fears as self-generated. In truth, they may be tapping into the energy of the collective.

I still was not clear about the benefit to the soul who had agreed to plant the bomb. "What does the soul of the bomber learn?" I asked Cassandra.

"The soul actualizes a depth of understanding that vibrates through all the etheric bodies." The etheric bodies are the generally invisible layers of energy that surround our physical bodies. Together, they comprise what many refer to as the aura. "That if he created something through what might have been felt as hatred at that time, that it be released and that he forgive himself for the activity. This may bring a deep conceptual understanding to the particular soul group and Earth plane group."

Cassandra's comment reminded me of the angel who had said that Jon (chapter 2) was healing himself in order to heal his entire soul group. Though Jon's role was to heal shame, the bomber's, it seemed, was to heal hatred—the hatred that had driven him to plant the explosive. If the bomber could transmute the energy of hatred through self-forgiveness, then both an energetic healing and a deeper understanding of hatred would come to those souls in his group. In regard to the Earth plane, any healing of hatred by the bomber would make it easier for others in body to overcome the hatred in their hearts, and any self-forgiveness by the bomber would make it easier for others to forgive themselves. Such are the energetic repercussions we have on one another; an increase in one person's vibration lifts everyone else.

"When he returns to the nonphysical," I asked, "what will be the reaction of other souls?"

"All events are looked at in a neutral fashion," Cassandra stated. "There will be an acknowledgment that the Divine Plan was carried out."

"So because this was an act of service that was planned before birth, this soul will not accrue any negative karma?"

"That is correct."

"Cassandra, is it accurate to say that on the other side, in spirit, there is love between Christina and the person who planted the bomb?"

"Absolutely."

"Have they worked together in past lives?"

"Yes. Some of their other activities have had to do with healing—mutual healing of other individuals and an aspiration to raise the consciousness of the Earth in other ways." I noted Cassandra's use of *other*. Like the other healing activities, the bombing, too, had been designed to elevate consciousness. The intent was the same!

"As I understand it," I said, "souls can choose to incarnate in any location at any time."

"Yes, that is correct."

"Why did Christina and the soul who planted the bomb choose the United States at this time in history?"

"It had to do with freedom," Cassandra said. "It had to do with an unconsciousness on the part of one and a consciousness on the part of the other. Christina was unconscious, somewhat, about the political situation of the Earth at that point in time. Christina was moving through her life in a way that was planned, but she was not making conscious decisions as much as was necessary. Her brother was in Vietnam in the middle of the war. This one [Christina] did not fully understand the essence of what he was going through until he returned and she had been through this accident."

"Did Christina plan this experience to wake herself up so that she could lead a conscious life?"

"That is correct."

"Was she given opportunities to awaken earlier in her life so that the accident would not have been necessary?"

"No, that consciousness was not made available."

"Cassandra, what I've seen is that the soul tries at first in subtle ways to awaken the personality. If the personality doesn't awaken, the soul tries in stronger ways. Eventually, something major, like a bomb explosion, may happen. But in this case, it seems to be the opposite — that the explosion was chosen in preference to the more subtle ways."

"In this particular case, that is correct."

"Why was that the preference of Christina's soul?"

"Because it had a higher purpose to awaken other people in order to provide hope and consciousness."

"Cassandra, when the explosion was planned, was it understood that it would definitely, probably, or might or might not happen?"

"That it might or might not happen. Free choice always exists. She could have chosen not to [participate], and the soul who set it could have chosen not to.

"Free will is the term that vibrates harmonically to each individual as they live on the Earth. You may change the lessons you have chosen by increasing your vibrational frequency, learning to be compassionate, and treating each person you encounter on the Earth as you treat your Messiah. You may not have a sense that you are making these changes, because the frequencies of your planet are quite dense, but if you always — and I mean *always* — take the higher road, the higher frequencies will lift you into more loving actions toward others.

"You may ascend to the place that holds all of your records past, present, and future — the Akashic Records — and access your life plan. This [plan] may be altered through loving thoughts and wishes that bring you into a thought-form for human good."

In using the term *thoughtform*, Cassandra was referring to the fact that thoughts are energy. When we first have a thought, it is energy in pre-physical form. If we (or others) think the thought often enough or with enough emotion, it eventually manifests in the physical realm. It is for this reason that negative thinking may create, for example, physical illness.

Cassandra continued. "Simply ask your guide at the Akashic Library to materialize your file in its current form, and meditate on the changes you have formulated to ascend you to higher planes of consciousness. You may not always be aware of those, but fear not—your angelic guides and beings are always present to log the fleeting moments of beauty you know in your heart. Ask them to emote those into your divine consciousness as you enter the Akashic Records.

"The Earth is currently moving up [in vibration] each day, and more souls are rising to the occasion of living out a higher thoughtform. Soon, there will not be room for those who do not act for the good of all. The challenges you chose to learn may no longer be appropriate to your soul as you have chosen to bring love and peace and light to the ones on your path. You may enact changes for yourself and the good of all by always seeing the best in all beings and lifting them to their highest good.

"Life challenges are simply a method to slow souls down so they may actualize the beauty around them. The slower you feel your movement on Earth, the higher the celestial vibrational frequency. Pain and suffering are some vehicles of choice, and some beautiful ones pick that because they are taking on the pain of others so they may live life on Earth free of pain. This is one of the highest forms of human sacrifice—to give your Earthly body so others may live a life of sensorial delight and freedom from pain and suffering. You are not given more than you can handle, but some souls choose to move more rapidly through the veils of conscious development in a particular lifetime. Miracles happen, and choices may be made to change things. Earth pain and suffering may not always transform on the physical plane, but the thoughtform of positive vibration chosen by the bearer of the pain may be altered. Those who live with challenges are sometimes the heroes and heroines who exemplify transcendence on the Earth. And so it is."

In the course of my research, I had not heard much about the post-birth altering of our life plans, but Cassandra's inspiring explanation rang true intuitively. Since we plan life challenges to experience and know ourselves as love in all its many forms, then such challenges are rendered unnecessary if we arrive at that self-knowing before the challenge occurs. In Christina's case, that knowing had not been available to her because she had a contract to experience the explosion as an act of service to others. She still could have chosen on some level not to participate, but such a decision would have been inconsistent with her desire to serve. To me, it seemed more likely that the bomber, for many reasons, might have decided not to cause the explosion.

"Cassandra," I asked, "if the person who planted the bomb had chosen not to, what would have happened later in Christina's life to awaken her? Were there back-up plans in place?"

"Yes," Cassandra answered. "Practices of consciousness would have occurred related to the vibratory patterns of the Earth where she lived. Other events would have occurred within her family structure."

Given that Christina's plan was to raise consciousness, it occurred to me that she and I might have agreed prior to incarnation to tell her story in this book. Certainly, a book would provide a second public format for Christina to transmit her message of hope.

"Cassandra, did Christina plan before birth to tell her story in the book I'm writing?"

"Yes," was her simple reply. Although part of me had anticipated this answer, I was nevertheless electrified by it. I had known Christina before I was born! Not only had I known her, but we had planned to locate each other at this time in our lives. I felt a sense of wonder at the way our plan had come to fruition.

"Have Christina and I worked together in other lives?"

"You have had contact before."

"How did she and I know we would find each other in this lifetime?"

"It is a sea of consciousness, and the vibratory patterns brought you together. You are of the same soul group." This information, though startling, struck me as correct, particularly given the similarities between Christina's work and the work in which I was now engaged. I felt joy at having found a kindred soul.

"Cassandra," I said, "some of the readers of Christina's story will be people who have had an accident. What would you like to say to those people?"

"The depression, the anger, the 'why me,' and the final state of acceptance are part of the lesson that has to be accomplished to reach a particular soul level of consciousness. It is a beautiful process. It is very important to forgive yourself in each stage of the process so that you can achieve your highest level of consciousness and then regenerate that beauty, compassion, and understanding out to all people who are going through the same thing."

Christina's Story — Part II

Wisely and with great insight, Cassandra helped me to understand both the purposes of the explosion and how Christina had been able to heal emotionally from it. Christina had planned the explosion in part so that she might heal herself and in so doing, help others to heal. Forgiveness had been the key to her inner healing, and forgiveness came more easily with the realization that she had planned the accident before birth and that it was an act of service to the world.

Christina formally embarked on a career as a healer shortly after completing her college degree. At that time, an acquaintance in the field of speech pathology invited her to observe patients. Fascinated by the experience, Christina developed an interest in neurological disorders and began working in hospitals. She quickly saw that she was in a unique position to be of service.

"People wanted to know what happened to my hand," Christina told me. "When I explained, they began to realize there was hope. That was the reason my soul made the contract to have such a horrifying event happen, because it gives other people hope. If someone can move through a path that brings them out the other end and makes them productive, then anybody can."

I asked Christina to talk about the patients with whom she works.

"The individuals I see become very conscious following injury," she said. "They have an understanding of their purpose. Every person without fail has told me that it's been a spiritual journey for them. If I ask if they would do it again, they all say yes. With the people I see, it frequently takes at least two to three years, sometimes five, to heal. Some of the final stages of spiritual growth have to do with endurance and patience. People learn those skills as they move through the injury.

"Many of them have multiple accidents, one after the other. Car accidents increase in occurrence. Once you have one, the chances of having another increase exponentially. These people don't cause the accidents [through negligent driving]; most of them are rear-ended. The message I've gotten is that it has to do with an advancement of spiritual growth and the soul. If they don't get the message the first time, then they get another opportunity."

"Christina," I asked, "have you received information from Spirit as to why, in addition to learning patience and endurance, they planned those challenges before they were born?"

"Sometimes it's self-love," she replied. "Some people—people who have lived their lives in a very unconscious way, doing many things as rapidly as possible—learn how to love themselves through having to slow their lives down. Other lessons have to do with the people in their environment. They're the ones learning. The person's soul has agreed to have that injury in order to give information to other people. The others are learning to love people who have injuries and to understand that what is invisible on Earth [such as brain trauma] really does exist.

"Part of the knowledge I've been given to pass on to people is that they made a pact to have this happen. When you tell people that, it's very calming to them. When they begin to understand that they did make this pact to learn specific lessons, then it's forward movement."

"Christina, as a healer what would you say to people who must endure great physical pain?"

"Draw a circle in front of yourself," she advised. "Step into the circle of pain and toward it, rather than trying to move away from it. It will then subside to levels you can handle."

As Christina offered this advice, I thought of my conversations with people who had experienced major accidents. In addition to physical pain, they often faced significant changes in their relationships.

"Christina, how did the relationships in your life change as a result of the explosion?" I asked.

"Some of my best friends left my life," she said quietly. "People understand that life is extremely fragile. If it can happen to someone they know, then it can happen to them, and that's frightening. Whoever is supposed to be in your life will be there. Sometimes, you're to walk the journey alone, and you don't need a lot of outside help. You may think you do. The people who think that and wallow in that become victims. If you look inside yourself, the pathway will be lighted for you, no matter whether you walk it alone or with other people. All you need to do is ask [Spirit] for help."

One of Christina's greatest changes took place in her relationship with her husband.

"My husband took particularly good care of me," Christina recalled. "He was supportive in a way that was like a father. Very protective. He believed he caused it by being late."

Yet despite the end of her marriage, and despite the years of physical and emotional pain, Christina had forgiven the bomber. I wondered if she had any additional wisdom to share with others who may be struggling to forgive.

"Bless that person, ask that they be forgiven, and allow it to occur by releasing them to a consciousness that's higher than ours," Christina suggested. "The best thing to do is release, because all they do is take energy, which you could be using to do good for the world."

"Beyond forgiveness, how did you get to the point of gratitude?"

"Layers unfolded like an onion. I was grateful to be alive. I was grateful as the pain started to lift. I was grateful if it was just thirty seconds that the pain would stop. I didn't feel that way in the beginning, because the pain was all the time, but there comes a time when being in the dark side is more than one can bear. Your choice is to move into the light."

And the bomber?

"He had been chosen to do that," Christina said. "I think it's a very high point of light to be chosen to do something we wouldn't consciously think of as goodwill."

Christina's Session with Staci Wells

To obtain further information about Christina's life blueprint and to listen to the conversation from her pre-birth planning, Christina and I talked with Staci Wells. I provided Staci with Christina's name and birthdate, and told her that Christina had been severely injured years ago in a bomb explosion. We waited expectantly as Staci listened for the first words from her spirit guide.

"As I started focusing on the year of the accident," Staci began, "what I heard was, 'That was the year of karma.' That accident was no accident. It was planned."

"Right," said Christina.

We paused for another moment as Staci's guide now took her to the actual planning session.

"I see you, Christina, standing up in this room in the middle of your soul group. There is a larger room where the soul group members gather, and a smaller, adjoining room where the spirit guides are. You're wearing an ivory gown. Very simple, flowing, natural in form. You are saying that you want to heal the world.

"There was much talk in this pre-birth planning session about spiritual growth. You are continuing in this lifetime a theme of spiritual empowerment that began during the Crusades. You were a woman who was short, verbal, and very smart, who worked unseen by the soldiers. You worked to protect others who could have come under suspicion. You ministered to them. You fed them. You housed them.

You told them safe routes they could go. When your friends were taken into prison and held captive, you handed them food and clothing through the grates. You did whatever it took to help. You were never captured in that lifetime, but many of your friends were. So, a desire to be of service and help people empower themselves in spiritual and practical ways is a continuing karmic theme.

"Of all things, the mind fascinates you. I see you having discussions with one particular spirit guide and three others in your soul group about how you wanted to study the mind and its implication in various body disorders in this lifetime. You wanted to empower people through better use of their minds.

"I'm asking to be shown a conversation regarding the accident. I sense that there is one individual responsible for this. I'm seeing you discuss things with this soul. I hear you agreeing to be part of this scenario.

Christina: It will herald a new opening in my life. It will act as a mental, unconscious reminder for me at that time to turn back to the path I want to walk. I need something like this so that I will make a course correction and be reminded of the greater purpose for my life.

"It's as if it physically blew a hole in a wall that you could walk through to enter the next phase of your life," Staci added. "I hear you explain that in your recovery from this explosion, you will empower yourself through the use of your mind, not just in terms of healing the body, but also in healing mentally and emotionally, and in willing yourself to heal.

"It would have been very easy for you to walk a different path, a path of familial responsibility, a path of putting your own needs last, if this accident hadn't happened. You're a woman of great energy. Your soul is vital and active. You seemed very enthusiastic, saying that you would be okay. On the soul level, you seemed jovial about it. Some of your soul group didn't say anything. They just listened impartially and observed. Others were surprised and shocked that you would choose such dramatic means of changing direction. You laughed about it, saying 'I need that kind of energy to make that kind of change.'

"This bomb," Staci asked, "was it in a brick building?"

"It was," Christina confirmed. "A very, very old building."

"Then I'm seeing the right thing," Staci replied. "I'm being taken again to when you sit down and converse with the man who built the bomb. He is a quiet individual. He only makes noises with bombs. At least on the soul level, he is oddly compassionate. He has had problems through several lifetimes with expressing himself through words, feeling at ease when he converses with people, and even being out in public where many people are gathered. In one lifetime, he had schizophrenia. He nonetheless manages to feel compassion.

"At the time you were talking about this, it was difficult for him to come face-to-face with you. His compassion makes him want to withdraw and hide. He would much prefer to work unseen. Your conversation with him is stop-and-go. You get some sentences said, and then there's silence. Then some other sentences. Then he starts to get up, and you pull him back. His concern seems to be with your well-being. You're almost acting like a spirit guide to him. He is part of your soul group, and you've seen him struggle with this issue through *many* lifetimes. I see you reach out to him.

Christina: It's all right.

Man: I never want to kill, injure, maim, or harm somebody. It is never my intent. I just want to make a statement. I just want to be heard clearly.

Christina: We hear you. We see you. All of us here see you and hear you. I'll help you with this. I will serve your purpose, and in serving you, I will also serve myself, don't you see?

"When you say 'this,' you mean his communication problems. He's wrestling with guilt about this. He doesn't want to hurt you or be responsible for anything that hurts you, but it's very clear as you plan your lives that his is going to become a jumbled entanglement, and that his ability to express himself will not be at the level he is trying to achieve. He will turn once again to doing things behind closed doors, in secret, that will have a large impact on people. It's all about communication for him.

"I feel coming from you, Christina, a great deal of love. I hear you making assurances to him, trying to get him to come out of his viewpoint to see your side and how it will serve your purposes. There's a lot of convincing and hand-holding here. You try to convey to him that you will be affected only positively.

Christina: It's okay. I want to do this. I will help you. I will help myself. I will see only light. Negativity does not always beget negativity. Sometimes negativity is the road to wholeness. We all have to start somewhere.

"So," concluded Staci, "this is a soul in your soul group and who you have great compassion for."

I now had a good understanding of how the explosion had furthered Christina's goals for this lifetime. Nevertheless, I was unsure how causing an explosion would help the bomber to overcome past life difficulties with communication.

"I'm not clear on what planting a bomb does for him," I said to Staci. "What does it help him to accomplish?"

Abruptly, Staci's speech slowed and became halting. Her spirit guide was now speaking directly through her.

"This soul has been stuck for millennia in a self-absorbed, self-defeating cycle and has resorted to violent tendencies throughout several lifetimes. In another lifetime he was a member of the IRA [Irish Republican Army] who often did violent things, who helped plan attacks, who helped make bombs. This has been his means of communication. Emotional intimacy is difficult for him. Through it all, there has been an underlying need to create self-esteem. This life and this intersection in time with this bomb and Christina are for him an extension of another lifetime where he is still trapped in this cycle."

As quickly as Staci had left, she now returned, her speech restored to its usual manner. She continued listening to the pre-birth conversation. "There is discussion with Christina about him getting caught or being trapped, that this bomb could be the thing that leads him to get help. We all spend various lifetimes repeating self-defeating behaviors before we finally understand that they aren't serving us and are then able to move on. Those are two different things: coming to the understanding that it isn't serving us and being able to correct ourselves. Christina is very much into helping people correct themselves. She volunteers to be at the effects of another one of his violent communications in the hope that it will help him correct himself. I keep hearing the word *peace* here. She hopes that it will help him eventually find peace.

"He has from time to time gotten a payoff for this behavior. The payoff in the IRA was that he was well respected, brought into the inner circle, and made to feel important. He's followed the same well-worn path for so many lifetimes that it's easier for him to go in that direction than anything else. Eventually, he's going to shift. Christina was hoping that this lifetime would be that time."

"Have I met him?" Christina asked.

"Not in this lifetime," Staci told her.

I then asked if we could hear the conversation between Christina and the three other souls Staci had first seen in the planning room. There was a long paused as Staci listened.

"Your father, Christina, was one of those souls. The other two souls are female [in this lifetime]. One has the appearance of an older, middle-aged woman — your mother — and the other has the appearance of a blonde, young woman." Staci was seeing the forms these souls would assume in their upcoming incarnations. "Both mother and father are concerned with your welfare. They're questioning you. 'Are you sure you want to do this?'

Christina: Yes, it is what I want. I can handle this. I'm very strong. You know that. I can take on the greatest of challenges.

"The younger female," Staci added, "is somebody who was in your life for two years prior to the accident."

"It might have been my friend Alice," Christina said.

"It wasn't in your mutual plans for her to be a lifelong friend," Staci responded. Staci's words reminded me that we often plan to be friends or even spouses with other people for finite periods of time. Since we have no memory of these agreements, we may view the end of a friendship or marriage as a negative event. It is not. We part ways with others when we have completed our plans with them.

"Right. She's not," Christina confirmed.

"It's definitely a before-the-accident friendship," said Staci. "I get the feeling that she was your closest friend at that time. Perhaps even a roommate?"

"That's exactly right," said Christina.

"I hear her saying, 'Are you sure this [the explosion] is what you want?' Oh, and I see your husband coming up to the four of you. He had been sitting and observing with the rest of your soul group. I see him put his arms around you.

Husband: I will ease some of your burden. I respect all that you do. I respect that you hold the light for many of us. I will support you as much as I possibly can while you go through your time of healing and build your strength.

"He kisses you on the forehead, Christina. You put your arm around him. There's a great deal of understanding and mutual respect between the two of you. That's all that's said."

The appearance of Christina's former husband brought to mind a question that had occurred to me when I first talked with Christina. "Staci," I said, "at the time the explosion occurred, Christina's husband was late picking her up from work because he was engrossed in reading. Could it be that one of his or Christina's spirit guides focused him to such an extent that it forced him to be late?"

Staci was silent for a few seconds as her guide took her to that critical moment.

"Absolutely. He was in an altered state of consciousness, removed from the reality of time. There's very much a spirit guide standing behind him, orchestrating this at the appointed time to make sure everything went right. This spirit was actually one of the guides I saw at the pre-birth planning session."

"Is it Cassandra or Leona?" I asked.

"Cassandra," said Staci, relaying the answer from her guide.

"Staci, I said, "please ask your guide to take us to any other portion of the pre-birth conversation in which Christina talks about how she will grow as a result of this experience or how the experience will allow her to do work that benefits humanity."

"I'm being shown the beginning of this pre-birth planning session," Staci announced. "Christina is with her highest guide, who is in male form. I've mentioned a checkerboard before in other sessions. I'm seeing it again. This is like an actual checkerboard, though, not the pattern on the floor. I see Christina taking pieces and skipping several squares. She is talking to her guide.

Christina:	I have made great leaps [in past lives]. I can continue in this life to make great leaps in growth. I want to do that. I am capable of that.
	I want to be relevant. Whatever the circumstances, I want to be relevant and help people in a relevant manner.

"There's talk about her teaching, lecturing, and writing. Those suggestions are coming from the spirit guides. Christina says, 'I need to be [more] hands-on with people.' There is talk about Christina's intellectual capacity and her ability to analyze people, situations, and family dynamics. These are skills gained in previous lifetimes and the interim between lives. Christina gestures to her heart and says, 'I want to make a difference.'

"Christina talks about working in the background in the Crusades and the French Revolution. In those two other lifetimes, it was getting food to people, getting them hidden, getting them to the next safe house.

Christina: I am tired of doing that. I want to be of service to others, but I don't want it to be as fundamental as it was. I want to do something more and different in a helping capacity.

Spirit Guide: You can become part of the brave new wave of people entering into physical embodiment at a time when the world is ready to embrace again the notion of using unseen energies and even magnetism in healing methods without it being thought of as witchcraft.

"Christina agrees to work in a healing capacity. Emotional healing, at the very core, often brings about the spiritual growth she wanted to help people with. She also wanted to help people in a way that would let them dictate their own journey and envelop them in a process of self-discovery.

Christina: Through so many lifetimes, I have known myself so well and so clearly. That has been the energy that empowered me to be so strong, to fight, and to help others fight. I want to embrace others and enable them to discover that same self-confidence and self-empowerment.

"Then there was talk about how Christina would have to rediscover this process for herself—in order to be reminded of it—so that she could in turn teach others.

"Now I'm being shown something," Staci said excitedly. "Christina, did you spend a period of time in unconsciousness after this accident?"

"I was in and out of consciousness, yes, for quite some time."

"I'm being shown—this is all in your pre-birth planning session—that there would be spirit guides and members of your soul group who would work with you during the time you would be unconscious. They would be trying on the soul level to remind you of the purpose of the accident. They also worked with you to heal you, to show you your healing abilities, and to remind you that you wanted to carry this forward with others. You had a lot of help."

"Yes," Christina said emphatically.

"In this part of the planning," Staci continued, "there is talk from your guides about reaching the masses. They encouraged you to involve yourself with large numbers of people, spread your wealth of knowledge, and infect people with your strength, purpose, and sense that anything can be accomplished. They talked with you a lot about doing something in your later years, such as writing a book, which would serve as a platform for you to travel and make public appearances. It was talked about as something you could do in your fifties. Have you ever felt you wanted to write a book?"

"Actually, I have," Christina replied. "I've even thought about what kind."

At that moment, I recalled Cassandra's reference to Christina's decision to participate in this book.

"Staci," I said, "Cassandra told me that Christina and I are in the same soul group and that we planned for her to tell her story in my book. Can you hear that conversation?"

A long quiet ensued as Staci shifted her attention to that part of the session.

"There are many, many authors in this soul group," Staci told us as the vision became clear. "I get [from my spirit guide] the phrase, 'a storehouse of intellectual knowledge among this soul group.' I see you, Rob, about four rows back from Christina and whomever she's interacting with. I see you with a letter-writing tablet in your hand and a stylus of some kind. You rise up from the soul group and walk to Christina. You're writing something as you do that. I pick up that you have long been—in several lifetimes, in other words—an observer and a chronicler. You have developed the powers of the observer.

"Although you play a small role in Christina's life, she seems delighted to see you as you come toward her. You sit down and talk to her about the details. She claps her hands together excitedly.

Rob:	I would like to chronicle your journey.
Christina:	Oh yes, please do!
Rob:	I'm going to write a series of books, beginning with the one I want your story in, that

will chronicle the journey of the soul, the journey we all take for lifetimes. I would like to include your journey as a way to represent cause-and-effect karma."

Although Cassandra had told us of our intended collaboration, hearing words that I had spoken before incarnating was entirely different—and quite thrilling. And the information was entirely consistent with what I had learned in personal sessions with other mediums; that I had, in fact, lived a number of lives as an observer and recorder of the human experience.

I was, however, perplexed by the term "cause-and-effect karma," as I had always thought of karma as a balancing. Though I did not know it at the time, my long-forgotten pre-birth use of this term would have a significant impact on my post-birth work. I now conceptualize karmic balancing *as* a cause-and-effect phenomenon.

"I am seeing an apple appear at this moment in the conversation," Staci continued. "You manifested the apple, Rob. You're using the analogy of planting seeds. That is the purpose you want your books to serve.

Rob: I want to plant seeds in the minds of many people—seeds of knowledge and awareness of the soul and the soul's journey—and explain the mysteries, or what so many people think of as the mysteries. In the process, *my* journey will include self-discovery. Your [Christina's] story will enlighten others about the process of cause-and-effect karma and the many paths a soul can take.

"There is a hug between you two and a mutual understanding," Staci added.

Another question came to mind. "Staci, can you hear any conversation between Christina and Cassandra?" Staci then repeated words from Cassandra to both Christina *and* me.

Cassandra: You [Christina] and I have worked together in other lifetimes to let people know that they are not alone, that there are always others who will help, others who have been through it before, whatever it is. This is part of the circle of life. There is no line between soul life and physical life. It is all one.

The involvement with you [Rob] and the book will further the principle that people go through the same thing even though their lives may seem different. When people feel they are the only ones to experience something, it is a selfish delusion. To wallow in delusional moments of self-pity disconnects one from the flow of life and the flow of eternity. It is by *not* cutting oneself off from life that people progress. By realizing the unity of all people, mankind moves to the next step in consciousness. This is part of the greater good, which we all serve.

And with that, Staci and her spirit guide finished their presentation of the conversation from Christina's pre-birth planning session.

While we were listening to the dialogue, I formed several impressions; one was that Christina had expressed great love and understanding to the soul who had created the explosion. I began the follow-up questions by asking Staci and her guide to comment on how members of the soul group interact with the soul of the bomber.

"The other souls aid and assist," Staci replied. "There is no judgment on the spirit plane. They simply reach out to him in love and allow him to do what he needs to do for his evolvement."

"Staci, I'd like to ask your guide what the relationship is between Christina's accident and cause-and-effect karma." Since my own terminology had been presented to me, I decided to make use of it.

Staci's guide spoke directly through her again. "As you have done with other case stories in your book, you are discovering that an accident is often not an accident, that it is simply the cause of a pre-arranged, agreed-upon shift in a person's consciousness. As souls cross the veil onto Earth, they forget the plans they made before crossing. Events such as this serve as very purposeful reminders, even on the subconscious level. The subconscious is the birthplace of change. In that manner, the accident can be seen as the cause—though we [spirit guides] view it as a reminder—that produced the effect of shifting to a new direction, a new focus.

"In unconsciousness after an accident, we have full access to the soul. We work to remind the soul of the soul's chosen purpose and destiny, thus embracing the soul and helping it to rise in vibration during that period in unconsciousness. When full consciousness returns, the soul would have the subconscious seed planted to produce the desired effect."

"That makes sense to me," said Christina.

The desired effect was for Christina to remember her plan to be a healer. Knowing that Christina wanted to bring healing to the world and that her story would be read by many who seek healing, I decided to broaden the scope of our inquiry.

"I'd like to ask about healing," I said to Staci's spirit guide. "Christina went through quite a bit of healing, both physically and emotionally. She forgave the person who planted the bomb. My understanding is that forgiveness literally alters the DNA of the forgiver and the person being forgiven. Is that accurate? If so, how does it change DNA?"

"It is accurate," he confirmed. "It produces change on the chromosomal level. This topic is covered in the Ayurvedic system of healing. Energy goes out from you, and a wave of forgiveness is felt on an unconscious level by the person you forgive. It's up to them whether or not they accept that forgiveness. Many times that person will continue to grieve and not forgive themselves, but it does free the person so they can progress."

"If the person accepts the forgiveness, what specifically happens on the chromosomal level?"

Staci stopped channeling for a moment to describe an image her guide was now creating in her mind: hard particles were falling away from chromosomes and were being replaced by something rounder and softer.

"That enables a better flow of energy—what you sometimes call chi—through the body and mind," continued the spirit guide. "With this greater flow, there is more energy available to move forward with purpose in life. It pervades the body and mind on something smaller than the cellular level."

"Does crying heal DNA?" I asked.

"When it is a release, not when it is self-pity," he answered.

"Does laughter heal DNA?"

"Laughter is very healing. It starts a cascade of hormones that wash over the body, wash out toxins, and promote circulation of fluids. Does it alter DNA? It prevents the toxic alteration of DNA. It is more of a preventive maintenance than an altering. There are times when people like cancer patients can engage in laughter therapy to heal on a cellular level, but it does not in and of itself produce changes on the DNA strand. It enables the body to function more positively and in harmonic resonance to itself."

"I'd like to ask the same question in regard to water," I said. "We've talked about crying as part of the healing process. Some people I've spoken with did visualizations in which they washed themselves in water or reclined in a stream. There's a book by a Japanese scientist, Emoto, who spoke certain words to water, then froze it and analyzed the crystals. He found that high vibration words, in particular, *love* and *gratitude*, resulted in the most beautiful crystals. What is the role of water in healing?"

"Water imbues all body parts and particles," said Staci's guide. "Water takes on vibration and releases vibration. Water can take on magnetism. It can dispel magnetism. It is a carrier and an enabler."

"If someone who has been hurt physically or emotionally speaks to water, 'programs' it with thoughts like love and gratitude, and then drinks the water, would that stimulate either physical or emotional healing?"

"Yes, it would. Speaking these things to it imbues it with a life force, an energy. Ingesting the water brings that life force into the body and helps the body release and cleanse itself of toxins through several organ systems."

I could hear in Staci's voice that she was tiring; channeling her guide was requiring a tremendous amount of energy. I decided to ask him for concluding remarks.

"What would you like to say to people who hear or read about something like a bomb explosion and then feel fear, judgment, and a greater sense of separation from others?"

"There is always a reason," he stated. "The true measure of a person's evolution is their ability to turn a negative into a positive. To dwell on the negative and use judgment and fear-based thought would not feed the truth of a matter such as this. The concern should always be how to make the most positive use of one's time, whether one's time is in a wheelchair or running a marathon. There is always a positive and negative. Such is the duality of Earth. Without the negative, you cannot experience or know the positive. Without the negative, you cannot be motivated to want the positive, because you forget when you cross the veil.

"We would ask those of you who find yourselves thinking judgmental thoughts about the perpetrators of what you see as harm to know that there is always a positive outcome to be served by the misery. We would say to you that misery is the illusion. We would say that people who open a newspaper or turn on their television, see world events, and judge them as negative are simply taking the easy road and not thinking things through. There is always something deeper. There is always something more. There is always meaning. We hope that the examples in this book will help to teach people to think two and three times about the meaning and value of diversity and how it is the catalyst to growth."

⤴

"I will see only light."

This seemingly simple statement, spoken by Christina before her birth about her life to come, means more, far more, than may be immediately apparent. It signifies an intent to be who she really is. The light she sees in others, including the soul who planted the bomb, mirrors the light within her. In others' faces does she glimpse her own reflection.

The central tenet of this book is that we are love. This is more than mere kind notion or pleasing sentiment. This is our nature as eternal souls. It is evident in our pre-birth desire to be of service to one another. It is expressed in the warm caresses and compassionate words among souls as they plan their lives together. And it is reflected in life plans that bless us with an opportunity to discover and know more deeply what it means to be love.

In our nonphysical Home, there is only light. Without darkness, without contrast to light, we cannot fully appreciate the light we see. Without contrast to love, we cannot know, fully and profoundly, who we really are. And so we script lives in which we forget our true identities, hopeful that challenges will awaken us to ourselves, certain that from the remembering will come a greater self-knowing.

In spirit, where there is only light, there is nothing to forgive. There, we know ourselves to be love and so express only that, for only what is known can be expressed. No soul conscious of itself as love would ever express anything else. No soul aware of itself as love would ever create cause for forgiveness.

Yet forgiveness is an expression of love. Without opportunity for it, we could not experience ourselves as love in this form. And so we create pacts in which some of us, forgetful of the love we are, will take actions that appear to call for forgiveness; others of us, equally unaware of ourselves as love, will be challenged to offer it.

Such is the agreement Christina and the bomber forged. Christina is not the intense anger and guilt she once felt in this lifetime; she is the love, the forgiveness, that emerged from those feelings. Nor is the bomber who we might imagine him to be. He is not the hatred that created the explosion but rather the soul who said, "I never want to kill, injure, maim or harm somebody. It is never my intent." His wish to be "heard clearly" is simply a desire to receive, while in body, the same love and understanding Christina showed him when, in spirit, they planned the intersection of their lives.

That intersection created both opportunity and motivation for Christina to remember. By design, part of that remembering was to occur while she was unconscious after the explosion, when her spirit guides and members of her soul group would remind her of her plan: self-healing followed by a life of healing others. To be of service to the world, remembrance is the greatest gift one can bestow.

Christina's is therefore the plan of a lightworker, a soul who intends before birth to recall her internal wisdom in order to, as Cassandra said, "regenerate that beauty, compassion, and understanding out to all people who are going through the same thing." Importantly, Christina first had to remember her natural focus on light before she could share it with others. By remembering, she raised herself to a vibration at which she can uplift and heal. It is her energy, not her words or actions, that does so, and the power of her energy stems from personal transformation. Only to the extent Christina truly sees beauty in the bomber can she help the aggrieved to forgive; only to the degree she genuinely feels gratitude can she foster it in the embittered.

Christina is able to offer these blessings because she forgave in circumstances that could have engendered unrelenting rage. Truly, it is her living of forgiveness, not her profession, that makes Christina a healer. Though she might have closed her heart, she instead opened it wide. Every person on a healing journey follows in her footsteps. If Christina played a different role in society, if those footsteps were rendered less visible, they would remain just as expansive.

If you would bring light and healing to humanity but believe your impact constricted by role, your power weakened by circumstance, your reach limited by injury from physical accident, rest assured that all the world knows you are here. You are heard. You are seen. And where your voice does not carry and your feet cannot tread, even so does every soul feel your presence on levels beyond conscious, human perception. And your impact radiates farther still, throughout the dimensions, dimensions that appear to be, but are not, far removed from you. The light you live, the forgiveness you extend, the healing you create, and the love you remember yourself to be are deeply felt by all in body and all in spirit. That you might bring hope and consciousness to them, Christina agreed before birth to bring hope and consciousness to you. That you might fulfill your pre-birth plan, Christina now fulfills hers.

And when Christina returns to spirit, the effects of her lifetime will continue to ripple across the physical plane. Like a hand on a clear window, each of our lives leaves fingerprints that endure long after the touch. Some of our energy lingers in the thoughtforms of which Cassandra spoke; all of it echoes across time and space, affecting not only those who share Earth with us when we are here, but also those who will follow.

To understand the indelible imprint each of us makes upon the world is to come face-to-face with a great responsibility. Christina knew of this responsibility before she was born and so planned a challenge that would leave profound healing as her legacy. Perhaps, then, Christina's ex-husband has found peace by understanding his role in her life plan. If he has awakened to the part he played, his guilt has been replaced by self-forgiveness, his remorse by acceptance and peace. If he has recognized the courage he showed in enacting a role of which he was unaware, then self-love has blossomed. If such awakening has not occurred, he remains immersed in an illusion of his own creation, an illusion that fosters the growth and learning he sought before he was born.

The same may be said of the bomber. How transformed his self-perception would be if he knew his role to be "a very high point of light." Though now he may believe himself to be anger and hatred, he might instead know that he intended no harm, sought only to be heard, and was the means by which Christina brought healing to the world. If he experiences such an awakening, he might then accept Christina's forgiveness, an energy so powerful that it permeates to the very level of human DNA.

When we return to spirit and recall the pre-birth plans we made with those who "wronged" us, their light becomes apparent to us once again. Until then, our challenge is to see their light while we are in body, behind the veil, screened from their true identities by our own self-selected amnesia. We can do so by realizing that the people in our lives are eternal, nonphysical souls playing temporary roles on a physical stage. Like the soul who planted the explosive, they are part of a larger plan that often remains concealed from us. Yet we can know that each person we encounter is a spark of Divine Light, a loving, transcendent being with whom we are one. Anything less is not real. Anything else is illusion.

To see only light is to see only Divinity in each person who walks on Earth.

It is then we remember who we really are.

CHAPTER 8

∞∞

Conclusion

I T HAS NOW BEEN THREE years since I embarked on the journey that created—indeed, the journey that *is*—this book. On this physical and metaphysical voyage, I have been blessed to hear the stories of many brave individuals. Truly, they have been my teachers. As well, I have learned from the wise nonphysical beings with whom I have spoken. Each has touched my heart and expanded my life.

Through them I now understand the immense power of this most elemental truth: that we are not our bodies. What could be more simple? Yet for someone in Jason's circumstances, this realization makes all the difference. If you are physically disabled and you believe this is your only life and you are no more than your body, then abject despair can result. If, on the other hand, you know—which is to say you *feel*—yourself to be an eternal soul, then an entirely different life is the consequence. If you also know that you planned your disability, that it indeed has deep significance, then your life may become a quest to uncover that meaning. Suffering is lightened, emptiness replaced with purpose.

In those three years, I have come to believe that everything has a higher meaning. I have grown in faith, trust, and willingness to surrender to the purposeful flow of life, even when I do not know where its current may carry me. I have come to see our world, despite its anguish and heartbreaks, as inherently beautiful. I sense a sweetness in life. I feel it—everywhere. At times elusive and obscured by pain, it is nevertheless always there, underlying every difficulty, behind every circumstance.

Our challenge is to find it in our challenges.

In the days before I knew of pre-birth planning, I felt sympathy for others who appeared to be less fortunate than I, pitying a homeless person on the street, for example. Now aware that this seemingly "bad" experience may have been planned, I feel only deep respect. I ask myself: What did this person seek to learn or contribute? I remind myself: She may be having exactly the experience she wanted. I tell myself: He shows enormous fortitude in living such a difficult life plan. Though I do not know why each soul chose that challenge, I do know that the life was designed in wisdom and based on love. Perhaps, I say to myself, the homeless person planned such a life so that I and others who pass by may offer assistance or a kind word in order to experience and thus know ourselves as compassion.

In this way I have come to recognize that little is as it seems. Before I learned of pre-birth contracts, I took much of life at face value. But now, having spoken with Jon, I understand that a soul may choose to experience AIDS so that I and many others may grow in tolerance. Having talked with Pat, I realize that an individual may plan alcoholism to reclaim his spirituality. Having learned from Sharon, I look at the unfailing love of so many mothers and fathers and wonder: Did you and your child plan a drug addiction to show us what love looks like?

And where I've judged, I now see a divine order to and in everything. Where I've seen flaw, I now see perfection — the perfection of lives unfolding just as we planned them. Such unfolding is evident not only in our challenges, but also in the most minute, seemingly insignificant aspects of life. Each leaf that falls from a tree, each blade of grass that bends in the wind ... nothing happens by chance, and all is in divine order. Always.

I have realized, too, that each of us has a divine purpose, a reason for being here, that includes but goes well beyond our own learning. That is, we plan life challenges not only to remember who we really are, but also to share ourselves, our unique essence, with one another. Jon teaches tolerance, Doris brings healing, and Jennifer offers lessons in truthful communication. We are gifted with Bob's gentle kindness, Penelope's egalitarian compassion, Pat's deep faith, and Sharon's tireless heart. Valerie shows us that love is eternal. Jason's resilience inspires our own, and Christina helps us to see light in seeming darkness.

Each of these souls came here to be the love they are.

Courageous souls, one and all.

Epilogue

Twenty-five years after the explosion, Christina returned to the place where her life had forever changed.

On this warm fall day, the fragrance of orange blossoms perfumed the air. Students chatted happily as they crisscrossed the campus on their way to class. Some sat quietly under eucalyptus or palm trees, reading, thinking, daydreaming.

Inside the building in which she had once worked, Christina stood in front of the basement mailboxes. Some were empty, others full with letters and papers. Someone came by to pick up his mail. He reached into his mailbox, grabbed a few envelopes, turned, and left.

Christina climbed the stairs to the main floor. She walked down a hallway, across the lobby, through the portico, and into the bright day.

In the distance, the Santa Ana Mountains stood like silent, immutable sentinels. Shafts of golden sunlight brushed their slopes, and a wind-whispered hymn of joy echoed through the canyons.

A Note to Readers

IF THE STORIES IN *Courageous Souls* have touched you, please let me know. And if you might like to share your story in my next book about the pre-birth planning of life challenges, please let me know that as well.

For all readers, which life challenges would you like to see addressed in the next book? What questions would you like answered? How can I make the next book more helpful to you?

I look forward to hearing from you. I can be reached at the e-mail address at the bottom of this page. Please indicate if you would like to be added to the e-mail list or if you would like me to speak with your book club by teleconference.

To order copies of *Courageous Souls*, please visit www.CourageousSouls.com.

A Note to Mediums and Channels

I INVITE YOU TO PARTICIPATE in my ongoing study of pre-birth planning. If you might like to lend your talents to subsequent books in the Courageous Souls series, please contact me.

Robert Schwartz
CourageousSouls@yahoo.com

Appendices

Appendix A:
Courageous Souls

Jon Elmore
Jonelmore3rd@net-wizardry.net

Doris
wordsvoices@capital.net

Jennifer Stewart
jstewart15@cfl.rr.com

Penelope
peepingthoughts@gmail.com

Bob Feinstein
harlynn@panix.com

Sharon Dembinski
sharond0317@yahoo.com

Pat
Patrickgene33@sbcglobal.net

Valerie Villars
vvillars@bellsouth.net

Jason Thurston
scilifechanges@yahoo.com

Christina
soulcomplete@gmail.com

Please understand that a personal reply to your email cannot
be promised.